TD
170
.C55
1992

$16⁰⁰

About Island Press

Island Press, a nonprofit organization, publishes, markets, and distributes the most advanced thinking on the conservation of our natural resources—books about soil, land, water, forests, wildlife, and hazardous and toxic wastes. These books are practical tools used by public officials, business and industry leaders, natural resource managers, and concerned citizens working to solve both local and global resource problems.

Founded in 1978, Island Press reorganized in 1984 to meet the increasing demand for substantive books on all resource-related issues. Island Press publishes and distributes under its own imprint and offers these services to other nonprofit organizations.

Support for Island Press is provided by Geraldine R. Dodge Foundation, The Energy Foundation, The Charles Engelhard Foundation, The Ford Foundation, Glen Eagles Foundation, The George Gund Foundation, William and Flora Hewlett Foundation, The Joyce Foundation, The John D. and Catherine T. MacArthur Foundation, The Andrew W. Mellon Foundation, The Joyce Mertz-Gilmore Foundation, The New-Land Foundation, The J. N. Pew, Jr. Charitable Trust, Alida Rockefeller, The Rockefeller Brothers Fund, The Rockefeller Foundation, The Florence and John Schumann Foundation, The Tides Foundation, and individual donors.

Lessons from Nature

The author is grateful for permission to include the following previously copyrighted material: Figure 3 appeared originally in William D. Nordhaus and James Tobin, "Is Growth Obsolete?" *Economic Research: Retrospect and Prospect,* Volume 5: Economic Growth (New York: Columbia University Press for the National Bureau of Economic Research, 1972). Used with permission of publisher and authors. Updated version published in Paul A. Samuelson and William D. Nordhaus, *Economics,* 12th ed. (New York: McGraw-Hill, 1985). Used with permission of publisher. Sections on designing with nature in Woodlands, Texas, and Boston, Massachusetts, in Chapter 8 and land-use planning in Chapter 10 adapted with permission from Daniel D. Chiras, *Environmental Science: Action for a Sustainable Future* (Redwood City, Calif.: Benjamin/ Cummings, 1991). Sections on greening the corporation in Chapter 5 and Denver's Better Air Campaign and the Timber, Fish, and Wildlife Agreement in Chapter 8 were adapted with permission from Daniel D. Chiras, *Beyond the Fray: Reshaping America's Environmental Response* (Boulder, Colo.: Johnson Books, 1990).

Chiras, Daniel D.
Lessons from nature: learning to live sustainably on the earth
Daniel D. Chiras.
p.   cm.
Includes bibliographical references and index.
ISBN 1–55963–107–4 (acid–free paper).—ISBN 1–55963–106–6 (pbk.:
acid-free paper)
1. Environmental protection. 2. Human ecology. I. Title.
TD170.C55 1992
304.2—dc20   91-39156
CIP

Lessons from
NATURE

Learning to Live
Sustainably
on the Earth

DANIEL D. CHIRAS

ISLAND PRESS
Washington, D.C. □ *Covelo, C*

*To the Earth and to those who work unselfishly
in her defense and nurturance*

The care of the Earth is our most
ancient and most worthy, and, after all,
our most pleasing responsibility. To
cherish what remains of it, and to foster
its renewal, is our only legitimate hope.

Wendell Berry
The Unsettling of America

Contents

Preface

Lessons From Nature is a book about the future of humankind and the Earth, intimately and mutually bound together, yet rarely considered simultaneously in most human deliberations. Drawing on the biological principles of sustainability gleaned from studies of nature, this book explains what we must do to place human civilization onto a sustainable course. It shows how we can—and must—alter ethics, economics, and government to create an enduring presence. It shows the wisdom of complying with the rules of nature.

In this book, you will notice that I have devoted scant space to the barriers that will inevitably obstruct progress toward a humane, sustainable future. This omission is intentional, motivated principally by my belief that at this point in human history guidance on how to build a sustainable society is far more important than a detailed discussion of the forces that will stand in the way. I believe that barriers to this revolutionary idea will fall as others have in recent years, suddenly and with little warning. Or, we will find ways around them in time.

Besides presenting a blueprint for a sustainable future, this book offers numerous examples of change already underway. These models provide direction and considerable encouragement in these troubled times.

A word of warning: what you are about to read will question a number of our society's cherished beliefs. While this may unsettle some readers, it is vital at this juncture in human history. The environmental crisis closing in on us is rooted in basic misconceptions about our place in the biosphere, fallacies that have spawned a dangerously unsustainable way of life. Not until we discover the folly of our ways and of the thinking that fostered them can we extricate ourselves from this crisis.

What follows is a journey of reorientation, divided into three parts. The first is a frank discussion of the unsustainability of human actions. The second is an exploration of ethics, economics, and government; it shows how the biological principles of sustainability can be used to refashion human society to honor the Earth's limits and avail itself of her opportunities. The third part examines critical systems—agriculture, energy, waste, and others—that have, over time, become grossly unsustainable. This part shows how to convert these systems into enduring human activities that benefit humankind *and* the Earth.

To some, many of the ideas in this book may seem utopian or theoretical or—worse yet—foolishly uneconomical, but I assure you that what is presented here is anything but theoretical. Most of the ideas you are about to encounter are not only practical but affordable. This course is far from utopian—it is essential to our survival on the planet. Most of the ideas set forth here are already being implemented throughout the world by people and nations that recognize the fundamental need to create a sustainable way of life.

Join me in this journey of discovery. There's nothing to lose and everything in the world to gain.

In keeping with the principles of sustainability, this book is printed on recycled acid-free paper. The manuscript was produced on recycled computer paper, using recycled printer ribbons that have been used and refilled for nearly a decade. All photocopies were made on recycled paper, and all early drafts were recycled.

Acknowledgments

This book is the work of hundreds of dedicated people who have devoted their lives to understanding the interaction between humans and the environment and to finding ways to live sustainably on the planet. I am deeply indebted to them, especially to those whose works influenced my thinking: Aldo Leopold, Paul Ehrlich, Garrett Hardin, Charles Southwick, Richard Wagner, Lester Brown, E. F. Schumacher, Hazel Henderson, Barry Commoner, Peter Russell, Rod Nash, Raymond Dasmann, and Donella Meadows, among others.

Many thanks as well to my wife Kathleen for helping with the research, for reading and rereading the manuscript and offering valuable suggestions along the way, for seeing me through the hard times and encouraging me at every stage. Her love and kindness have meant a lot over the years.

A warm thanks to my perceptive friend and inspiring colleague Alan AtKisson of the Context Institute for his insightful comments and suggestions on the second draft. His expertise on sustainability has helped immensely. Thanks also to Arianthé Stettner, another insightful friend and colleague who read and commented on the second draft. Her questions and shared thoughts helped to shape my thinking, and I am indebted to her. A very special thanks to my editor and friend Barbara Dean, who diligently pored over all three drafts and helped me to polish the final one. Barbara's dedication to excellence and her cheerful input were invaluable. I am honored to have worked with such a fine, capable person.

To all the folks at Island Press who made this book possible, my deepest appreciation. The service they render to the environmental community and to society deserves far greater recognition. May they keep up the fine work!

Finally, although he is too young to read these words, a debt of gratitude to my son Skyler, whose love and affection have filled my life with joy and given me even more reason to work on behalf of the Earth's future.

Lessons from Nature

1 Can the Human Race Survive the Human Race?

The optimist proclaims that we live in the best of all worlds, and the pessimist fears this is true.

J. B. CABELL

IF THIS IS A TYPICAL DAY on planet Earth, 116 square miles of tropical rain forest will be destroyed. In the Third World, where much of the cutting occurs, only one tree is planted for every ten cut down; in the tropics of Africa, the ratio is one to 29.

If this is a typical day, 70 square miles of desert will form in semi-arid regions subject to intense population pressure, overgrazing, and poor land management. Already, one-third of the world's cropland is threatened by desertification.

As if that is not bad enough, today 250,000 newborns will join the world population. Each new resident requires food, water, shelter, and a host of other resources to survive.

On this day, at least 1.5 million tons of hazardous waste will be "disposed of"—released into our air, water, and land—and Americans will throw away enough garbage to fill the Superdome in New Orleans two times. By various estimates, 10 to 40 species will become extinct today, mostly as the result of tropical deforestation.

At day's end, the Earth will be a little hotter, the rain a little more acidic, the water a little more polluted. The world's already crowded cities will be more crowded and the air in and around them, now choked with pollution, will be a bit dirtier. At day's end, the web of life will be a bit more threadbare.

Tomorrow, it starts all over.

Outlines of the Environmental Challenge

A survey of global environmental problems suggests what many have feared for some time now: the fate of the Earth and our own survival are on the line. The next ten years could determine the future of humankind. It's time to mobilize to save the Earth and save ourselves.

The first step in finding a solution is understanding the problems. What are they? How serious are they? How do they interact?

Since many books on the environment present the wide array of problems facing the modern world, I'll only highlight a handful of the 16 or so major environmental trends that are foreclosing on our future (see table 1). First, however, let me hasten to note that this discussion is intended to lay the groundwork for a frank discussion of solutions, not to add to the current gloom and doom. There's no better place to start than with agriculture. (If you already understand

---

TABLE 1: Sixteen Major Environmental Trends

Population growth
Species extinction
Deforestation
Destruction of wetlands
Desertification of farmland
Soil erosion
Salinization of farmland soils
Farmland conversion
Groundwater contamination
Groundwater depletion
Declining oil supplies
Declining mineral supplies
Water shortages
Global warming
Acid deposition
Ozone depletion

---

the problems, you may want to skim the following sections on pages 5–9, then move on to the analysis.)

· *Soil erosion is destroying cropland and rangeland throughout the world.* In the past 100 years, one-third of the topsoil on American farms has been stripped from the land by wind and rain. Each year, nearly two billion tons of soil is blown off or washed away from farms and ranches. If this trend continues, U.S. crop production could decline by 10 to 30 percent in the next 50 years, a time when world demand for food and alternative fuels from crops like ethanol is on the rise.

Unfortunately, Americans are not alone in their plight. Worldwide, an estimated 24 billion tons of topsoil is eroded from farms and ranches each year. If this soil could be captured, it would fill a freight train that could encircle the equator 170 times.

The loss of topsoil is important because it destroys farmland. At the current rate of loss, 7 percent of the world's cropland will be forfeited to erosion in the next ten years.[1] Making matters worse, valuable cropland and rangeland are also being destroyed by other forces such as the spread of desert and cropland conversion—the loss of arable land to airports, highways, housing developments, and so forth.

· *Hunger and starvation exist in epidemic proportions and are likely to worsen as the human population expands.* Despite three decades of agricultural research to increase the world's food supply, one of every five Third World inhabitants cannot find enough to eat. They are literally starving to death.[2] Worldwide, 12 million people will succumb to starvation this year, and 30 million more will perish from diseases aggravated by hunger. Forty-two million people dying each year is equivalent to 300 Boeing 747s, each carrying 400 passengers, crashing every day of the year with no survivors. Almost half of the victims are children.

Although efforts to feed the world's people are impressive, hunger and starvation will likely worsen as the world population swells. In addition to these problems, continued growth of the human population could double or even triple deforestation and other environmental damage already occurring at intolerable levels today. It won't be long before we have eaten ourselves out of house and home.

· *Rapid deforestation threatens the long-term ecological stability of the planet.* Rain forests are a rich source of diverse wild species, new medicines, and useful products. Once covering an area the size of the United States, tropical rain forests have been reduced by a least a third, perhaps as much as a half. In some areas, deforestation has nearly wiped out the forests. The forests of the island nations of Borneo and Sumatra, for example, have been nearly decimated. Forty years ago Ethiopia was 30 percent forest; 12 years ago, only 4 percent of the nation was covered with trees, and today it is less than 1 percent. Before the turn of the century, India was 50 percent forest; today about 14 percent of the area is covered with trees.[3]

Each year, a region of tropical rain forest the size of the state of Washington is cleared to make room for farms, ranches, roads, and human settlement. Despite increased efforts, timber cutting is clearly not being matched by replanting. Compounding the problem, current replanting efforts usually create plantations or tree farms that are a mere biological skeleton of the complex forest ecosystems they have replaced.

· *Oil supplies could be depleted by the year 2018 if oil consumption continues to increase at current rates.* The industrial world depends heavily on oil. At the current rate of consumption, however, known world oil supplies will only last about 40 more years. Undiscovered oil—that is, oil thought to exist—might last another 25 years.[4] Unfortunately, oil consumption has increased at a rate of 5 percent a year since its discovery. If demand continues to increase this quickly, world oil reserves could be depleted by 2018.

Some geologists in the oil industry believe that global oil supplies are much larger than those currently thought to exist (about 1,400 billion barrels). It is possible, they say, that an additional 3,000 billion barrels of oil could be had. Although this is a massive amount, a quick calculation taking into account a 5 percent annual growth in demand reveals that even this seemingly vast supply will only last an additional 20 years. By 2038, that is, the world could be completely out of oil.

Without carefully developed alternatives, the decline in oil supplies could spawn an inflationary spiral that would cripple the industrialized world. Unfortunately, in many countries relatively little effort is currently being made to use oil more efficiently. Even less effort is focused on developing environmentally safe alternatives, such as hydrogen, ethanol, and solar energy.

· *Many crucial minerals are bound to fall into short supply in the near future.* Current estimates of world mineral reserves and projections of consumption suggest that about three-quarters of the 80 or so economically vital minerals are abundant enough to meet our needs for many years—or, if they are not, there are adequate substitutes available. However, at least 18 economically essential minerals—gold, silver, mercury, lead, sulfur, tin, tungsten, and zinc among them—will fall into short supply, some within a decade or two. Shortages will occur even if nations greatly increase recovery and recycling.

Don't count on new discoveries and improved extraction technologies to save the day. Even if we could mine five times the currently known reserves of these 18 endangered minerals, they would be 80 percent depleted on or before the year 2040.[5] Their depletion, combined with declining oil supplies, could bring the world economy to its knees—unless we make significant changes in consumption, and soon.

· *Acid rain and snow are destroying lakes, rivers, forests, and farmland.* Today, over 230 lakes in the Adirondack Mountains of New York have become critically acidified from sulfuric and nitric acids, produced from sulfur dioxide and nitrogen oxides released by the combustion of fossil fuels. In lakes and rivers, acids kill fish, algae, and aquatic plants. In 1988, the National Wildlife Federation published a list of U.S. lakes that have high acid levels or are sensitive to acid precipitation. The report notes that eastern lakes have been particularly hard hit by acid deposition, with one-fifth of the lakes in Massachusetts, New Hampshire, New York, and Rhode Island containing enough acid to threaten aquatic life. The report adds that one-third of the lakes in Florida are acidic enough to be harmful to aquatic life.

Throughout much of the developed world, the story is the same. In southern Sweden, 20,000 lakes are without or—some think—soon to be without fish, in large part because of widespread acidification. In Canada, the prospects for lakes and rivers are also dimming. Nine of Nova Scotia's famous salmon-fishing rivers have already lost their fish populations because of acids deposited in rain and snow. Eleven more are teetering on the brink of destruction. In southern Ontario and Quebec, acid deposition has already destroyed 100 lakes, and by the year 2000, scientists predict, nearly half of Quebec's 48,000 lakes will be destroyed.

Acids also affect cropland and forests and are implicated in the widespread destruction of statuary and historic buildings in Europe and North America. Much of the once-lush Black Forest in Germany has died as a result of acids deposited from the sky.

· *Hazardous waste continues to be dumped in the environment.* Each year, American factories produce an estimated 250 to 270 million metric tons of waste considered hazardous by state and federal standards. That's over a ton of hazardous waste each year for every man, woman, and child in the United States. Despite tighter regulations and concerted efforts to reduce the generation of hazardous waste, a lot of toxic chemicals still end up in our groundwater, rivers, lakes, and landfills. Other industrial nations produce equally impressive amounts of hazardous waste. It is unlikely that the world can continue to absorb such an enormous output of waste without creating massive problems in the long run.

· *Greenhouse gases and deforestation are causing the planet to heat up.* Addicted to fossil fuels, modern industrial nations may well be setting the stage for a disastrous global warming. Global warming results from at least three atmospheric pollutants, carbon dioxide, methane, and chlorofluorocarbons, all produced by modern industrial societies. These gases absorb heat escaping from the Earth's surface and radiate it back to us, much like the glass in a greenhouse.

Global atmospheric levels of carbon dioxide have increased 25 percent since 1870 as a result of increased fossil fuel combustion and deforestation. Scientists predict that global carbon dioxide levels could double in the next 40 years, raising average global temperature by 4 to 9°F. A decrease in global temperature of only a few degrees means the difference between an ice age and today's relatively liveable global climate. A 4 to 9°F increase would have devastating effects. Much of the United States and Canada would be warmer and drier. The agriculturally productive Great Plains states could very likely become too arid to support farming. The United States and Canada, both major exporters of food, might face severe food shortages.

Global warming could eventually melt the polar ice caps and many of the world's glaciers, raising the sea level by as much as 200 to 300 feet and flooding 20 percent of the world's land mass. Much of the state of Florida and many coastal cities throughout the world would be under water. Without an extensive system of levees to hold back rising seas, New York and Los Angeles would cease to exist. Farmland, already threatened by lower rainfall and searing temperatures, would shrink as displaced coastal residents moved inland to avoid the rising seas.

Signs of global warming are already evident. In fact, seven of the hottest years in over a century of record keeping have occurred since 1980. If the temperature continues to rise as it has in the past 20 years, the Earth will soon be warmer than it has been in the last 100,000 years.

The trends in environmental deterioration and resource depletion paint a rather ominous picture of the present state of affairs. Lest we forget, many of the changes currently under way could act synergistically, producing far greater damage than anticipated. For example, environmental harm caused by increased greenhouse gases will likely be worsened by deforestation, an expanding population, and acid deposition.

Taken together, these trends point to one inescapable conclusion: the current course of human society is unsustainable. It cannot continue much longer the way it has for the past 200 years.

Overshooting the Earth's Carrying Capacity

What's happening on planet Earth? From an ecological perspective, human society has slowly and inexorably pushed beyond the means of the Earth's life support system. The massive multibillion dollar human economy is destroying the intricate economy of nature, which is, unbeknownst to many, not just the source of human wealth but also the source of all life.

In the language of ecologists, humans have exceeded the Earth's carrying capacity. The environmental problems we face are signs that we have transgressed critical ecological thresholds.[6] Unfortunately, few people in positions of power understand the meaning of carrying capacity and the limits it places on human endeavor. Even fewer understand how far we have overstepped ecological boundaries and the long-term consequences of continuing to do so. An understanding of the term carrying capacity is therefore vital to solving our problems.

Reduced to its basics, carrying capacity means the number of organisms an ecosystem can support year after year, decade after decade, century after century. To many people, however, the phrase "exceeding the carrying capacity" brings to mind pictures of starving African children. It is often taken to mean too many people, too little food.

Others see carrying capacity as a matter of living space. Flying over the vast unpopulated expanses of the Earth, it is hard for them to imagine that humankind could have exceeded the Earth's capacity to sustain human life.

Carrying capacity does indeed refer to the ability of our environment to provide food and living space, but the term also encompasses at least two additional factors: resource supply and waste assimilation.

Consider resource supply first. Modern society requires many resources. In industrial nations, economies depend chiefly on our ability to draw sustenance from a finite natural world—that is, from nonrenewable resources such as oil, natural gas, and minerals. Given trends in population growth, nonrenewable resource supplies, and demand, our continued existence will depend on our ability to shift from finite nonrenewable resources to renewable resources. This includes wind, hydropower, solar energy, forests, and crops. Today's challenge, then, is to refrain from destroying forests, grasslands, and other resources that can provide a continuous supply of food and materials, and to rebuild (restore) what has already been lost.

Unfortunately, heavy timber cutting in tropical and temperate forests, overhunting, and overfishing are destroying renewable resources at a rapid rate and, in the process, undercutting the resource base upon which the future of humanity depends. From the viewpoint of long-term sustainability, the destruction of these resources is

far more dangerous than the quick depletion of nonrenewable resources—oil and minerals—now under way.

Another key determinant of carrying capacity is the ability of the
environment to assimilate and degrade waste. In ecosystems, waste is
"handled" by dilution, decomposition, and recycling. Although
these natural mechanisms have been adequate throughout most of
human history, the advent of industrialization and rapid population
growth over the past 100 years have begun to overwhelm them. Today, for example, many nutrient cycles have been overpowered by
the effluents of our factories which, lest we not forget, turn out a
variety of products that support our way of life. The global carbon
cycle, which has for centuries ensured a constant concentration of
atmospheric carbon dioxide through the interaction of plants and animals, is one of the best examples of a natural system thrown out of
balance by human activity. Nitrate and phosphate pollution in our
oceans, lakes, and rivers, which result in algal blooms, also show
how the sheer volume of waste from human activity can overwhelm
nature.[7]

The advent of synthetic chemicals, moreover, has also sabotaged
nature's innate mechanism of waste control. Since naturally occurring bacteria do not contain the enzymes needed to decompose many
of these molecules, synthetic chemicals often persist in the environment. They may hang around for decades, entering food chains and
poisoning a wide range of species, or, as in the case of plastic, may
persist for centuries, providing a perpetual reminder of human care-
lessness.

On all three counts—food, resources, and pollution—the Earth's
carrying capacity is stretched thin and in places ripping. Living sustainably means learning to live within limits.

Why Have We Failed?

In the past two decades, governments the world over have generated
a blizzard of rules and regulations to protect the environment. Private
industries—some under duress, some on their own accord—have
taken many initiatives to reduce pollution and use resources more

efficiently. Tens of billions of dollars are spent each year on environmental protection by governments and private interests.

Unfortunately, most of the policies and actions that have resulted from this steady outpouring of legislative mandate and private initiative are fundamentally flawed. This is not to say that environmental protection efforts have been ineffective. Surely without them the condition of the environment would be much worse than it is today. My contention, however, is that many of our efforts are really nothing more than stopgap measures. Consider a few examples that point out the flaws in the environmental response.

Smokestack scrubbers have been a major element in pollution control. Installed on power plants, they reduce sulfur dioxide emissions, helping to decrease acid deposition. Unfortunately, scrubbers generate a highly toxic ash, which is typically dumped in landfills where it may leach into groundwater. Scrubbers are symptomatic of an end-of-pipe control strategy that merely shifts pollutants from one medium to another and has resulted in nothing more than an elaborate and costly toxic shell game.

In other cases, pollution control efforts mandated by legislative bodies have been too narrowly focused. Catalytic converters in automobiles, for example, have been added to reduce carbon monoxide and hydrocarbons in exhaust gases. But the catalytic converters in use today do nothing to reduce carbon dioxide emissions, a major contributor to global warming. Nor do they limit nitrogen oxides, a component of photochemical smog, which plagues most cities, and acid rain. Catalytic converters are successful in what they do, but they don't go far enough.

Finally, many improvements achieved by pollution control efforts are being offset by increases in population and consumption. Expensive sewage treatment plants, for instance, have helped to reduce pollution entering many rivers and streams in the United States, but increases in human population have resulted in an offsetting increase in nonpoint pollution—chemicals from lawns, streets, and so on—that frequently negate gains from sewage treatment plants.

The important point is that in most cases, environmental policy in the United States and elsewhere has been crafted to reduce environmental pollution and destruction, not to end the erosion of our life support system. That is to say, environmental policy was designed to clean up the mess a little, not to ensure a sustainable way of living and doing business on the planet. Policymakers have given little thought to the long-term sustainability of human activities.

If environmental policy is flawed, then, it is because the wrong questions were asked early on. Instead of "How can we reduce pollution or environmental destruction?" a more appropriate question might have been "What do we need to do to live sustainably on the planet?" As you shall see, this is a fundamentally different question that leads to fundamentally different strategies.

Besides ignoring the question of sustainability, the environmental response the world over has focused on the symptoms of the crisis, such as air pollution, hazardous waste, and deforestation, while overlooking the root causes. This approach to environmental protection is not unlike that of a physician who prescribes nitroglycerine for a patient suffering chest pains but who fails to address the issue of lifestyle changes—a better diet, a reduction of stress, an active exercise program, and so on.

Today, more than ever, environmental policy requires strategies that address the underlying causes of the crisis. Anything else is inadequate.

At least six factors lie at the root of the sustainability dilemma (see figure 1). First and foremost is overpopulation, a problem to which I have already alluded. It can be summed up as too many people reproducing too quickly.

The second root cause is excessive resource consumption. Overconsumption is particularly evident in the industrial world, and especially in North America, where energy, timber, food, water, and a host of other resources are consumed in a mad frenzy to support an economy predicated on rapid throughput—that is, excessive production and consumption.

The third root cause is linearity. In most countries, resources follow a straight line from mines to manufacturing plants to consumers to landfills. Enormous amounts of waste are generated along the way and at the end of line, and very little of it is recycled.

The fourth root cause is our addiction to fossil fuels. A host of environmental problems, including urban air pollution, global warming, acid deposition, oil pollution, and habitat destruction, stem from our heavy dependence on coal, oil, and natural gas. Few can deny that fact.

The fifth cause is inefficiency. Although there are encouraging improvements, most of us waste extraordinary amounts of energy, water, and other resources.

The sixth and final root cause of environmental deterioration is our values. As you shall see in the next chapter, most industrial countries are driven by a frontier mentality. With its view of the Earth as an unlimited supply of resources for human use, the frontier mentality places humans apart from nature and suggests that we are immune to natural laws. It also asserts that success stems from efforts to domi-

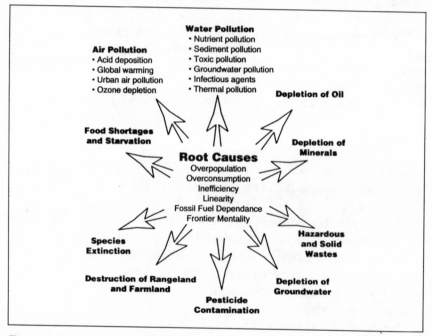

Figure 1: Root Causes of the Environmental Crisis. Progress toward sustainability requires efforts to address the underlying causes of the environmental crisis, not merely the symptoms. Root-level solutions are cross-cutting, solving a number of problems at once.

nate or control nature. A growing body of evidence argues otherwise.

Steering a sustainable course will require systemic changes that confront the underlying causes of the environmental crisis head on. Ironically, the best advice in this area comes not from political science but from biology, where studies of undisturbed ecosystems yield simple yet timely advice to those of us who will step back from the din of modern life and listen.

The lessons we can learn from nature comprise the biological principles of sustainability and form the foundation of this book. These principles explain why undisturbed ecosystems persist in the absence of human intervention or in the absence of major geological change, and they offer a ray of hope in a world being ravaged by the frontier ways.

Applying biological principles to human civilization may seem outlandish. It is not. In fact, it may be our only hope of weaving the human economy and the human way of life back into the economy of nature and ensuring our survival in the long run. Applying these principles to ethics, government, industry, and our own lives can help us end the destruction and heal the massive damage already wrought in the name of progress.

In Search of Instructions

Buckminster Fuller likened the Earth to a giant spaceship. Equipped with intricate recycling mechanisms that provide its inhabitants with a continuous supply of nutrients, this celestial ball of rock, ice, and water is home to at least three million species, although the number is probably more likely 30 to 50 million.

Over a brief time span, one species, *Homo sapiens,* has become the dominant life force on Earth. But the assumptions and instructions that have brought us to this place of domination are ruining the world we depend on. Standing on the brink of disaster, we ask ourselves what it is we need to do.

Clearly, we don't need an operator's manual, a set of engineering instructions that tell us how to manage the Earth; we need a *co-operator's* manual that teaches us how to fit into the cycles of nature's economy. Applying eco-logic to human endeavor, the co-operator's manual will teach us to live within the limits of the Earth's carrying capacity.

It has been said that people and nations behave wisely once they have exhausted all other alternatives. Many believe that the time for wisdom is at hand. If we are smart, we will follow the logic and laws of nature and remake our world according to its patterns, which have proven successful throughout evolutionary history. The Earth's wisdom is irrefutable. And, as a student of mine recently reminded me, nature is the master of sustainability.

2 Healing the Earth, Healing Ourselves: Toward a Sustainable Earth Ethic

Measure your health by your sympathy
with morning and spring.
                HENRY DAVID THOREAU

SOME TIME AGO, Father Guido Sarducci of Saturday Night Live fame invented the Five-Minute University. For a paltry $25, you can enroll in his school that, in five glorious minutes, teaches you everything you will remember two years after graduating from a traditional university. In his Introduction to Business course, you learn the central tenet of successful business: buy something and sell it for more than it cost you. In Introductory Economics, you learn the law of supply and demand, which says, if supply exceeds demand, you'll never make a buck, but if you can turn things around, you are certain to be wealthy.

Were it offered at the Five-Minute University, a course on the environment might be similarly distilled. Its lesson would be: we live in a world of rapid environmental change governed with remarkable shortsightedness.

A Tale of Two Graphs

The Five-Minute University environmental science lesson can be summarized in two graphs. The first graph is an exponential growth curve, or J curve (see figure 2). Put simply, exponential growth is a fixed-percentage growth. A familiar example is a bank account where the interest is automatically reinvested (added to the principal) so that interest is earned on interest.[1]

Exponential growth is deceptive. It begins slowly, producing a long flat line on the graph. During the early growth phase, the principal (or base amount) edges up almost imperceptibly.

As an example, imagine that your parents invested $1,000 in a 10 percent savings account on the day you were born. During the first

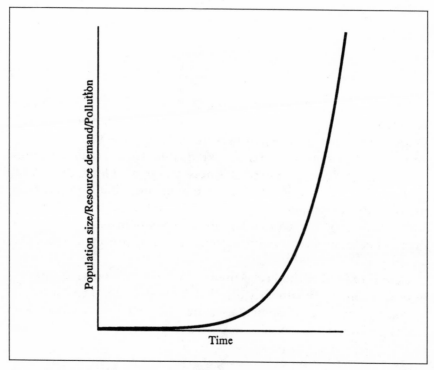

Figure 2: Space-Time Values and Exponential Growth. The graph on the left illustrates the nature of exponential growth of human population, resource demand, and pollution. The graph on the right depicts human values and indicates that most people are concerned with the immediate. Limited space-time values hinder long-range thinking and planning and do a disservice to humankind given the exponential growth of pollution, resource depletion, and population growth. Expanding our space-time values is essential to put society onto a sustainable course.

seven years of your life, the interest earned would increase your balance from $1,000 to $2,000. In the next seven years, you would earn an additional $2,000 in interest, bringing the account balance to $4,000. Every seven years, the account would double and, by the time you turned 42, the account would hold $64,000.

Suddenly, the curve rounds the bend and the balance begins to skyrocket. For instance, in the next seven years, your account would grow to $128,000. If you waited seven more years, the balance would reach $256,000. By the time you were 63, the account would have doubled again, giving you over $500,000. By the time you were 70, the account would be worth over one million dollars.

Looking at it another way, over the first 49 years, your account increased a measly $127,000—from $1,000 to $128,000. In the next 21 years it increased nearly $900,000, even though the rate of growth was constant over the entire period.

This example illustrates a key concept about exponential growth: once the base amount reaches a certain size, growth in absolute numbers accelerates, even though the growth rate remains the same. The reason is simple: when the base amount becomes extremely large, even small-percentage increases are substantial.

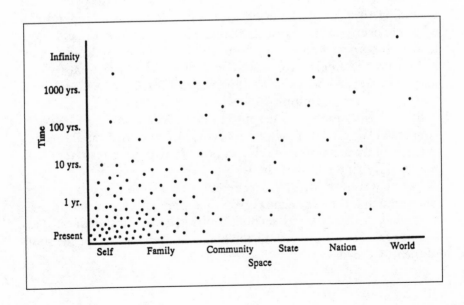

World population growth is another example of exponential growth. Today, the world population of 5.4 billion is increasing at a rate of about 1.8 percent a year, but we have rounded the bend of the J curve. Thus, while this rate of growth appears small, it translates into nearly 90 million new people each year.

Population growth is one of the key forces driving resource demand. The acquisition and use of resources, in turn, are largely responsible for pollution and environmental destruction. Thus, the exponential growth of the human population is often paralleled by exponential growth in resource demand, pollution, and environmental destruction. In fact, the J growth curve representing population growth could just as easily be the plot of species extinction, pollution, deforestation, desertification, or any of a dozen growing environmental problems. In other words, as the population goes, so goes the planet.

The second graph helps to illustrate why exponential growth is of such concern at this time in human history. This hypothetical graph plots space-time values—or human values related to space and time. The horizontal axis begins with the individual, then proceeds outward in order of decreasing concern: family, community, world, and universe. The vertical axis plots time, beginning with the present and extending to infinity. A dot on the graph represents an individual's ethical concern on any particular issue. The aggregation of dots in the lower left corner of the graph suggests what most of us already know to be true: that most people are concerned with the present (what's going to happen today and tomorrow), with themselves, and with their immediate community of friends and relatives.

Side by side, these two graphs tell it all. Mired in the immediate, concerned largely with their own needs, humans are catapulting forward, rapidly increasing in number, swiftly depleting resources, and unwittingly ripping apart the web of life in the process. Creating a sustainable way of life therefore requires two simultaneous changes: first, reducing the exponential growth in population, resource depletion, and pollution, and second, shifting space-time values. This chapter focuses on the second challenge, addressing one of the roots of the modern-day crisis.

The Frontier Mentality

Unfortunately, we live in a frontier society that acts as if the Earth were endowed with limitless resources. Founded on a narrow view of the role of humans in the world and an even narrower view of nature, the frontier mentality is characterized by three principles. First, the world is an unlimited supply of resources for human use— that is, there is always more, and it is all for us. Second, humans are apart from nature and are immune to her laws. Third, human prosperity and well-being flow out of efforts to master the environment.

· *The first tenet: There's always more and it is all for us.* The view of the world as an unlimited supply of resources for human use undoubtedly evolved in prehistoric time when human numbers were small and the Earth's resources did indeed appear inexhaustible. The massive increase in economic activity and the surge in population over the last 200 years, however, have brought us face to face with the limits of our finite world.

Despite growing evidence that the unbounded frontiers have vanished, many people still adhere to the idea of the Earth as an unlimited resource bank. In his nomination speech at the Republican National Convention in August 1988, New Jersey Governor Thomas Kean spoke of the dream of a bountiful American future. Senator Phil Graham proclaimed, "There is no limit to the future of the American people." Speaker after speaker echoed this sentiment. A month earlier at their convention, the Democrats expressed a similar view, suggesting that shortsightedness knows no party allegiance. Why not promise unlimited opportunity if there is an unlimited supply to draw on—and an election to win?

Many among us, especially those in positions of power and influence, have failed to grasp the fundamental reality of limits. In failing to do so, humanity has mortgaged the Earth's future and the future of our children, taking the goods and leaving the bill for them to pay.

· *The second tenet: Humans are apart from nature and are immune to its natural laws.* Since the agricultural revolution, humankind has sought to position itself outside the realm of nature. Albert Camus summed it up best when he wrote that "man is the only creature that refuses to be what he is." Ecologist Raymond Dasmann reminds us, however, that "a human apart from environment is an abstraction—in reality no such thing exists." Day after day, nature affirms Dasmann's assertion, flooding homes and farms built in floodplains, gobbling up vacation homes on the ever-shifting sands of barrier islands, and filling reservoirs with sediment washed from denuded hillsides. To think of ourselves outside of the realm of nature and immune to her laws is pure folly.

· *The third tenet: Human success stems from the control and domination of nature.* Throughout much of human history, people lived in a wilderness amidst real danger. Against nature our ancestors battled and won. The war against the world, however, reached its zenith in the industrial era. One of England's nineteenth-century poets, Matthew Arnold, observed: "Nature and man can never be fast friends. Fool, if thou canst not pass her, rest her slave!"

Believing in the need to reign supreme, humanity has become a conquering army. Today, thousands of dams tame the world's rivers. Millions of miles of highways cut through the once-thriving wilderness. Breakwalls restrain storm surges and levees hold back the floods. Resource "managers" manipulate wildlife, soils, fisheries, and forests like so many pieces in a board game.

Unfortunately, even though much of the natural world is under human subjugation, efforts to control continue unabated. Meanwhile, the results suggest that the war is over: we are no longer vanquishing nature, we are beating her to death. Ironically, many of the environmental problems we face today stem from our success at dominating the environment.

Nowhere is our attempt to control more evident than in "modern" agriculture. Today, many farmers increase crop production through the heavy use of chemical fertilizers, irrigation water, and pesticides, an approach that is riddled with problems. Experience with synthetic pesticides, for instance, shows that farmers are losing their battle against insect pests. Since World War II, chemical pesticide application has increased tenfold, while pest damage has doubled. Today, well over 450 species of insects are resistant to at least one chemical pesticide, and a dozen insect pests are resistant to every pesticide known to science. In the war against insects, the bugs have emerged the victors.

Modern agriculture creates other problems as well. One is that it tends to increase erosion and it robs the soil of vital nutrients, for example, organic matter. Organic matter acts as a kind of biological sponge, absorbing water and reducing erosion. It also feeds soil bacteria and fungi that are essential to the cycling of inorganic nutrients. Over time, efforts to increase productivity have ignored the need to retain this vital component.

Attempts to manipulate farmland endanger the life of our soil—and the future of agriculture. Euripides once said, "Chance fights ever on the side of the prudent." For humankind, prudence is cooperation, not domination.

Frontier Thinking, Frontier Living

Frontier ethics cloud our thinking. Projections of declining fossil fuel supplies, for instance, elicit little concern among residents of industrial countries steeped in the frontier tradition, because most people are convinced that there is always more. The belief in unlimited resources, as well as the faith that technology will allow us to extract even marginal deposits, prevents many among us from finding ways to use energy more efficiently and blocks efforts to tap the Earth's generous supply of renewable resources.

Frontierism also influences how we go about solving environmental problems. The solution to impending oil shortages, for example, is to step up our search for more, even if it means venturing into pristine Arctic or Antarctic wilderness.

Nowhere is the frontier mentality more evident than in the continued interest in macroengineering projects—gargantuan plans to supply water and energy to meet growing human needs. At a huge cost to the environment, we turn to new hydroelectric projects and power plants to satisfy demand. Until quite recently, little thought had been given to simple, cost-effective measures such as efficiency, which could supply us with enormous amounts of resources by tapping into our abundant waste. Efficiency wasn't an option in part because supplies seemed so vast.

In an article in *The Futurist*, MIT's Frank P. Davidson proposed a massive tree-planting effort to replace the Earth's vanishing tropical rain forests.[2] Typical of frontier strategists, Davidson suggests that replanting occur in the world's vast stretches of unused desert. All that's needed, he says, are water, which could be transported by extensive pipeline from distant sources, trace elements, also available from afar, and the political will. Besides ignoring the massive environmental consequences of altering the desert biome and of diverting billions of gallons of water from distant lakes and rivers, this proposal overlooks the elegant simplicity of one sustainable alternative: preventing the destruction of tropical rain forests in the first place.

Lest we forget, the frontier mentality also permeates our own lives, influencing personal decisions. As consumers we ask, "Can I afford to buy this?" not, " Can the planet afford it?" Because nearly all of the social and political institutions of the industrial world function to maintain the continued pursuit of unlimited economic growth, dislodging this pernicious notion from the human psyche will be no easy task.

The Low-Synergy Society

Over the years, the unquestioned acceptance of frontier ethics has spawned an industrial world that, while successful in many ways, is quickly wearing out its welcome on planet Earth. One of the most obvious outcomes of frontierism and one of the reasons our time on Earth may be limited is the loss of synergy. Synergy can be defined in social and ecological terms. In an ecological sense, it is a measure of cooperation between humanity and nature. A low-synergy society, for example, grows crops at the expense of soil, birds, and beneficial insects. It destroys the habitat of fish and wildlife, endangering our own food supply. It builds homes and offices in floodplains. It levels forests, replanting only a fraction of what is removed. It replaces diverse ecosystems with monocultures that are often highly vulnerable to infestation and disease.

In contrast, a high-synergy society satisfies the needs of people without subtracting from nature's capital. That is, it grows crops without depleting soils or poisoning wildlife and beneficial insects. It harvests trees while protecting forests, without clogging nearby streams and lakes with sediment eroded from the land. It designs communities that exist in harmony with nature—not in floodplains.

A high-synergy society does not merely prevent destruction from occurring, it seeks ways to enhance nature. That is, it reaps the benefits of the Earth but also promotes the long-term health and welfare of the ecosystem. A good example is an organic farm. Many organic farms increase the organic content of their soil by adding compost and by taking other measures. Over time, the land becomes more productive without a heavy investment in chemical fertilizers and pesticides.

In the social context, synergy is simply a measure of cooperation in a society. A low-synergy society like ours is characterized by bitter conflict over resources and often by inefficient use of those resources. Consider an example. Many Colorado communities have ventured into the mountains in search of water for farms, factories, and homes. Long convinced that the snow-capped Rockies could supply unlimited water, Colorado's Front Range communities have constructed a vast network of dams and canals to deliver this precious liquid. Today, in fact, 300 special water districts serve cities, towns, and farms on the semiarid plains of eastern Colorado. In the words of Colorado Governor Roy Romer, Coloradans have produced "a crazy-quilt system" of water supply. Because there seemed to be so much water available, little thought was given to sharing it or using it efficiently. In Colorado and elsewhere in the West, the lack of social synergy, spurred by frontier notions, has wrought unnecessary damage to mountain ecosystems from dams and diversions. It has destroyed precious riparian habitats and dried up streams vital to many species of wildlife.

An undisturbed ecosystem is a kind of high-synergy society. Life in an ecosystem exists without ravaging the soil, air, water, and plants. In undisturbed ecosystems, organisms evolve to fill vacant niches with a minimum of overlap. Where competition is great, evolution eliminates one or the other. The hawk and the owl, for example, evolved to fill niches that minimize their competition for food. The hawk hunts by day, feeding on animals active then, and the owl feeds by night, dining on those that frequent the darkness.

Billions of years of evolution have created an elegant synergy in nature. In a brief span of time, however, humans have begun to unravel the fabric of ecological synergy, replacing it with a system that is out of step with nature and torn by vigorous competition for limited resources.

Creating sustainability means greatly increasing the level of social and environmental synergy. That's possible only with a new value system that respects limits, offers a more equitable share to other species, recognizes our place in the natural order, and favors cooperation over domination.

Sustainable Ethics: The Directive Principles

In 1982 Paul Hawken, James Ogilvy, and Peter Schwartz of the Stanford Research Institute published a book called *Seven Tomorrows*.[3] It outlined seven possible scenarios for the 1980s and 1990s, ranging from a continuation of present trends ("the official future") to a scenario of despair and destruction ("chronic breakdown") to one that probably represents humankind's greatest hope for long-term survival ("living within our means"). In this last scenario, people consciously change their way of life and of doing business because they have come to realize that the old ways simply aren't working any more. What emerges is frugality, cooperation, and attention to community.

Living within the Earth's means is the bottom line in a sustainable society. But this goal will not be met without acquiring a new ethic, a sustainable ethic. The sustainable ethic holds that (1) the Earth has a limited supply of resources, and they're not all for human beings; (2) humans are a part of nature, not apart from it, and not immune to its laws; (3) success stems from efforts to cooperate with the forces of nature, not dominate them; and (4) all life depends on maintaining a healthy, well-functioning ecosystem.

Any ethical system that calls for human restraint will be viewed as subversive to those who persist in believing in unbounded material progress, unlimited growth, separateness, and control. Sustainable ethics, however, should be viewed more as an attempt to reestablish synergy in an era of unprecedented social and ecological disruption than as an effort to subvert. It seeks to redirect human progress, not stop it.

A sustainable society is based on two sets of principles. The first, the directive principles, provide broad guidelines for human behavior. The second, the operating principles, provide specific advice on ways to put into effect the directive principles. We begin with the directive principles.

· *The first principle of sustainable ethics: The Earth has a limited supply of resources for all species.* In 1948, the noted British astronomer Sir Frederick Hoyle predicted that "once a photograph of the Earth, taken from the outside, is available . . . a new idea as powerful as any in history will let loose." A few years later, the picture came to us and Hoyle's prediction came true. All of a sudden, it seemed, the world awakened to the fact that our home, which we had always seen as an inexhaustible supply of resources, is indeed finite.

The reality is being driven home even more vividly in the form of depleted fisheries, extinct species, vanishing rainforests, shortages of landfill space, and declining agricultural land. These rude facts of life suggest the first principle of sustainable ethics: the Earth has a limited supply of resources. There is not always more and it's not all for us.

The decline of resources underscores the practical importance of this principle and suggests the need for us to act much more responsibly. The most important step in building a sustainable society is to learn to use all resources—renewable and nonrenewable alike—more efficiently and to devote greater care to renewable resources, which could supply our future demands for fuel, food, and building materials ad infinitum if carefully managed.

The first principle of sustainable ethics also claims that the Earth's resources belong to all species, not just humans. Instead of defining resources as "materials from the Earth that provide for human needs," it boldly asserts that "the goods and services of nature's economy are here to benefit all species." This definition widens our ethical boundaries, making us not self-interested stewards of the planet but rather active participants in maintaining its health for all those who share in the wealth.

· *The second principle of sustainable ethics: Humans are a part of nature, subject to its laws.* In 1972, British scientist James Lovelock suggested that the Earth behaves as if it were a living organism.[4] Like an organism, the Earth contains many mechanisms that maintain relative constancy. This idea, called the Gaia hypothesis, is drawn principally from observations of the Earth's atmosphere. Lovelock noted that although the atmosphere contains a mixture of highly reactive gases, such as oxygen and methane, its composition has remained relatively stable for millions of years. Atmospheric stability, Lovelock notes, is controlled by homeostatic mechanisms akin to those in our bodies, which maintain constant levels of glucose, salts, and other nutrients. The Earth also maintains constant levels of salt in the ocean and oxygen in the atmosphere. And for years, the Earth has kept global temperature more or less constant.

All organisms, including humans, unwittingly help to ensure constant global conditions. Plants and algae, for example, absorb carbon dioxide from the air and release oxygen. Animals, in turn, consume this oxygen and produce carbon dioxide, which, as any high-school biology student knows, is used by plants to make organic molecules that feed the rest of the living world. This give and take helps to keep levels of oxygen and carbon dioxide in the Earth's atmosphere steady.

The Earth's organisms participate in dozens of similar cycles, each functioning to preserve constancy. Thus, all living things—including humans—are part of a single collective known as the biosphere, the Earth's equilibrator. One of the biggest mistakes we humans can make is to think of ourselves as independent from the biosphere. We are not. We are intricately tied to the rest of the living world.

Besides being part of the biosphere's nutrient cycles, and thus intricately linked to nature, we are also dependent on nature. Everything around us comes from our environment: the cereal we eat for breakfast, the plastic, the metal, the wood. Noted conservationist Norman Myers once pointed out that from our morning coffee to the evening nightcap, our lives are enriched by plants and animals that make this Earth their home. Nowhere is our dependence on nature more evident than in the air we breathe, for each year, plants and algae replenish half of the oxygen in the atmosphere. Without them, all animal life would quickly vanish from the Earth.

Nature is also a source of information. Reportedly, the idea for the steel I-beam used in constructing bridges and skyscrapers came from the giant water lily, which grows in the heart of the Amazon.[5]

From the rich world of living things we reap countless economic benefits: fish from the sea, medicines and other products from plants, genes to improve domestic crops and livestock, and so on. U.S. trout and salmon anglers annually spend an estimated five billion dollars on equipment, transportation, food, and lodging, while hunters and bird-watchers spend billions on tennis shoes, supplies, books, gasoline, food, and lodging. Billions of dollars pour into companies that cut timber or extract valuable medicines from plants. Each time we take a prescription drug, chances are one in two that it owes its origin to a wild plant. The commercial value of such drugs is around $15 billion per year in the United States and about $40 billion worldwide.

The U.S. Department of Agriculture estimates that each year, genes introduced into commercial crops in the United States from wild species yield over one billion dollars' worth of food. Similar gains can be documented for Canada, Great Britain, the Soviet Union, Australia, and other agricultural nations. About one-half of the increased productivity in corn over the past fifty years has resulted from "genetic transfusions" from wild relatives of corn found only in isolated regions.

Finally, plants, microorganisms, and animals provide innumerable services free of charge, day after day, including pest control, nutrient recycling, local and global climate control, and flood control.

Without question, our lives are tightly linked to nature, and at the very least, it is foolhardy to think of ourselves as independent of the biological world. Some would say it is suicidal.

It is equally dangerous to think of ourselves as immune from nature's laws. Almost 400 years ago, the poet Edmund Spenser said that nature is both a mother and a judge. She gives us life, but she insists on justice. If we destroy the ozone layer, for example, we destroy ourselves. If we pollute our groundwater, we pollute our bodies. If we deplete our forests, we foreclose on the entire human race.

· *The third principle of sustainable ethics: Our future depends on cooperation.* For years, humans have wrestled to make nature do their bidding. Today, it is becoming clear that domination often leads to desecration. Even though conflict will always exist between the human and the natural world, it cannot continue at the current pitch without a heavy cost to nature and to human survival. In a sense, humans have become victims of their own crimes. But if dominance and conflict are inappropriate, what is the proper relationship with nature?

Creating a sustainable future depends on finding ways to enhance cooperation. Today, more and more people and their governments are seeking a peace with the planet based on cooperation. Consider just one example. Over 50 years ago, Texas roadworkers began sowing wildflowers along the state's many highways.[6] Today, over 5,000 species of wildflowers grace the 70,000 miles of roadways. Wildflowers are uniquely adapted to the Texas climate. They eliminate the need for mowing, watering, and fertilizing of roadside grass, and they also seem to deter people from littering. Following this example from the Lone Star State, the Federal Highway Commission now requires 25 cents of every dollar spent on landscaping federally funded highways to be used to plant native species.

Cooperation is a tall order for a society whose sense of vulnerability to nature's forces has created a powerful urge to control. In a cooperative society, one that lives within the limits of nature, this sense of vulnerability should cause us to challenge our basic assumptions, says Lester Milbrath in *Envisioning a Sustainable Society*. Recurrent flooding, for example, usually leads to the construction of dams and levees, a frontierist strategy to gain control. In a sustainable society, it might lead to efforts to revegetate barren land within a watershed, or to protect watersheds from careless timber cutting and other activities that increase surface runoff and flooding. Cooperative solutions to flooding are, in the long run, far more effective and less costly.

· *The fourth principle of sustainability: All life depends on a healthy environment.* Maintaining the integrity and proper functioning of the global ecosystem should be a fundamental value in a sustainable society.[7] Since human health depends on a healthy environment, planet care is the ultimate form of self-care.[8] But a healthy ecosystem is paramount not just to our own survival but also to the survival of all species.

To ensure a healthy environment, we must act with compassion. The Iroquois Indians offer a model of great importance. When making decisions, the Iroquois gathered all of their people together to discuss proposed actions. Before commencing discussion, however, the chief instructed his people to consider the impact of present actions on the needs of the next seven generations. In so doing, they helped to ensure the welfare of future generations. Modern society can gain much by learning to do the same.

The Operating Principles of a Sustainable Society

The directive principles expand our time-space values. They suggest the restraint so vital to shifting the human economy and way of life onto a sustainable path. Arne Naess, a Norwegian philosopher, argues that "a philosophy, as articulated wisdom, has to be a synthesis of theory and practice."[9] In other words, a sustainable ethic requires more than a set of lofty guidelines; it requires action to manifest them. Without a set of operating principles, the directive principles outlined above become just so much useless philosophy. What actions are needed?

LESSONS FROM NATURE

Some years ago, I began a lengthy deliberation to address this issue. The central question in my quest was, Why is it that natural ecosystems persist for tens of thousands of years—perhaps longer, if undisturbed by humans—but human society seems to be on the path to self-destruction? In other words, why is it that nature sustains while humans destroy? Are there secrets we can learn from nature?

My examination revealed a simple answer. Ecosystems persist for four major reasons: conservation, recycling, renewable resource uses, and population control.[10] A deeper analysis has since suggested one additional factor—self-healing. Ecosystems persist because of natural mechanisms that restore damage from a variety of causes. Together, these five factors constitute the biological principles of sustainability. If we're wise, we'll make them the operating principles of society.

Conservation (efficiency). Nature's first secret is conservation, the efficient use of resources. The antithesis of conservation is waste. In nature, virtually nothing is wasted. For the most part, species use what they need. No more, no less. Mature ecosystems persist in part because they do not waste.

In sharp contrast, humans overeat, overconsume, waste, and deplete. Americans are by far the most wasteful of all Earth's people. The average New Yorker, for example, discards nearly four pounds of trash each day. In Rome, the average citizen throws out only one and a half pounds. As noted in chapter 1, Americans produce enough garbage to fill the Superdome two times every day of the year. Citizens in the developed world also produce enormous quantities of hazardous waste and waste vast amounts of energy. The Soviets, Americans, and Canadians are the most wasteful people on the globe, letting escape unused about half of consumed energy.

Energy-efficiency expert Amory Lovins of the Rocky Mountain Institute believes that the United States could cut nationwide consumption of electricity by 75 percent simply by replacing inefficient appliances, lighting, motors, and other electrical devices with efficient models. This change would not result in a decline in services one iota; we would still be doing the same things, just doing them much more efficiently.

Although many despair about the enormous waste of modern society, there is hope. Where there's waste, there's opportunity for vast improvement. By closing the loops, becoming more conscientious consumers, and using energy and other resources more efficiently, we can move toward a sustainable state.

Recycling. Nature's second strategy is recycling. In nature, everything is used over and over again. New generations are built from the old. Nutrients from soil, water, and air support plants. Plants feed herbivores. Herbivores are eaten by carnivores. The death and decay of these organisms return nutrients to the air, soil, and water, permitting the cycle of life to repeat itself ad infinitum.

As noted earlier, even humans are a part of the global recycling network. The carbon atoms in the protein in your muscle, for example, may have been part of the protein molecules of dinosaurs that lived 300 million years ago. These atoms will live on long after you are gone, becoming part of a continuous line of organisms you will never know. Even body cells recycle worn-out parts, grinding them up to generate new building materials.

Recycling not only eliminates waste but helps to guarantee sustainability. Human success, indeed our survival, depends on following a similar path. But modern society has not yet begun to fulfill the potential of recycling. In the United States, for example, only about 13 percent of trash was recycled in 1990. Although many other countries boast a higher rate of recycling, there's much room for improvement. Based on the model of Japan and on studies by other leaders in this area, Americans could recycle and compost an estimated 80 to 90 percent of all municipal garbage.

Renewable resources. Nature's third secret is the use of renewable resources. As I pointed out earlier, industrial society draws life from a vast array of nonrenewable substances: fossil fuels, chemicals derived from oil, synthetic fabrics, metals, and the like. Approximately 90 percent of the energy consumed in the United States comes from nonrenewable fossil fuels—oil, natural gas, and coal. Nuclear fission, another nonrenewable resource, supplies 7 percent of our energy needs, leaving only a tiny fraction from renewable sources such as the wind and the sun.

In the long run, human success depends on shifting more and more to renewable resources, as many as possible and as quickly as possible. Renewable resources are no panacea, however, for improperly managed timber cutting, farming, and ranching can result in severe erosion and marked decreases in the productive capacity of land. A sustainable society, therefore, depends not just on shifting to renewable resources but on the careful management of the Earth's regenerative gifts.

The potential of renewable resources is mind-boggling. Renewable energy resources could provide virtually all of the energy needed by the world. According to Robert L. San Martin of the U.S. Department of Energy, total global fossil fuel reserves (including all oil, oil shale, natural gas, and coal) are equivalent to about 8.8 trillion barrels worth of oil.[11] In contrast, renewable energy resources such as wind, solar, and hydroelectric could provide nearly ten times that amount each year. That is, renewable energy sources could provide the equivalent of 80 trillion barrels of oil *per year!*

Population control. The fourth secret of nature is population control. Through sometimes simple, and other times elaborate, systems nature controls its numbers. Predators control populations of their prey, assisting in holding numbers within the carrying capacity of the environment. In nature, competition and disease limit population. Inclement weather also helps hold populations in check. Whatever the mechanism, population control in ecosystems helps to ensure their preservation, sacrificing individuals for the sake of the whole.

Humans behave dangerously (and desperately) in this regard. To many of us in the West, individual human life is paramount. We fight to save starving children, but oppose funding to help support family planning in needy countries.[12] In 1965, Pope Paul espoused a view that holds sway today in certain circles. Speaking to the United Nations, he argued, "You must strive to multiply bread so that it suffices for the tables of mankind, and not, rather, favor an artificial control of birth, which would be irrational, in order to diminish the number of guests at the banquet of life." Paul Ehrlich, author of *The Population Bomb,* argues that we cannot let humanity be destroyed by a doctrine of individual freedom or by religious beliefs conceived in isolation from the biological facts of life. Reckless population policies have no place in nature.

Although many people side with Ehrlich, recognizing that unlimited population growth is the seed of our ruination, control efforts remain insufficient. Many women who want birth control in Third World countries can't get it. Making matters worse, at present nearly 35 percent of the world population is under the age of 15. Soon to enter their reproductive years, the world's children hold the fate of the world in their hands. Their decisions about childbearing are crucial. Conservation, recycling, renewable resource use, and restoration will have little effect unless this group acts responsibly.

Restoration. Self-healing is nature's fifth strategy. The ability of the human body to survive the many assaults it endures depends on innate mechanisms of repair. Without them most of us would bleed to death in early childhood. Nature also possesses a remarkable self-healing ability, which contributes significantly to sustainability. In the language of ecology, natural mechanisms of repair are known as ecological succession. A forest leveled by a tornado will regenerate over time if left alone as will grassland scorched by fire.

Unfortunately, in the relentless quest for material wealth humans have frequently altered conditions of ecosystems so drastically that natural restoration cannot occur. In the absence of human intervention, millions of acres of the Earth's surface have been laid barren. If humans are going to create a sustainable presence on the planet, we must restore ecosystems that have been grossly damaged over the course of human civilization. In all future resource extraction, restoration must be a primary objective.

It is one of the supreme ironies of modern living that at this point in human history, despite our impressive level of scientific knowledge and vast technological achievements, we must go back to nature for guidance to plot a sustainable course for our future. But let me hasten to add that however humbling this may be, building a sustainable society does not mean reverting to a primitive existence. The challenge is to find a new synthesis that melds the wisdom of nature with human institutions and technologies and lifestyles. The benefit of such an approach can be told in one world: survival.

The Core Values of a Sustainable Ethic

The principles outlined above, if enacted, would help create a kinder, gentler society. These principles are underpinned by two core values: ecological justice and social justice. Let's begin with the more familiar concept of social justice.

In an article in *Environment* magazine entitled "In Fairness to Future Generations," Edith Brown Weiss, a professor of international and environmental law at Georgetown University, proposed a doctrine called intergenerational equity. The doctrine of intergenerational equity asserts that humans hold their natural and cultural environment in common with all other generations, past, and future.[13] Each generation is a custodian of the planet for future generations; each

generation is a beneficiary of the previous generation's stewardship—
or a victim of its lack thereof. Thus each generation has certain rights
and obligations. We have, for instance, a right to use the Earth's resources for our benefit. However, because we hold the natural and
cultural environment in common with all past and future generations, we also have an obligation to take care of the gifts of the Earth.

Intergenerational equity assumes, and rightly so, that each generation wants both to inherit a planet in as good a condition as it was in
previous generations, and to have access to its resources. Intergenerational equity therefore calls on us to view the natural world much
like a priceless heirloom. Passed to us from previous generations, this
heirloom must be preserved and protected so that it can be delivered
to future generations in the same or better condition. Intergenerational equity requires a view of the human community as a partnership of generations.

Social justice is ensured in part by intergenerational equity, but social justice has an intragenerational dimension as well. Intragenerational equity insists that because all members of the present generation live on the same planet, they must act responsibly. Deforestation
in the African rain forest, for example, reduces rainfall as far north as
Europe. Carbon dioxide pollution released by the Western world will
surely influence the lives of Africans of the already-parched Sahel.
Intragenerational equity calls on each of us to take care of the Earth
not just for future generations but for all people, no matter how distant or unrelated.

Together, intergenerational and intragenerational equity constitute
social justice. They expand human concern into the future and across
a wider geographic range. Also needed, however, is a doctrine of ecological justice.

Ecological justice asserts that the Earth is held in common by all
species, past and present. Accordingly, we have an obligation to protect it, not just for people but for all living things. Ecological justice
is essential to the health of the planet and the health of human society.

How Do We Achieve Social and Ecological Justice?

One of the barriers to social justice is a lack of rights for future generations. In our society, Weiss points out, full rights belong only to

living human beings ("identifiable individuals"); the rights accorded to other species are even murkier.

Traditional legal bias ignores future generations because they have no identifiable individuals, and it ignores other species because they are not human. Weiss maintains, however, that the rights of future generations are not individual rights, they are class rights. Each generation is a class. In some cases, she argues, generational or class rights should supersede individual rights.

Do other species have class rights? Can those rights supersede the rights of humans? Why not? Who holds the original deed to the land, air, and water? Who trod the distant shore long before *Homo sapiens* arrived? In a legislature composed of a representative of all species, humans would have only one vote in 50 million.

Weiss argues that we need a formal mechanism to establish social justice. One way of incorporating the doctrine of intergenerational rights and obligations into our ethical framework, says Weiss, would be to make a formal declaration of them. Drawn up by the United Nations and endorsed by its members, this declaration would set forth the concept of intergenerational equity and outline its key tenets. It would also describe duties associated with the use and care of the Earth's resources.

Weiss is quick to point out that such a declaration would not be binding, but it could have profound effects on international law. Ultimately, it could shape the thinking of policymakers, government leaders, and business people, influencing many day-to-day decisions in business, government, and individual lives.

One tangible effort to promote intergenerational equity comes from the environmental movement. In September 1989, the National Wildlife Federation (NWF) presented a proposal to amend the U.S. Constitution, which stated: "Each person has the right to clean air, pure water, productive soils, and to the conservation of the natural, scenic, historic, recreational, aesthetic, and economic values of America's natural resources. There shall be no entitlement, public or private, competent to impair these rights. It is the responsibility of the United States and of the several states as public trustees to safeguard them for the present and for the benefit of posterity." This amendment would help not only to ensure social justice but also to protect the environment, thus serving ecological justice.[14] However, ecological justice would better be served if the document read: "*All living creatures* have a right to clean air, pure water, productive soils. *The world's natural resources are the common property of all living things,* including generations yet to come. As trustees of these resources, the United States government shall conserve and maintain them for *the benefit of all*." Like a UN declaration of intergenerational rights and responsibilities, a constitutional amendment could have a profound influence on judicial decisions and U.S. policy and actions.

The NWF proposal is one of several similar proposals now circulating in the United States.[15] Another complementary effort that could help promote social and ecological justice would be for each legislative body—state, national, and international—to elect one or two "representatives of the future," whose job it would be to ensure that the voice of those to come is heard over the din of partisan politics. These representatives would speak for other species as well. A formal representative of the future would be compelled to side with and argue for the needs of the unborn and of the various species, thus helping us end the pilferage of the Earth for immediate gain.

Solving Interspecies Conflicts

Ecological justice requires a balancing act, a weighing of the needs of the present against those of the future. This is made difficult by the lack of representation of all parties and by the disproportionate power of those in charge. To facilitate this elaborate balancing act, we need a set of rules that will fairly resolve conflicts between present generations and future.

First and foremost, it is essential to establish if there really is a conflict, or if it is just a presumed conflict based on human paranoia about losing something valuable. If there is a real conflict, then it is necessary to settle it justly. Philosopher Paul Taylor offers five principles for fair resolution of conflicts between humans and nature. These principles could also help us solve potential intergenerational conflicts. Taylor's principles are self-defense, proportionality, minimum wrong, distributive justice, and restitutive justice.[16]

THE PRINCIPLE OF SELF-DEFENSE

The principle of self-defense states that in any real conflict, it is permissible for an organism to defend itself if attacked by another organism. Under such conditions, it is acceptable for an organism to protect its own life by killing the attacker. Unfortunately, self-defense is often abused. For example, a female grizzly bear that mauls a back-country visitor who comes between her and her cubs will usually be killed. In this situation, human error or stupidity has little bearing on the bear's future—the principle of self-defense has clearly been distorted.

Acts of self-defense may also be motivated by paranoia. In many parts of the world, people kill snakes out of fear. If the truth be known, fatal snake bites are rare, and people are rarely bitten unless they fail to heed warnings.

Economic self-defense is often used to justify ecologically destructive behavior. Ranchers, for example, often slaughter predators like coyotes to defend their livelihood. Numerous studies, however, show that there are ways to live in harmony with coyotes and other predators. The state of Kansas, for example, has a healthy coyote population and a healthy sheep population; only troublesome coyotes are killed. Sheep ranchers can introduce guard dogs or llamas to their herds to reduce coyote predation. The annual cost of a good sheep-dog is about the cost of one ewe.

Self-defense is permissible, as long as it's honest.

THE PRINCIPLE OF PROPORTIONALITY

The principle of proportionality applies in situations in which non-vital human desires conflict with vital needs of other organisms. Cutting tropical rain forests to make disposable chopsticks for the Japanese fast-food market is a good example of a nonvital activity conflicting with vital needs of others. Still another is the slaughter of African rhinos to acquire horns used to make aphrodisiac for Chinese men.

The principle of proportionality helps temper the impulse to treat other organisms and ecosystems as instruments to serve human fancy. This principle gives greater weight to the essential needs of an organism than to the nonvital needs of a human.

THE PRINCIPLE OF MINIMUM WRONG

The principle of minimum wrong or harm asserts that if you must do something, incur the least damage. Put another way, it means finding the least damaging way of meeting human needs. In tropical rain forests that means replanting forests and creating a sustainable timber harvest instead of just cutting down trees and moving on.

Minimum wrong asks us to find the least polluting forms of energy. Energy efficiency measures and some economical solar energy options, for example, would provide us with energy while doing minimum harm to the environment. To feed the human population, the principle of minimum wrong suggests vegetarianism, because it is the most efficient way to provide food. It uses less land, requires less water, and demands less energy than a meat diet. Finally, for urban transportation, the principle of minimum wrong suggests mass transit in preference to private automobiles, because it uses far fewer resources.

THE PRINCIPLE OF DISTRIBUTIVE JUSTICE

The principle of distributive justice is, in some ways, related to the principle of minimum wrong. It recommends choosing options that free up resources for other people and wild species. By meeting our needs more efficiently, we leave more for others. By recycling wood and wood products and by building smaller homes, for example, we reduce timber cutting, leaving more forest for other species. Efforts to reduce population growth also represent a kind of distributive justice, for they free up resources for wildlife.

The principles of distributive justice and minimum harm underlie one of the first rules of living sustainably on the planet—notably, that a license for resource acquisition is not granted to those who live inefficiently. If you're driving a car with a leaky gas tank, wisdom would suggest plugging up the leak rather than making frequent stops to gas up. That's not a bad metaphor for life.

The Principle of Restitutive Justice

The final principle, that of restitutive justice, says that humans must pay restitution for past wrongs. According to the principle of restitutive justice, remaining old-growth forests in the Pacific Northwest should be preserved as special compensation to the spotted owls and other species that have lost so much over the years. Restitutive justice requires that we restore the peregrine falcon population and save the grizzly and wolf. Restitutive justice suggests that we've been living rent free on the planet for too long. The time to pay is now.

3 Healing the Earth, Healing Ourselves: Developing the Ecological Self

It is not enough to have a handful of heros, what we need are generations of responsible people.

RICHARD D. LAMM

RESIDENTS OF SOUTHERN INDIA devised an ingenious device to capture monkeys. Consisting of a hollow coconut filled with rice and chained to a tree, the trap operated on a deceptively simple principle: the hole drilled in the shell was large enough for a monkey to insert its hand, but too small to extract it once it had clutched a handful of rice. Instead of letting go of its booty the monkey would hold on tenaciously, only to be captured in a net cast by villagers. In a sense, the monkey was captured because of its own refusal to let go.

Modern society is trapped in a similar predicament. Despite growing signs of environmental deterioration, we cling tenaciously to an unsustainable way of life and an unsustainable way of thinking, frontier ethics. Releasing ourselves from the monkey trap requires a new world view. This chapter furthers the discussion of this new world view and points out what a sustainable ethic requires of us, how we can "create" it, and the many benefits of adopting it. We begin with an overview of what sustainable ethics requires of each of us.

The Ecocentric View

In general, sustainable ethics calls for a much deeper understanding of nature and a much wider appreciation and respect for it. To adherents of sustainable ethics, nature is not a stage upon which all human activity takes place, but rather the fabric into which human life is woven. This ethics, therefore, contrasts sharply with the prevalent frontierist view of nature as a source of human wealth and the repository of our waste. It stands in sharp contrast to frontier thinking because it places humans within the realm of nature, rather than the hub of a wheel with everything else—birds, mammals, insects, plants—lying outside of our narrow ethical range. As such, sustainable ethics is a philosophy of inclusion and participation, markedly different from the philosophy of alienation and domination of frontierism.

Unlike frontier ethics, in which nature has worth only insofar as it serves us, sustainable ethics bestows intrinsic value on nature. It is not wrong to decimate tropical forests and millions of species because we rid ourselves of the forests' free service; it is wrong because it harms living things that have a right to live. This alternative vision of humankind's place in the biosphere is part of a rich body of thought sometimes referred to as ecological philosophy, an ideology that is clearly ecocentric or Earth-centered.

Though foreign to the thinking of mainstream American society, ecocentrism is not a revolutionary idea. It has been an integral part of the philosophy of Native Americans, Zen Buddhists, Taoists, and even some pre-Socratic Greek societies. For thousands of years, in fact, mystics have spoken of the unity of all things, living and nonliving. Chuang-Tzu, writing over 2,000 years ago, proclaimed, "I and all things in the universe are one."

Ecocentricity is seen in the rituals and ceremonies of many hunting and gathering Indian societies that revered the animals that gave them life. Ecocentricity is found in the writings of the Dutch philosopher Spinoza.[1] It is evident in the written works of some American transcendentalists, including Ralph Waldo Emerson and Henry David Thoreau. More recently, it appears in the poems and essays of such luminaries as John Muir, D. H. Lawrence, Aldous Huxley, Robinson Jeffers, Gary Snyder, Aldo Leopold, and Rachael Carson.

Today, ecological philosophy lives on in a movement called deep ecology. The deep ecology movement urges us to respect the Earth and all living things and to act on this deep and abiding respect. It emphasizes the inherent right of all species to live. Deep ecology calls on us to find a way of life that is ecologically sustainable. It requires a long-term, holistic outlook and suggests that humane treatment of the planet means reducing the size of the human population to let other species live.

Unquestionably, deep ecology prescribes a major realignment in our thinking. Many times, it puts ecological interests above economic self-interest, and it stresses the importance of looking at the long-term needs of all species. As such, it often finds itself on the side of nature.

The Case for an Ecological Philosophy

In the spring of 1989, a professor of resource economics came to my office at the University of Washington where I was teaching a course on environmental science. He had recently read an article of mine on sustainable ethics and was puzzled by my claim that other living things had inherent rights. He wanted to know how this notion could be justified.

In an effort to rationalize my position, I talked first about all the things we are granted from nature, using the human-centered (utilitarian) argument for preserving species. I went on to talk about children and how they seem to value other living things without being told to. As children get older, however, I noted that their compassion for other species often wanes. In geography and history classes, they learn that nature is a source of products for the use of human society. In the process, they frequently lose their inherent sense of the inherent right of other living things to exist. That is to say, their ethical realm shrinks as their view of nature becomes more pragmatic.

When I finished, I realized I hadn't gotten through to my colleague. He seemed as convinced as ever that only humans have rights, and offered elaborate proof. At that point, though, in a moment of melodrama, I put my hand to my heart and said, "The answer won't be found in your head, it will be found elsewhere." Ethics do not always emanate from the head.

Efforts to devise an elaborate proof to validate ecological philosophy will only end in frustration and confusion. Clearly, no logical arguments are available to explain why other species should be granted rights. As author and deep ecologist Bill Devall points out, in the context of mainstream Western society, ecological philosophy cannot be completely justified. On the surface, in fact, ecological philosophy appears to contravene human interests.

In human society, values often spring from human priorities and needs. The frontier ethic is a fine example. Largely a utilitarian ethic that serves immediate human interests, the frontier ethic lays claim to the Earth's resources, essentially declaring the Earth a garden for exclusive human use. It grants rights to one species—the human rule maker—and gives heed to no other. It is important to remember, however, that the frontier ethic is merely a mental construct albeit so deeply ingrained in our thinking that many of us think it inviolate. We could just as easily believe that other species have rights—although it wouldn't be as self-serving.

It is also important to point out that modern ethics are not entirely self-serving. The ethics that governs the way we treat one another, for instance, is based on a humanitarian concern—interest in treating one another equitably. Most of us don't rob and murder others, because we view these actions as unjust. Upon closer examination, though, even humanitarian-based components of our ethical system serve our society—for example, by fostering social order.

In frontier ethics there is little, if any, compassion for the natural world. In the long term, frontier ethics does not serve society well. Thus, what *appears* utilitarian is actually counterproductive to our own well being.

In contrast, sustainable ethics calls on us to have a "humanitarian" view of nature. While this may *appear* counterproductive or nonutilitarian, it is truly not. Treating nature equitably will pay enormous dividends to present and future generations.

Broadening the Self

Deep ecology calls for unity with nature. Arne Naess, whom many consider the father of that movement, notes that a oneness with nature arises from a conscious process of broadening the self. Extending the boundaries of what we call I often occurs naturally as we mature, that is, discover connections with family, friends, community, and Earth.[2] In the process, the interests and well being of others (including the Earth's creatures) begin to coincide with the interests of the self.

Broadening the self is really a process of widening our individual ethical realm—expanding our space-time values. "Higher unities," writes Naess, "are created through circles of friends, local communities, tribes, compatriots, races, humanity, life, and, ultimately . . . unity with the world."

Developing the Ecological Self

One of the first steps in developing an ecological consciousness is to explore the concept of the ecological self, that which identifies with a broader community—the Earth and all living things. During this intellectual and spiritual exploration, one comes to question the boundaries that artificially exclude humans from the larger whole. One questions the conventional notion of individual responsibility, seeing that it reaches far beyond home and family and encompasses the entire living Earth.

When we identify with nature, something interesting happens. First, we see that it is actually in our own interest to use resources efficiently, to recycle, to tap renewable resources, to restore damaged ecosystems, and to limit family size. These actions become a way of caring for the self. We aren't sacrificing for some abstract idea. In fact, we don't give up at all; we end up giving *to*—the Earth, to fellow species, to future generations, and of course to ourselves. If our definition of self embraces other beings and the Earth, what we do for the Earth we do for ourselves. If we endanger the Earth, we endanger ourselves.

Developing the ecological self requires study, thought, and participation in nature.[3] Study ecology and learn the lessons nature whispers to us. Participate by getting out of the city and tramping through the mountains for a day or many days, weeks, months, if need be. Get in touch with the region in which you live. Learn the rivers, the trees, the birds, and the landforms. Learn to watch the subtle changes of the seasons. Read ecological poetry and listen to the music of Dana Lyons and Raffi, among others.[4] Several modern poets like Gary Snyder can assist you on your journey. A New Mexico poet who calls himself Lone Wolf notes that the ecological poet can stimulate our hearts to new ways of seeing. He says that such poets can drop a monkey wrench into the mind, halting the gears of preconception and alleged reality long enough for a sense of the oneness with all living things to emerge and take hold.

Cultivating the ecological self means blending into the landscape. In so doing, we develop a sense of union and empathy with other beings.

PUTTING ETHICS INTO ACTION

Sustainability was the original economy of our species, writes William Ruckelshaus in an article in *Scientific American*.[5] People lived a sustainable lifestyle because they had to. If they did not, he says, they answered to nature, either starving or being forced to migrate to new territory. During the agricultural and industrial revolutions sustainability was discarded for a new way of life, one that has pushed us to the brink of ecological ruin and made it imperative to establish new patterns of living.

Returning to the sustainable lifestyle of our ancestors is not the goal of the sustainability movement. Creating a sustainable consciousness suitable to the modern era is. But we must also put into practice our beliefs—stop talking about the environment and start acting in ways that manifest our new world view.

Individual acts of kindness. In 1990 Earth Day 20 inspired a rash of books, each listing ways individuals can help save the planet—installing energy-efficient light bulbs, driving the speed limit, walking or bicycling instead of driving to the convenience store, and a variety of other measures.[6] Surely no single act will save the planet, but the actions of each of us combined with those of millions of others could dramatically reduce our devastating impact on the environment and improve our chances of living sustainably. As such, individual actions are the seeds of global change.

Individual action and responsibility may seem futile given the size and complexity of the human economy and of the environmental crisis. I want to be very clear about this: I'm not proposing that individual actions are *the* answer, but that they must be part of any strategy for sustainability.

Historically, individual responsibility and action have been excluded from efforts aimed at protecting the Earth. Many environmental groups, for instance, labored long and hard over the past two decades to pass legislation to further their goals, or sued in court to compel environmentally friendly behavior.[7] Few groups attempted to inspire individual action, encouraging citizens and businesses to act responsibly. Recent efforts to inspire individual action and responsibility fall far short of what is needed.

Developing the ecological self requires consistency of thought and action. Today, however, too many people think globally, but act vocally. Put another way, many profess respect for nature, but act otherwise.

For guidance on ecologically responsible living, the many how to save the planet books are a must. Readers often complain, however, that they get lost in the sheer number of ideas and are overwhelmed by the task. As an antidote to this problem, I suggest readers remember the five operating principles of a sustainable ethic: conservation, recycling, renewable resources, restoration, and population control. Let these be a guide for all human action.

Becoming a conscientious consumer. One way of putting sustainable ethics into action is to become a conscientious consumer. In 1977, the Simple Living Collective of San Francisco proposed four questions to help us become more conscientious consumers:

1. Does what I own or buy promote self-reliance and involvement, or does it induce passivity and dependence? Do I buy a chainsaw instead of a hand saw, a power broom instead of a hand-held broom?

2. Does my buying satisfy my needs, or do I buy much that serves no real need? Do I buy to boost a deflated ego?

3. How are my present job and lifestyle dependent upon installment payments, maintenance, and repair costs? If I'm working hard to keep up with payments, I'm often not enjoying life.

4. Do I consider the impact of my consumption on other people and on the Earth?

Extracting oneself from the culture of mass consumption. Becoming a conscientious consumer is fraught with difficulty because it goes against the mainstream of our society and requires fending off the constant barrage of advertisements on television, in magazines, and in newspapers. The modern advertising blitz fuels excessive consumption principally by undermining self-confidence and promising false hope. If we use a certain toothpaste, advertisers imply, we will have a brighter, more appealing smile. If we wear a certain pair of jeans we will be more popular. If we exercise at a certain health club we will melt away the flab and become instantly appealing. The message behind the advertising is that we are all fundamentally inadequate. That is, there is something keeping us from achieving love, happiness, wealth, pleasure, and power. A weak ego falls victim to rapacious campaigns, from which the economy presumably benefits.

Modern advertising also promises personal success through consumption. If we buy one type of computer, for example, our businesses will improve. If we use a particular airline, we will meet up with potential customers that will make us rich beyond our dreams. Riches equal success. Success and happiness go hand in hand.

The culture of mass consumption, says Andrew Bard Schmookler, has developed around a core of unfulfilled longing.[8] The goods we buy are supposed to induce the states of consciousness we desire— such as happiness—but the more we buy to offset personal inadequacy the more damage we cause to the environment. Soon we find that the new clothes and cars and electric gadgets that promised personal salvation did not change much. In fact, many of the things we purchased to bolster our egos end up in the dump, along with our feelings. Still clinging to hope, we remain willing to try another round. The broken promise of each purchase, says Schmookler, leads to new yearnings.

The pursuit of happiness through material wealth is like trying to fill a sieve. Instead of looking for more materials to pour through the sieve, we would be better served by looking for ways to fill the holes. Healing the self is essential to healing the Earth.

It is not necessary to have expensive houses, cars, and clothing to live well. Virtually all that's necessary is a sound mind and food, shelter, friends, community, and nature. A simple yet elegant life can be rich and rewarding. Conversation and personal activities can enrich our lives, replacing the mesmerizing glare of television and videos. A life lived in conscious pursuit of relative simplicity is called voluntary simplicity and is the subject of a book of the same title by Duane Elgin. What Elgin makes clear is that voluntary simplicity is not to be viewed as a life of self-denial but rather a sane and manageable way of living that shows consideration for the needs of other creatures.

When individuals begin to practice sustainable ethics, they move from an abstract to a practical world. Here they make choices with very real consequences, choices that affect their own lives and the lives of countless other species. Experience, however, shows that developing an environmentally sustainable lifestyle may take years. Most individuals will act in contradictory ways at first—fighting to save forests but not recycling paper, or recycling but driving a gas-guzzling car. The important goal is to live consistently with your values, to strive to align principles and actions. Gandhi would remind us that if we take care of the means, the end will take care of itself.

Pursuing work consistent with one's principles. Another challenge that faces those of us who want to live consistently with our values is choosing the right livelihood, that is, an occupation that is environmentally and socially constructive—for example, finding employment in a company that is developing energy-efficient technologies or renewable resources. It means working for companies with good social and environmental records. If these options are not possible, an individual can promote sustainable practices within the company in which he or she is employed.

Becoming an earth-wise investor. Right actions also include right investments—choosing environmentally and socially conscious companies. Environmental investing is one way individuals can vote in the marketplace for companies that care about the Earth. One of the best avenues is to invest in mutual funds such as the New Alternatives Fund, the Calvert Social Investment Fund, the Pax World Fund, and others that select businesses with good environmental records. Of these, the New Alternatives Fund stands out because it invests in companies that work on alternative energy sources, energy conservation, recycling, and pollution cleanup—companies that are helping to pave the way to a sustainable society.

Environmental investing can be quite lucrative. Some funds earn as much as 12 to 16 percent per year. Today, approximately $500 billion of investments is screened to avoid companies that make weapons, are involved in nuclear power, or don't abide by fair employment practices, notes Worldwatch Institute's Cynthia Pollock Shea.[9]

In closing, the late (sometimes great) Edward Abbey once said that, "Sentiment without action is the ruin of the soul." Unless we heal our souls, all progress toward healing the Earth will be crushed. It won't be an easy task. Changing the mindset of the world's people will very likely make the moon landing seem like a weekend fix-it job.

Replacing the outmoded frontier ethic so prevalent today will require a continuation of the revolutionary rethinking and reshaping of human values fostered, in part, by the present-day crisis and by far-seeing environmental educators, writers, poets, musicians, politicians, business people, and citizens. If widespread and implemented quickly, this effort, which seeks to confront one of the root causes of unsustainability, could translate into a dramatic change in government that is essential to the task of building a sustainable society.

4 Commerce with a Conscience: Reshaping the Human Economy

Be great in act, as you have been in thought.

WILLIAM SHAKESPEARE

IN 1989, GENERAL ELECTRIC Corporation secured a $150 million loan from the U.S. Overseas Private Investment Corporation to refurbish 13 incandescent light bulb factories in Hungary, a country recently out from under the crippling rule of communism. On the surface, this effort may seem economically and socially praiseworthy, but from an environmental and economic standpoint it leaves a great deal to be desired. Why?

According to Representative Claudine Schneider, the $150 million could have been used to build 20 new compact-fluorescent bulb factories.[1] Compact fluorescent light bulbs screw into ordinary light fixtures and use only about one-fourth of the energy of a standard incandescent bulb. A 13-watt compact fluorescent bulb produces the same amount of light as a standard 60-watt incandescent. Over its lifetime, a high-efficiency compact fluorescent will save a homeowner $30 to $50—the bulb is not only inexpensive to operate, it pays for itself in reduced energy costs.[2]

High-efficiency light bulbs benefit the environment by reducing the demand for electricity generated from oil, coal, natural gas, and uranium. Reducing the consumption of these fuels, in turn, has a ripple effect on the environment, lessening damage caused along the production/consumption cycle, starting with power plants and extending back to the mines. According to Amory Lovins of the Rocky

Mountain Institute, widespread use of high-efficiency light bulbs in the United States could eliminate the need for 100 to 120 large (1,000 megawatt) power plants, significantly reducing air pollution, water pollution, and waste.[3] In addition, he notes, the widespread use of energy-efficient compact fluorescents would save American consumers about $90 billion a year.

In Hungary, investing the $150 million in compact-light bulb factories would have prevented the need for future investments in new power plants that will eventually cost the country an estimated $10 billion. From a long-term economic and environmental viewpoint, then, the General Electric project is an economic blunder. This example, of course, is not an isolated case of economic shortsightedness. It is just one of many myopic decisions made every day of the year in the board rooms of the world's corporations, decisions that in their sum have committed us to an unsustainable path of development. Like a ship bound for distant lands, our economy has been steered off course by minor navigational errors. Over time, the sum of these small mistakes has steered us way off course. If we're going to get back on course, some major corrections are needed.

This chapter looks at the human economy—what's wrong with it from an environmental point of view and, perhaps more important, how the economy can become more compatible with the environment. Let me be clear from the outset that my critique is not a damnation of capitalism or a call to dismantle our economic system. My purpose is not to criticize those who partake in the economy, which is most of us. Rather, I would like to point out some serious problems and outline ways to bring the human economy back in line with the economy of nature.

What Is Wrong with the Economy?

When viewed through the lens of sustainability, the human economy reveals four major flaws: it's shortsighted, it's obsessed with growth, it promotes dependency, and it tends to exploit people and the environment.

ECONOMIC SHORTSIGHTEDNESS

The science of economics concerns itself with the production, distribution, and consumption of goods and services. Modern economics is largely governed by the law of supply and demand, which describes the interplay of three factors: supply, demand, and price. Basically, the law of supply and demand says that the price of products or services results from the interaction of two factors, supply and demand. Reduced to its basics, the law says that when demand for a good or service outstrips the supply, prices rise, and when the supply exceeds demand, prices fall.[4] Supply and demand are therefore the principal determinants of price in a free-market system.

Price plays an important role in the demand side of the economic calculus, and here is where the law of supply and demand manifests its weaknesses. The law says that as the price of a commodity or service rises, the market will generally respond by increasing the supply. Rising prices generally stimulate manufacturers to produce more goods. Rising prices for minerals and timber compel mining and timber companies to extract more minerals and cut more trees. Many economists, politicians, and consumers, however, put blind faith in the power of price to stimulate supply indefinitely. Most of us are convinced that as supplies run low and prices rise, companies will find more supplies or will develop suitable substitutes. Our faith in supply and demand would be justified if the world had unlimited resources. Unfortunately, it does not.

The fundamental weakness of the law of supply and demand, in other words, is its blindness to resource limits. Proponents of supply and demand fail to take into account long-term depletion of resources and are convinced that rising prices will result in a successful search for substitutes, permitting society to continue its endless growth in production and consumption.

Unfortunately, rising prices cannot expand the supply of nonrenewable resources indefinitely. Nor can rising prices expand the supply of renewable resources far beyond nature's ability to regenerate. Like a machine with a faulty part, sooner or later the economy is bound to malfunction. It is just a matter of time.

The challenge today is to build an economy with vision, an economy that does not grind up nature to achieve short-term gains. One of the most important tasks is to modify supply and demand economics to reflect the finite nature of many resources.

THE SUCCESS OF OUR ECONOMY IS MEASURED BY GROWTH

In July 1990, the evening news reported on the economic health of the United States. According to the report, the states fit into four groups based on their economic growth. The first group of states was reported to be doing well economically, which is to say they were experiencing robust growth. The second group of states was doing less well but was still deemed healthy: their economies were growing slowly. The third group was more or less stable, and the fourth was doing poorly, experiencing a phenomenon paradoxically called negative growth.

Measuring the health of a state's or nation's economy by assessing its economic growth is like measuring your well-being by your heart rate. It is simply not enough.

A nation's economic health is assessed by the growth of the gross national product or GNP, the value of all the goods and services of the nation. The GNP is a nation's economic heartbeat. Even a superficial analysis suggests that the GNP is a less than satisfactory measure of economic health. Why? The GNP of many countries is inflated and sometimes grossly distorted by the inclusion of negative economic factors. For example, the cost of cleaning up an oil spill, or of health care for people dying from lung cancer resulting from urban pollution, is included as a contribution to U.S. economic output when, in fact, it should be listed as a cost.

The GNP fails to distinguish between expenditures that advance society—for example, the publishing of a book—and expenditures like the cleanup of the Exxon Valdez, which, while important, could have been avoided.

Separating the "good" economic output from the "bad" shows that much of America's increase in GNP in recent years has resulted from a whole host of economic negatives—pollution control, cleanup, and cancer.[5] A good example of this on a statewide scale was the Exxon Valdez oil spill and subsequent cleanup, an effort that greatly boosted Alaska's economic output, or gross domestic product in 1989 and 1990. In economic terms, 1989 and 1990 were banner years. Standing on the shores of Prince William Sound today, however, one might come to a far different conclusion.

Another example worth noting is a study by economist Christian Leipert showing that between 1970 and 1985, West Germany's spending to protect or restore the environment increased from 5 percent to 10 percent of its GNP.[6] Measures to check environmental deterioration were a significant contribution to economic welfare.

Growth in the GNP as a single measure of economic welfare also fails to take into account accumulated wealth—the goods people in a society have amassed over the years. That is, by measuring our economic success strictly in terms of its *growth* in GNP, we're ignoring present prosperity.

GNP also pays no attention to the distribution of wealth in a society, a fact that has important implications in Third World development. As you shall see in chapter 6, many projects that improve the GNP of a nation fail to improve the lives of the masses they were designed to help. And in developed countries, the GNP hides frightening inequities. In the United States, for example, a country deemed rich by GNP standards, one-fifth of all children live in poverty and 37 million have no health insurance.[7] Looking at the GNP alone, one would be compelled to think that all was well within America's borders.

The nearly singular focus on growth in GNP as a measure of economic success has another downside: over time, residents of industrial nations have become addicted to growth. We have become economic junkies, dependent on the rise and fall of the stock market. And what is more, we have imposed the growth imperative on Third World countries.

With the growth-is-essential logic so deeply imbedded in our thinking, modern society has evolved a rather lopsided view of human progress. In many ways, we are seized by economic-growth paranoia. Racing into the future, we see only one viable option: to produce and consume more and more, regardless of the cost to the planet or to future generations. Few among us recognize that progress based on continued economic growth is incompatible with nature's economy. In nature, unlimited growth occurs only in the cancer cell, which reproduces uncontrollably before killing its host.

In his book *Poverty of Affluence,* Paul Wachtel observes that we see growth as an omnipresent symbol of good. It is very difficult for us to accept limits to growth because they imply stagnation. Contentment, says Wachtel, suggests complacency. The main challenge today is to find a way to end this dangerous obsession, a process that will require new measures of economic success.

Our Economic System Promotes Dependency

The current economic system also creates and fosters dependency between individuals, localities, and nations. Economic dependency began during the agricultural revolution. During that time, rising productivity resulting from technological advances such as the plow reduced the demand for human labor on farms. Farm laborers migrated to cities and towns where they took up trades. Thus, people who once consumed the food they produced suddenly became dependent on farmers. Tradespeople became more and more dependent on one another for goods and services.

Today, the modern consumer is dependent on a legion of specialists, so many, in fact, that most of us have become virtually helpless in the conduct of our affairs. Lawyers untangle legal affairs; accountants keep our books; an army of technicians repair our appliances, computers, and TVs; teachers educate our children.

More relevant to the environment, economic interdependence separates producers from consumers, blinding us not only to the source of human wealth, the Earth, but to the massive environmental cost of satisfying our seemingly endless wants. The partitioning of producers and consumers fosters a process of decision making where one's ability to pay becomes the chief determinant in purchasing decisions; little thought is given to the hidden environmental costs of individual purchases.

Nations are highly dependent on one another for energy, minerals, food, and many other resources, but international reliance does not come without a cost. The OPEC oil embargo in the early 1970s illustrated this point well. Rising prices resulted in crippling inflation, which brought the industrial world to its knees.

Besides separating producers from consumers, economic interdependence has allowed regional populations to grow beyond the carrying capacity of the environment. Water imports to the southern Arizona desert from the Colorado River, for example, have resulted in explosive and unsustainable population growth. Food imports have had a similar effect, allowing human populations in high-mountain regions and deserts to flourish in fragile environments that might otherwise be inhospitable to humans. Without imported fuel, food, and water, many regions simply could not survive. If Phoenix had to rely on indigenous water supplies, it would probably be a smaller, cleaner, more manageable city.

All this is to say that economic dependence has created pockets of humanity living in unknown peril. If resource supplies should dwindle, many of these "outposts" of civilization would very likely suffer extreme economic and social hardship. For example, projections of global warming suggest that water flow in the Colorado River, which serves approximately 20 million people, could decrease by 30 percent. A decline such as this would devastate water-dependent cities of the West and could cripple farming in the near-desert of southern California, which depends on Colorado River water to irrigate cotton, rice, and oranges.

Despite the problems, interdependence is often viewed as a desirable economic relationship. Business economists cheerfully describe the global marketplace as if it were a poultice for ailing economies. From an ecological viewpoint, the global marketplace and the rising interdependence that accompanies its development are a prescription for future hardship and environmental despair.

From a long-term, sustainable vantage point, the future of the human economy lies not in globalization but rather in local or regional self-reliance—communities living within the means of their immediate environment. Regional and local self-reliance means living more independently, or less dependently, by using a region's resources in a sustainable fashion, a strategy that will be outlined below and in more detail in chapter 10.[8]

OUR ECONOMIC SYSTEM TENDS TO EXPLOIT NATURE AND HUMAN BEINGS

The human economy is exploitive of human beings and thus often inhumane. Modern economic practices, for example, tend to widen the gap between the rich and the poor, the powerful and the weak. Consider some statistics that support this contention. In 1980, the average salaries of the chief executive officers of the 300 largest companies in the United States were 20 times greater than the average salaries of manufacturing employees; by 1990, CEOs were earning 93 times more than the average manufacturing employee.[9] Since 1950, the gulf between America's upper and lower classes has continued to widen.[10] From 1980 to 1990, the income of the top 1 percent of the U.S. population (those earning over $250,000 a year) has doubled, while middle income has increased only slightly. Meanwhile, the poor have gotten poorer.

Economic exploitation is also part of the reason Third World nations remain so poor. As in colonial times, the rich nations often continue to reap the harvest of natural resources in Third World nations, paying very little in return. Gold mined in African countries, for example, swells the already bulging coffers of wealthy American and European companies but provides little economic benefit to poor miners and their local economy. Poverty caused by exploitation is an environmental problem of grave importance. According to many analysts, it is a key element in the complex equation of rapid population growth in many Third World nations, and population growth is one of the root causes of the environmental crisis.

On another front, the human economy also exploits the environment, taking much but often giving little in return. In the 1800s, for example, timber companies began cutting forests in the northeastern United States to supply lumber to resource-hungry cities and towns. When those forests were depleted, the companies moved westward across the northern states, felling trees as they advanced toward Minnesota and Wisconsin. When they had depleted the supply of white pine in these states, the companies moved southeast and northwest, cutting with wanton disregard for long-term sustainability of the forest. The exploitation and near extinction of many whale species is another example of economic exploitation. Commercial fishing, which has depleted two dozen ocean fisheries in the North Atlantic in the past 40 years, is a more contemporary example.

Economic exploitation of natural resources continues today, as witnessed by the massive deforestation of tropical rain forests, global loss of topsoil, and the spread of desert land. This dangerous undermining of nature results from many factors, one of the most important of which is time preference.[11]

Time preference is a measure of one's willingness to give up some current income for sustained and perhaps even greater returns in the future. A farmer, for example, may choose to plant wheat or corn year after year because they offer high economic return. Over the years, though, wheat and corn deplete soil nutrients and organic content.[12] Modern farmers have also come to depend heavily on pesticides and artificial fertilizers to bolster productivity. These measures, which may poison soil and diminish its long-term productivity, say critics, result in a temporarily high yield at the cost of a long-term sustainable yield and are a clear expression of a farmer's unwillingness to give up current income for sustained returns. This is referred to as an immediate time preference.

The alternative approach to agriculture is the conservation strategy. It involves crop rotation, heteroculture (planting two or more crops in the same field), natural methods of pest control, and other techniques that preserve and protect the soil and protect wildlife and water supplies. Alternating crops from year to year, for example, reduces insect damage and reduces or eliminates the need for costly pesticides. If properly executed, crop rotation helps to maintain the soil's organic and nutrient content, thus reducing the need for fertilizers and effectively reducing soil erosion.

Conservation strategies such as these favor long-term, sustainable use of the land. The choice between conservation or depletion hinges solely on the time preference of the farmer, which is determined in large part by his or her economic pressures. In their effect on the environment and future generations, these approaches couldn't be more different.

Building a sustainable society requires strategies that favor the long-term health of the world's soils, forests, oceans, wildlife, fish, rivers, and air. At times, this may mean choosing techniques that offer lower immediate return. The farmer who shifts to organic farming, for example, may go through several transitional years during which yield and profit suffer.[13] And after the transition, yield is likely to be lower. This decrease, however, is offset by lower input costs, making organic farms as profitable as their counterparts. When the loss of soil on traditional farms is figured in, it becomes evident that organic farms are far more profitable. That said, it is important to remember that many sustainable strategies, such as energy efficiency, offer immediate economic returns that substantially outweigh any reaped by current methods.

Correcting Flaws in the Economy: A Long-term Environmental Perspective

Jim MacNeill, secretary general of the World Commission on Environment and Development, points out that the rapid increase in economic development has produced a world with strikingly new realities—realities that are not yet reflected in human economic, political, and personal behavior.[14] Since 1900, the world's industrial output has increased by a factor of 50 and the global economy has expanded 20 times over. Interestingly, 80 percent of the increase in economic and industrial activity has occurred since 1950. Thus, the so-called flaws in our economy are partly the result of the rapid expansion of human economic activity, an increase so swift that we have had little time to adjust to the environmental realities. Fortunately, efforts are now under way to understand those realities and to reshape human economic systems according to ecological laws.

To be sustainable, the human economy must be compatible with nature. To make it so, we must all learn to think not just logically, but eco-logically. There is no fudging allowed, says critic David Haenke.[15] All economic systems must be designed for long-term ecological resonance. One way of making the human economy consistent with the economy of nature is to convert linear processes to cyclical ones—instead of dumping our waste into landfills, for instance, recycling and composting it.

In an environmentally compatible economy, then, the bottom line is not money but rather the wise stewardship of resources and the preservation of ecological integrity. The chief goal of a sustainable economy is to provide goods and services for people while protecting, even enhancing, a well-functioning ecosystem. How can this happen?

BUILDING AN ECONOMY WITH VISION

The first step in creating a sustainable economy is to infuse economic institutions, key economic players, and important economic laws with a vision that transcends the narrow boundaries of space and time that frequently lead to short-term profiteering. This will invariably require drastic alterations in one of the key economic principles, the law of supply and demand, forcing it to take into account the Earth's limits.

Business and economics professors can assist in this effort by pointing out the limitations of supply and demand and encouraging students to think in the long term. Recognizing that renewable and nonrenewable resources cannot expand indefinitely could temper human desire and inspire a move toward greater efficiency, recycling, renewable resource use, restoration, and better management of renewable resources.

A new view of the law of supply and demand that takes into account the finite nature of resources will also require public policy measures that establish alternative pricing structures—that is, a system of pricing in which the costs of goods and services are determined, in part, by long-term supplies, and not just by immediate supply and demand. One prime candidate is the user fee.

User fees typically involve some form of tax on raw materials (for example, coal), which is generally paid by producers (mining companies), then passed on to consumers. User fees artificially raise the price of raw materials and of finished goods produced from them, discouraging waste and helping to protect resources for future generations.

The revenues generated from user fees can be spent in a variety of ways. For example, money collected from oil producers might be invested in nationwide energy conservation programs, efforts to pro-mote the use of renewable alternatives, or measures that stimulate recycling. They can also be used to help fund family planning.

Currently, a number of states assess user fees—called severance taxes—on natural resource extraction. Revenues generated from sev-erance taxes pay for infrastructure such as new roads and sewage sys-tems required in rural regions to accommodate resource develop-ment. Severance tax revenues are also used as recompense to future generations. The constitution of Montana, for example, imposes a severance tax on coal mining. Approximately one-quarter of the sev-erance tax is used for a trust fund "to compensate future generations for the loss of a valuable and depletable resource and to meet any economic, social, and environmental impacts caused by coal devel-opment." The trust fund money can also be used to help develop a stable, strong, and diverse economy.

Hazel Henderson, author of *The Politics of the Solar Age* and one of the world's leading advocates of a humane, sustainable economy, calls user fees "green taxes" and notes that they may be applied to a variety of products and activities, including disposable items, inefficient au-tomobiles, factory pollution, airplane travel, international tourism, and oil transportation.[16] Some European nations have embraced the idea that present generations have an obligation to future generations and are developing green taxes. Green taxes, they have found, can be a major source of new revenue. Henderson notes that many business executives find green fees more palatable than excessive, complex regulation, and most economists approve of them.

According to the principle of intergenerational equity, each gener-ation must compensate future generations for the costs it imposes on them. Compensation requires money to develop alternative re-sources. Some economists are quick to point out, however, that part of the compensation future generations receive from present genera-tions comes in nonmonetary forms. Knowledge, technology, infra-structure, investments, and institutions, they say, are part of our leg-acy to future generations, perhaps more important than conserving resources or protecting environmental quality.[17]

This view, however, fails to take into account that technology is useless without energy and other natural resources. What good is a technologically advanced automobile if there is no gasoline to power it? What good is a jet airplane if there's no place worth flying to?

Improving cost-benefit analysis. Another way of building vision into the economic system is by improving cost-benefit analysis, one of the chief decision-making tools of modern corporations. Cost-benefit analyses generally concentrate on the immediate and most obvious costs of doing business, including expenditures on labor, materials, and energy, which are then weighed against the most obvious and easily quantified benefits, increased profits and jobs. If benefits outweigh costs, the activity is deemed acceptable.

In this tidy little exercise, the hard-to-quantify but very real social, ecological, and health costs of business are often ignored and thus passed on to the public at large. A good example is the tens of millions of dollars spent by the United States to give the Statue of Liberty a facelift, a project necessitated by acid rain and urban air pollution. Crop damage caused by ozone in photochemical smog is another example, and so are the health bills of the thousands of individuals suffering from emphysema and lung cancer caused by urban pollution.

To discourage the transfer of discernible business costs to the public, the environment, and future generations, all costs, environmental and otherwise, should show up on the balance sheet of the producer. This is referred to as full-cost pricing.

Attempts to narrow the gap between the market price of goods and services and their full cost began in the United States with the passage of environmental laws and regulations in the 1960s and 1970s, laws that require companies to reduce emissions of harmful air pollutants by installing pollution-control devices. Pollution-control devices help to internalize economic costs, so instead of taxpayers footing the bill for pollution damage, companies and consumers pay for pollution control.

Further tightening of environmental laws and regulations could reduce pollution more. This would save money in environmental cleanup while raising the cost of goods and services, making price a more accurate reflection of the economic and environmental cost. But many pollution-control strategies are economically inefficient ways of minimizing external costs. Far more economical and effective are pollution prevention measures that eliminate pollutants altogether while saving producers large sums of money.

By modifying manufacturing processes, finding nontoxic substitutes, and recycling waste, companies have found that they can dramatically reduce their output of pollution, sometimes eliminating it altogether, and at the same time decrease production costs. In the process, external costs are greatly reduced or eliminated. Pollution prevention is therefore a win-win-win strategy. The environment wins, the consumer wins, and manufacturers win.

Economics and business professors can play a major role in teaching their students, future entrepreneurs and business people, full-cost pricing. Companies can also help by studying the environmental impacts—not just local, but global—of all their projects and processes and by taking steps to reduce or eliminate these impacts. Corporate environmental-impact statements would help company officials to recognize the true cost of their activities and to implement procedures to avoid them or, at the very least, to fold them into the price of their products or services. A company that wants to build a new office building, for example, might determine the amount of carbon dioxide its heating and cooling system will produce, then assess how much it would cost to offset the additional carbon dioxide production by planting trees. The cost of the tree-planting program could be included in the cost of products the company makes. Better yet, the company might decide to redesign the facility to make use of passive solar heating and natural cooling, thus greatly reducing carbon dioxide pollution.

Government can assist in the development of full-cost pricing by applying green taxes. Revenues from green taxes can be used to pay for environmental damage. According to a recent study by the Department of Energy and the New York State Power Authority, the environmental damage caused by generating a kilowatt hour (kwh) of electricity from 1.2 percent sulfur coal is about 5.9 cents—more than the cost of the electricity itself, which averages 5.5 cents per kwh. A tax levied on electricity from high-sulf coal, then, could be used to pay for revegetating acid-rain-damaged forests or bringing acidified lakes and rivers back to life.

Full-cost pricing helps to ensure social and ecological justice, but it is really only an ideal to be moved toward. Economic critic David Haenke points out that if large-scale economic enterprises were made to pay their way in terms of the full, ecologically audited cost of raw materials, production, and distribution, most of them would go broke in a matter of days. Supporting this contention, Hazel Henderson estimates that the *true* cost of one CFC aerosol can—factoring in its contribution to the destruction of the ozone layer, cancer rates, and so on—would be about $12,000.[18] Clearly, businesses would not be able to absorb such long-term costs, but the closer a society is to full-cost pricing, the better its chances of ensuring sustainability.

Shifting the time frame. For many business economists, the dividing line between the near term and the far term is no more than five years. One-, two-, and three-year plans are the norm. Sustainability, however, requires a longer time frame for business decisions—20, 50, and perhaps even 100 years.

Many businesses are reactive, responding almost daily to shifts in competition, pricing, and consumer demand.[19] Practicality seems to require the flexibility of a short time frame. But by attending to the immediate, businesses set aside important long-term considerations that often come back to haunt them. Actions (like selling off profitable business operations) that appear to be practical in the short term often turn out to be economically disastrous in the long run. Modern farming is an example of an industry with a short-term outlook on production. Unfortunately, many farmers are finding that the measures they use to boost crop production in the short term (pesticides, fertilizers, and monoculture) incur high costs. Heavy chemical use, for instance, has poisoned their own drinking water. Deforestation of the tropics is another short-term activity that brings immediate economic gain but long-term environmental and economic costs that far outweigh any immediate gains.

In a sustainable economy, practical actions are those that serve human needs without bankrupting nature. If economic options fail to withstand scrutiny in this context, they are simply not practical.[20]

Shifting the time frame of business and government will require striking changes in our world view. A world view centered on sustainable ethics will require education on a massive scale, reaching children and adults alike. Science teachers can help by exploring the biological principles of sustainability. History and government teachers might examine ways those principles apply to law and government. Environmental groups can contribute too, but their message must reach far beyond their own members. To become an agent of change, the environmental movement may need to forgo direct mail as its main organ of public outreach in favor of television, radio, and print ads, which reach a much larger audience.

ENDING OUR OBSESSION WITH GROWTH

To temper our all-consuming passion for economic and material growth, we need better measurements of progress—new state and national report cards that include economic and noneconomic data reflecting a nation's true well-being. The new report card must take into account a wide range of social, economic, environmental, and health-related factors, such as life expectancy, infant mortality, the general health of the population, literacy, crime, accumulated wealth, income distribution, air quality, water quality, and recreational opportunities.

Designing an economy that looks at progress holistically. One measure of economic health that may prove more useful than GNP is the net economic welfare (NEW). NEW is the GNP minus the economic negatives described earlier. Figure 3 plots the NEW and the GNP of the United States. As shown, the NEW is considerably lower than the GNP and is increasing at a slower rate.

In a sustainable economy, nations would strive to reduce the difference between GNP and NEW—in other words, strive to prevent pollution and environmental destruction in the first place, eliminating the need for costly pollution control and environmental restoration projects.[21]

In their book *For the Common Good,* economist Herman Daly and philosopher John Cobb present still another measure, the index of sustainable economic welfare (ISEW), which includes factors such as income distribution, pollution, the loss of farmland, and the external costs of development.[22] Comparing the changes in the ISEW to the GNP over the past 20 years, they show that the per capita GNP increased about 2 percent per year in the 1970s and about 1.8 percent per year in the 1980s. In contrast, the per capita ISEW increased only about 0.7 percent in the 1970s and actually declined 0.8 percent per year in the 1980s, a decrease largely attributed to the rapid deterioration of the environment.

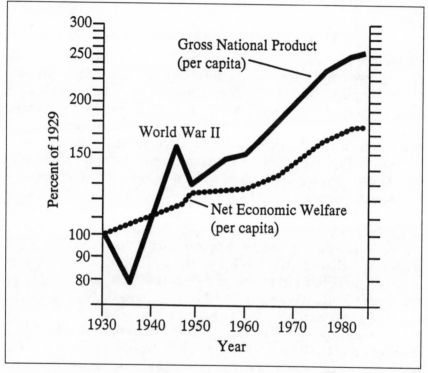

Figure 3: Net Economic Wealth vs. Gross National Product. GNP measures the value of all goods and services of a nation. NEW subtracts economic negatives from GNP, giving a truer accounting of economic and social progress. As this graph indicates, NEW is considerably lower than GNP and grows more slowly, indicating that much of our supposed progress is a result of negative economic factors, such as the rising cost of pollution cleanup.

Measures such as these provide a much more accurate and useful picture of human economic activity and permit us to assess progress as a physician might assess the health of his patient—by looking at many separate but related factors simultaneously. New indices of social, economic, and environmental welfare are vital to current efforts aimed at forcing a radical rethinking of human progress. The hope is that these indices will help politicians, economists, CEOs, and others set sounder social, environmental, and economic goals.

Hazel Henderson argues that an economic report based on a wider range of measures such as literacy, health, environmental quality, and income distribution would provide a view of genuine progress and genuinely sustainable economic activity. Never one to shy away from an issue, Henderson is now in the process of establishing a service that will provide such a multidimensional indicator. It will be published in *World Paper,* which reaches a million readers worldwide, and will also be made available on satellite for anyone with the technological capacity to receive it. Each telecast report will take three minutes. "Broadcast media," says Henderson, "will have to understand that this report card . . . isn't one of those things you can dash off like GNP." [23]

In 1991, a group of Colorado economists, environmentalists, educators, and businessmen, of which I am a member, began preparing a progress report for Colorado. It contains data on economic, social, and environmental conditions in the state. It will be published in short form in newspapers and in a more comprehensive form that will be available to legislators, business people, and concerned citizens. One of the most valuable sources of environmental data for the Colorado report was the *1991–1992 Green Index* written by Bob Hall and Mary Lee Kerr. This book contains a wealth of information—all told, 256 measures of environmental conditions and environmental policy in the 50 states—and will prove invaluable to individuals interested in creating their own quality indicators for progress.

If they are to make a difference, the new economic indicators must be more than academic exercises; that is, they must be put to use by those who influence the economic life of a nation. In addition, they must be used on a global scale by the UN, by development agencies, and by international lending agencies, such as the World Bank, that control the direction of development in the Third World.

. There is good news to report on this front.

- In Jacksonville, Florida, the chamber of commerce developed an alternative measure of success called Quality Indicators for Progress.[24] Its annual report presents numerical and graphical data on activities and conditions in nine areas, including the economic environment, health, public safety, and the natural environment.
- Recently, the Dutch government asked one of their leading economists to produce an alternative system of national accounting that reflects damage to air, water, soil, and animal and plant life, and to account for the cost of maintaining or restoring them.[25]
- Sweden's parliament has sent a delegation to the Netherlands for advice on establishing an alternative national accounting system.
- Germany is currently working on a alternative measure of economic output that more accurately reflects economic negatives.
- Indonesia, Thailand, and the Philippines have asked the Netherlands for technical assistance in environmental accounting.
- The UN statistical commission has agreed to set up guidelines for countries that want to draw up their own alternative measures of progress.

Even if governments only use alternative indices as a supplement to GNP, says economist Roefie Hueting of the Netherlands, they will help to clarify "our mistaken accounting and demonstrate how we are squandering air, water, ground, trees, spaces, silence, as if they were free goods instead of assets. . . ." They would suggest the need to "abandon the GNP as the main indicator of economic progress. . . ."

CREATING A HEALTHY ECONOMY WITHOUT GROWTH

A new economic report card for states and nations is essential to loosen the grip of economic growth on the industrial world, but it is not enough to end the mad frenzy of activity we sometimes mistake for progress, activity that undercuts our future. This section will describe three strategies that could help to reshape economics and help build stable, healthy economies in industrial nations without requiring growth in material production and consumption. Chapter 7 examines strategies for building stable, healthy economies in Third World nations.

Restoration. One of the first steps in creating a sustainable economy is to restore damage. Because of past abuses, the prospects for restoration are abundant. For example, hundreds of miles of salmon stream could be restored in the Pacific Northwest, an effort that could rebuild fish stocks and, over time, increase the supply of food for human populations. Throughout the world, millions of acres of forest that have never reseeded after clear cutting could be replanted, then harvested sustainably, reducing the pressure on virgin stands. Millions of acres of grassland denuded by overgrazing could be fertilized and replanted, then managed carefully to ensure long-term productivity. Millions of acres of farmland could be slowly replenished by applying organic compost from paper and other organic wastes collected in cities, then shipped to nearby fields. Millions of acres of wetland lost to development could be restored, along with populations of commercially important fish and wildlife.

Restoration of renewable resources would provide ample employment opportunity in the coming decades and could help create a sustainable resource base, which, if properly managed, could supply abundant resources for future generations and for wild species. Where would the money come from? And would these efforts be worth the investment?

One extraordinary example of restoration that speaks to the economics of this idea began in California in 1978. Then–Secretary for Natural Resources Huey Johnson launched an ambitious program called Investing for Prosperity. Johnson rallied support from industry, banks, agriculture, labor, and environmental groups to convince the state legislature to appropriate $400 million over a four-year period for investment in California's economic future. One of the projects financed by the state was a massive replanting effort on private forestland. At that time, the state of California had 13 million acres of timberland, only about 8 million of which were forested. The remaining acreage needed planting, but for one reason or another owners could not afford to borrow the money. The state provided $5 million to private landowners to turn barren hillsides highly susceptible to erosion into productive forest once again. A recent study showed that, over the next 50 to 75 years, the initial $5 million investment will return more than $400 million in timber sales and $100 million in tax revenues. This project, which will provide a sustainable source of income to many local communities, is a model of restoration that other states could follow.

Plugging the leaks. Another important effort in building sustainable economies is known as plugging the leaks.[26] This strategy seeks to make businesses, cities, towns, counties, even nations much more efficient in the use of resources such as energy, water, and building materials. For businesses, simple yet cost-effective measures often result in impressive reductions in operating costs; many businesses find that there is no faster way to increase profits than by becoming more efficient in the use of resources. To promote social equity, increased profits could in turn provide businesses with money to pay employees better wages, thus reducing economic disparities in our economy. Increased profits might also permit employers to hire more workers, reducing the tireless appeal for "economic growth to create more jobs"—a rally cry of government officials that often leads them to recruit new businesses or to build new projects (airports, dams, highways) despite questionable need.

Plugging up the leaks is vital to sustainable economic development because it reduces the waste of resources and stops the outflow of dollars from communities. Keeping dollars within a local economy builds economic stability and reduces the community's dependence on outsiders for resources. Before the 1973 oil embargo, a dollar used to circulate 26 times in the United States before leaving the country. Now it circulates about 10 times before making its way to the OPEC nations.[27]

Plugging up the leaks strengthens economies while protecting, even improving, the environment. In addition, economic development occurs not only without an increase in material consumption, but while reducing it.

The Japanese probably understand efficiency as well as anyone in the world today. On average, the Japanese use about 5 percent less energy than U.S. manufacturers, which gives them a slight advantage in pricing. According to the Worldwatch Institute, the relatively inefficient use of energy costs the U.S. economy about $220 billion a year in lost sales.

Finding hidden opportunities. The third development strategy useful in strengthening economies and improving the condition of the environment is finding hidden opportunities. Translated, that means tapping into our waste. In this strategy, waste from homes, businesses, and factories is put back into the production cycle or recycled. That is, waste becomes the raw material for industry, greatly reducing our need to harvest and mine resources and lessening our impact on the environment.

Consider an example. Residents of Denver and its suburbs discard approximately 4.5 million plastic milk jugs each month. Milk jugs can be melted down and reused for a variety of useful products. Denverites also discard nearly 700 tons of trash a day loaded with recyclable materials, enough to support a variety of businesses. Discarded newspaper, for instance, could be used to produce newsprint, egg cartons, animal bedding, cereal boxes, map tubes, drywall, ceiling tiles, and insulation. Discarded cardboard could be composted and sold to gardeners or farmers, or used to make cardboard boxes for local businesses.

A study in New York showed that recycling 10,000 tons of trash through curbside programs produces, on average, 36 new jobs.[28] If the city of Denver recycled half of its waste, over 400 new jobs could be created. Add the suburbs to the equation and the employment potential would increase substantially.

Clearly, there are jobs in our trash and enormous opportunities to create businesses by recycling the materials we ordinarily throw away—the stuff we disparagingly call garbage. In our shortsightedness, we are overlooking an enormous business opportunity and a great way of improving environmental quality.

The lesson of these three strategies is relatively simple: we can improve our economy and create economic stability without increasing our demand on resources. Moreover, we can put people to work while improving environmental quality. These strategies would obviously help to build a sustainable, enduring economy.

CREATING AN ECONOMY THAT FOSTERS INDEPENDENCE

Because of impending resource shortages, especially oil shortages, history could mark the current trend toward a globalized economy as a rather short-lived exercise in futility. In the coming decades more and more economic activity will, by necessity, shift back to the regional level principally because of a decline in world oil supplies that makes oil more and more expensive and transportation of goods increasingly costly. To avoid high transportation costs, many communities, states, and nations will inevitably begin to produce more of their own goods or purchase them from nearby, regional sources.

Over time, an increasing number of communities will become dependent on local resources. As a result, regional economies will likely diversify, providing a larger share of day-to-day goods and services such as food and energy required by local people and, in the process, becoming more self-sustaining.

It is important to point out that not all products and resources we need will come from local sources. Activities such as steel and automobile manufacturing will probably remain centralized for economic reasons.

Regional or local self-reliance in industrial nations could have an enormous impact on Third World countries now dependent on food exports from the West. As many industrial nations shift to renewable energy sources such as ethanol, farmland once used to grow wheat and other grains for export could shrink. Present-day grain surpluses now available in agricultural nations, and often donated or sold cheaply to Third World nations, might begin to dwindle. Should it materialize, a decline in food exports would require concerted efforts on the part of Third World nations to achieve agricultural self-sufficiency.

Local self-reliance is not a pipe dream; it is already beginning to emerge. In Brazil, for example, a government-subsidized ethanol program has helped cut the country's dependence on foreign oil. California's public utilities have in recent years become champions of energy efficiency and renewable energy, such as wind and geothermal, in an attempt to reduce dependency on outside sources of fuel. Efforts to promote state-produced goods are another sign of emerging self-reliance.

The transition to a sustainable society can be made smoother by consciously increasing regional self-reliance—that is, taking active steps to make it happen before it is forced upon us by decreasing oil supplies and rising transportation costs. For the United States, this means ending our dependency on foreign oil. For individual states, it means finding ways to diversify their economies, producing more and more of the goods and services needed on a day-to-day basis. Many products can be made from regionally recycled materials.

Besides promoting self-reliance, diversification makes communities and states more recessionproof, creating a much-needed buffer against the economic roller coaster.

CREATING AN ECONOMY THAT IS NONEXPLOITIVE

Ideally, a sustainable economy exploits neither the Earth, its people, nor its wealth of domesticated and wild species. Making the transition from an exploitive to a nonexploitive economy and way of life is a monstrous task that all of the efforts described so far in this chapter facilitate. A summary of ideas is presented in table 2.

A New Eco-nomics

Calvin Coolidge once remarked that "the business of America is business." For a sustainable society to emerge from the economic clamor of the industrial world, the business of nations like America must change. The age of self-interested economic behavior is past, says Natural Resources Defense Council's Peter Borrelli.[29] The zealous pursuit of growth is wrecking the planet. A new way of business that seeks to establish a partnership between humans and nature, a new eco-nomics, is necessary. The business of America is creating a

TABLE 2: Measures Required to Make the Transition to a Sustainable Society
Reduce population growth, then gradually reduce population size, through attrition
Reduce resource consumption and waste by reducing demand, increasing product durability, increasing efficiency, recycling, and reusing products
Increase national self-sufficiency by relying on local resources and renewable resources whenever possible
Protect and conserve renewable resources, such as farmland, fisheries, forests, grasslands, air, and water
Improve renewable-resource management to ensure sustainability
Repair past damage by replanting forests and grasslands, restoring farmland, reseeding roadsides, restoring streams, and cleaning groundwater
Cut pollution by 50 to 75 percent
Support sustainable development projects in Third World nations that draw on appropriate technology and local knowledge and are inspired by enlightened policy
Work for global peace and cooperation
Promote sustainable ethics and individual responsibility and action

healthy, enduring economy that not only supplies our legitimate needs but also promotes a long-lasting relationship with nature.

Happily, many of the changes prescribed in this chapter have already begun to take place in industrialized nations. Don't, however, be lulled into complacency by early signs of progress: the job has just begun. Our economic ship is off course. Unless a major course correction is made, and soon, we're bound to find ourselves grounded on a reef.

5 Greening the Corporation, Greening the Consumer

Take care of the means and the end will take care of itself.

GANDHI

BUILDING A SUSTAINABLE SOCIETY requires a transition from overconsumption to appropriate consumption. For many years, however, the goal of American society has been to do "more with more"—to expand our wealth with ever larger withdrawals from the Earth's bank account. Lured by the twin goddesses convenience and luxury, we equated bigger with better. This climate of self-satisfaction gave rise to the gas-guzzling automobile and the four-bedroom suburban home with its formal living room, formal dining room, and three-car garage. Big cars, big houses, big lawns—these were status symbols few could resist. Unfortunately, almost no one paid attention to the natural resources required to fulfill our ambitions.

Then came the oil embargoes of the 1970s. Sending shock waves through the economy, they put a chill on America's consumer fever and ushered in a new era—one still obsessed with luxury and comfort and status, but nonetheless marked by a commitment to do things a bit more efficiently. The chief impetus for this move was the price of oil, which skyrocketed from around $3 to $35 per barrel. With the cost of energy and virtually everything else spiraling upward, the days of doing more with more gave way to a time of doing more with less. Most of us believed that slight improvements in efficiency would save the day. We could still have our spacious homes, we could still commute alone in our cars, so long as they were efficient.

Despite what many think, doing more with less is only a step in the transition to a sustainable society. To become truly sustainable, we must become even more efficient in our use of the Earth's resources, and we must learn to be happy with less. The third phase in the transition to a sustainable world requires us to learn to do the *same* with less. Fostering a sense of contentment among those of us who have had so much in the past will require new avenues of fulfillment, and much of the change will come from inside.

But even this is not enough in the long run. A truly sustainable society cannot be achieved without a fundamental change in outlook—learning to do less with less. This means consuming less and using all resources with maximum efficiency.[1] It may mean smaller homes that are many times more efficient than those built today. It may mean using a fraction of the water we consume today as well as widespread use of mass transit in the urban environment. Trash service would be a thing of the past, since virtually all of our waste would be recycled or composted in backyard bins and municipal composting yards. Additional thoughts on the transition are offered in chapters 10 to 12.

This chapter concentrates on efforts already under way to make the transition to a sustainable society happen: demand-side management, green products, changes in corporate policy and management, and finally, ways to create an industrial ecosystem. These efforts help to put into action the operating principles of a sustainable society, to create an economy that is more visionary and less growth oriented, to promote regional self-sufficiency, and to reduce our exploitive ways.

Demand-Side Management

One of the operating principles of a sustainable society is conservation. Conservation means reducing consumption either through direct action, like turning off the lights when one is out of a room and buying less, or by using resources more efficiently, for example with high-efficiency light bulbs and low-flow showerheads. While both efforts conserve resources, they differ markedly in their approach. One depends on behavior, the other on technology.

For years, business and government leaders have looked at conservation measures with skepticism and even hostility, perhaps perceiving them as roadblocks to economic wealth. President Ronald Reagan summed up their disdain when he remarked that conservation meant "freezing in the dark."

Fortunately, the truth about conservation is a long way from what President Reagan might have hoped you would believe. A well-insulated house with weatherstripping and caulk to block air infiltration, in fact, is much cheaper to heat and far more comfortable than its drafty counterpart on a cold winter night. In addition, more and more electric utilities have found that conservation is one of the most economical and profitable ways of supplying energy to their customers. In an effort to avoid the negative connotations of the word conservation, to give it a suit-and-tie respectability, energy consultants now refer to it as demand-side management (DSM).

Utility DSM programs generally operate by improving the efficiency of the end use of electricity through a variety of technological means.[2] Energy-efficient lighting systems in office buildings and energy-efficient appliances are good examples. Electrical demand can also be decreased by altering the timing of customer use through technology. For example, utilities can install devices in air conditioners that automatically turn them off for short periods during peak energy demand. Utilities can also call on customers to conserve energy through behavioral changes—that is, by turning off lights, lowering thermostats, and the like. Thanks to the efforts of the Rocky Mountain Institute's Amory Lovins and others, businesses and electric utilities throughout the world are recognizing that conservation is sound business policy.

DSM programs work in large part because they eliminate the need for new electrical generating capacity to meet demand at peak periods. In years past, peaks in energy demand during certain parts of the day and during certain times of the year frequently led utilities to build expensive nuclear and coal-fired power plants. Today, companies are looking for ways to reduce peak demand and thereby avoid the expense of new construction. Interestingly, studies show that by implementing DSM programs, utilities can actually achieve a higher return on investment than they can by expanding their generating capacity.

New England Utilities Learn to Love Efficiency

In 1988, Northeast Utilities applied for permission to build a new power plant to meet projected electrical demand in Connecticut.[3] This proposal was challenged in a court of law by the Conservation Law Foundation (CLF), an environmental group based in Boston, which claimed that the utility could satisfy demand by conservation measures. To the surprise of many, the CLF prevailed, and the court ordered it to work with the utility to implement a demand-side management program.

Environmentalists first suggested a program to reduce electrical consumption in new buildings, in some cases by as much as 70 percent. This was an important development in the northeast, since about 80 percent of the growth in electrical demand resulted from new construction. Projected energy savings on a typical 60,000-square-foot office building proposed by CLF would free up enough electricity to supply approximately 2,500 homes. The CLF also proposed that the utility retrofit homes, businesses, and factories with energy-efficient appliances, lighting, and insulation. The final recommendation of the CLF was that the utility pay for the redesign of industrial plants to make manufacturing facilities and processes much more energy efficient.

The programs proposed by CLF have helped to reduce the demand for electricity in the northeast and made a new power plant unnecessary. The program has been so successful, in fact, that companies in Massachusetts, Rhode Island, New Hampshire, and Vermont have joined forces with the CLF to develop demand-side management programs. In 1990, New England utilities spent about $200 million in efficiency measures for consumers. In 1992, the figure is projected to be as high as $400 million.

One key to the success of the DSM program in the northeast was the regulators' decision to reward utilities for investments in efficiency. For example, in Rhode Island, utilities are permitted to receive a 17 percent annual return on conservation investments—considerably higher than the typical 10 percent return on a new power plant.[4]

USING DSM TO REDUCE ENERGY DEMAND IN RURAL AREAS

One of the first DSM programs in the United States began in Iowa long before Northeast Utilities and the CLF began working together. In 1974, the manager of Osage, Iowa's municipal utility projected that energy demand in the town of 3,800 people would double in the next ten years, putting a severe financial strain on this small rural town.[5] Instead of letting electrical demand climb, the utility took evasive action, opting to conserve their way out the crisis.

Soon utility officials embarked on an aggressive campaign to become more efficient. They began by setting rigorous home insulation standards for their customers, then convinced customers to take action. Articles in the local newspaper and the utility's bimonthly newsletter encouraged Osage residents to conserve energy and explained how it could be done, easily and inexpensively. Public lectures by employees of the utility company also spread the word. As evidence of the success of this program, today 75 to 85 percent of customer homes meet the utility's standards, and all new homes built since the 1970s have exceeded its recommended specifications.

In 1979, the utility launched a load-management program in which customers were asked to install small devices on their air conditioners that would turn off the compressor for seven and a half minutes each half hour during periods of peak demand. Peak demand occurs only five to eight days a year, during the summer, and lasts only about three to four hours each day. Switching off an air conditioner for this short period has little effect on the residents' comfort, but it has helped prevent electrical demand from exceeding the utility's generating capacity. Today, about 75 percent of the people eligible for the devices have had one installed.

In 1980, the utility purchased an infrared scanner that detects heat loss from buildings. Energy auditors use the scanners to show where energy is leaking out of homes and businesses. Free audits offered by the utility convinced many residents to take active measures to cut the loss of energy. Thanks to these and other efforts, 95 percent of the homeowners in the town have installed insulation blankets on their water heaters. Many customers have installed weatherstripping and sealed leaks in doors, windows, and foundations.

The success of the Osage experiment can be summed up in a few sentences. First, because of a cutback in demand, the utility has actually lowered the price it charges for electricity and natural gas. Unlike other utilities trapped by costly new construction, the Osage utility has been free of debt since 1984. By utility estimates, conservation efforts save the local economy $1.2 million a year. The economic benefit is obvious to anyone who travels down Osage's Main Street. Instead of the boarded-up storefronts typical of many small rural towns, you will find nearly all of the shops and stores open for business.

The economics of demand-side management are so compelling that a new industry has been born. In many major cities, new companies that specialize in energy efficiency offer advice and technical assistance to other businesses. Simple steps often save larger companies tens of thousands of dollars a year in energy bills.

Despite the benefits of DSM, there are some barriers standing in its way. Perhaps the most significant is that many utilities are still dominated by engineers and financial planners who have little experience in implementing efficiency programs. When it comes to meeting need, they're committed to building new plants, but as the successes of DSM spread, more and more utility officials will see the logic and benefits of this simple idea.

MEETING OTHER RESOURCE NEEDS THROUGH DSM

If we are to build a sustainable society, we must apply DSM to other areas. One excellent candidate is water.

For years, little attention was given to water conservation. Rising demand for industrial, agricultural, and municipal water was answered by large and costly projects. The era of big dams, however, is grinding to a halt for at least three reasons. First, federal financial support for major water projects has declined dramatically in recent years; this, in turn, has resulted in a reduction in demand for such projects. Second, many Americans now recognize that rivers are more than a supply of drinking and irrigation water; they are a source of natural beauty, they offer recreational opportunity, and they are vital to fish and wildlife. Furthermore, fishing, kayaking, and rafting represent sustainable economic activities that help diversify and strengthen local economies.[6] Third, many of the best locations for dams have already been used; developing potential locations will invariably be more expensive and more environmentally objectionable.

Because of these constraints and the favorable economics of conservation, water policy has shifted from development to management—finding ways to use existing facilities and supplies more efficiently. Water conservation through demand-side management can help to offset shortages and help many regions meet much, if not all, of their future demand at a far lower cost than that incurred by new dams.

In the agriculturally productive San Joaquin Valley of California, irrigation water currently costs farmers about five dollars per acre-foot, thanks to lavish federal subsidies and a failure of the government agencies that sponsored projects to include economic externalities (such as the loss of fisheries and recreation opportunities) in the cost of water.[7] The Environmental Defense Fund calculates that in the San Joaquin Valley, recycling water and scheduling water application according to crop and soil needs costs about $10 per acre-foot of water. Switching from irrigated crops such as cotton to dryland crops costs farmers about $40 per acre-foot in lost crop yield. Water conservation by more efficient drip and sprinkler systems costs about $175 per acre-foot. Thus, at first glance, farmers have little if any incentive to conserve water.

Like energy conservation, water conservation makes sense because it prevents costly new construction. At current rates, water from new projects costs up to $500 per acre-foot. The conservation measures described above, although costly, are far cheaper than the cost of developing new water supplies.

In rural areas, reducing the loss of water from irrigation ditches and other measures can free up water needed by growing municipalities. The major user of water, agriculture, can become a source of future water for cities and towns. In January 1989, the metropolitan water district that serves the greater Los Angeles area (including San Diego) entered into an agreement with the Imperial Valley irrigation district to the north. Under the agreement, the metropolitan district will finance water conservation measures on farms. Water saved by these efforts will be diverted to Los Angeles, San Diego, and neighboring cities at a cost far lower than that of a new dam.

In agriculture, DSM may also take another form, which I call geographic relocation—moving water-intensive activities to areas with abundant water supplies. Although controversial, this method is worth considering.

California's Central Valley, for instance, receives only about four inches of rain a year, but it is used to grow water-intensive crops like cotton and rice. Rice requires the equivalent of 100 inches of rainfall a year, and cotton, which needs less, still requires large amounts of moisture to grow successfully.

California's cattle industry also consumes inordinately large amounts of water. Approximately one million acres of California grassland is currently irrigated for cattle production, consuming one-seventh of the state's water while generating only 1/5,000 of the state's total annual earnings.

Shifting crop and cattle production to more suitable climates could free up enormous amounts of water, not just for human use but also for fish and wildlife. Relocation therefore helps to reduce demand while tailoring economic activities to the natural environment. It's one way of cooperating with nature.

Demand-side management is just as effective in cities and suburbs as it is in farming regions. Lawn watering restrictions at the hottest time of day and building codes that require low-water toilets, faucets, and grass, for example, cut municipal water demand, preventing the need for new dams and reservoirs.

Consider the following successful DSM programs:

- Under a newly amended plumbing code, the state of Massachusetts now requires that all toilets installed after March 1, 1989, use no more than 1.6 gallons of water per flush—approximately half as much water as current models use and two-thirds less water than older models. Because toilets generally account for 30 to 40 percent of the indoor water consumed by a family, reducing this amount can have an enormous impact on urban water demand.

· To conserve water and reduce the volume of waste handled by its wastewater treatment plant, the city of Santa Monica, California, is replacing 12,000 conventional toilets with ultra-low-flow fixtures. This will save the city over 800,000 gallons of water a day. Old porcelain toilets will be used to construct an artificial reef for fish and other marine organisms off the coast of California. In nearby Santa Barbara, California, old toilets are being ground up and used for roadbed, the layer under an asphalt or concrete road surface.[8]

· A hotel in Michigan installed water-efficient toilets, faucets, and showerheads, which saved the facility nearly $250,000 alone in construction costs and will save an estimated $45,000 per year in water and sewer bills. In the first eight years, savings are estimated to be an impressive $750,000.

In conclusion, DSM holds extraordinary promise in our quest for a sustainable future. It is environmentally sound and can, as the previous examples show, be highly profitable. Tapping current waste to meet future demand represents one of our best long-term hopes for plugging up the leaks in wasteful economies and lifestyles. If practiced widely, it will boost society's efficiency in the use of all resources, helping us create a better balance with nature.

Conscientious Consumerism: Green Products

Another promising change in recent years is the dramatic upsurge in green products. Green products include goods made from recycled material (for example, recycled toilet paper and paper towels), goods packaged in biodegradable and recyclable boxes or bags, goods made of less toxic materials or from nontoxic substitutes (such as cleaning agents or varnishes derived from plant materials), and a wide assortment of resource-efficient products (low-flow showerheads and high-efficiency light bulbs, for instance).

Richard Lawrence, president of Marketing Intelligence Service, of Naples, New York, estimates that more than 200 green products were introduced in the United States in 1989. In 1990, he says, the number doubled.

One of the first green products to hit the market was an environmentally friendly coffee filter manufactured by a West German firm, Melitta, with North American headquarters in Cherry Hill, New Jersey. Early in 1988, the company learned that white paper filters for coffee contained dioxin, a potentially carcinogenic chemical produced during the bleaching process. In response, Melitta decided to produce an unbleached coffee filter, which it began to market in the United States in the summer of 1989.

Another early arrival was a line of cosmetics sold in a chain of stores, The Body Shop, started in Great Britain in 1976.[9] With an investment of $12,500, Anita Roddick began producing cosmetics that were not tested on animals and were packaged in inexpensive, refillable containers. Today, wherever possible, Roddick uses raw materials and finished products from environmentally sustainable cooperative ventures in Third World countries. Besides offering information on health, The Body Shop's employees also give lessons on environmental conservation. Today, the chain consists of nearly 400 stores in 34 countries with a gross income of $125 million a year.

Still another example is Ben and Jerry's Ice Cream in Waterbury, Vermont. Founded by Ben Cohen and Jerry Greenfield, Ben and Jerry's sells among other products a nut-brittle ice cream and candy made from nuts harvested in the Amazonian rain forest. In the future, they hope to develop a market for other sustainably harvested products from the rain forest, thus offering Brazilians an economic alternative to deforestation.

GREEN PRODUCTS: JUST A BEGINNING

Green products may seem like the answer to a lot of the world's problems; unfortunately, they're not. First of all, even though a whole host of such products are now available to consumers, they represent only a small fraction of the goods available in our stores. The green products available today are, at this stage at least, little more than a symbol of our good intentions. To have a serious impact on the environment, many more environmentally friendly products must be introduced. In addition, many green products are not as green as you might think.

In an article in *Greenpeace* magazine, Andre Carothers, the editor, and Debra Lynn Dadd, editor of *The Earthwise Consumer,* argue that American business may be selling the public a false bill of goods.[10] Given the mood of the nation, they assert, many companies are pushing their products as environmentally sensitive or benign when in fact they are not.

Biodegradable diapers are a good example. While they may seem like a good thing, in reality the only advantage they have over their nonbiodegradable counterparts is the satisfaction they give the consumer. In a landfill, sealed off from air and water, they probably never biodegrade.

Another example is when Volkswagen and Audi ran ads bragging about their cars releasing harmless carbon dioxide. If they had done their homework, the two auto manufacturers would have found that carbon dioxide is a leading greenhouse gas. At current levels it won't affect human health, but it is clearly affecting the health of the planet and therefore, in the long run, human health and well-being.

"The environmental advertising bandwagon offers companies an opportunity to spruce up their images at relatively low cost," argue Dadd and Carothers. In support of this contention, they note that many of the recycled paper products currently on the market are produced by companies with reprehensible environmental records. To avoid being taken in by misleading campaigns, consumers should scrutinize so-called green products to ensure that they're really as green as manufacturers suggest.

GREEN SEALS OF APPROVAL

A truly green economy would require that *all* products be audited for their environmental impact from cradle to grave, say Dadd and Carothers. Audits should include a full ecological accounting: the amount of energy and materials used to produce and transport an item, the pollution generated in its manufacture and transport, the role of a product in the economic and social health of the country of origin, the investment plans of the company in question and all its subsidiaries, and the final disposal of the product. Performing a full environmental audit is an extraordinarily complex process, but it yields a more accurate picture of a product's environmental impacts.

Over a decade ago, the government of West Germany instituted a green product–labeling program, known as the Blue Angel program, which was designed to provide at least a partial environmental audit. Since its beginning, the program has passed judgment on over 3,500 products in 50 different categories.[11] A far more complete analysis is available in a German magazine called *Okotest* ("eco-test"), first published in 1985. The environmental equivalent of *Consumer Reports, Okotest* analyzes the impact of a variety of products from cradle to grave, offering consumers a much more detailed environmental assessment than they would get elsewhere. With a subscription base of about 87,000, *Okotest* is gaining credibility as an authoritative source for environmental impact information on products.

The Blue Angel program and *Okotest* have had a profound influence on manufacturing in West Germany. In many cases, companies have responded to poor ratings by altering their methods, making the production of paper, paint, and other products cleaner. Companies have also made radical changes in their products in order to receive a Blue Angel seal of approval.

Eco-labeling programs have sprung up elsewhere in Europe and in Canada and Japan in recent years.[12] Two independent nonprofit groups have launched national programs in the United States to rate products. The Green Seal program, under the direction of Denis Hayes, relies on criteria similar to those used by Canada's Environmental Choice. A second group, Green Cross Certification Company, employs a more rigorous set of criteria.

GREEN CONSUMING IS STILL CONSUMING

Some months ago I was leaving a book signing in Boulder, Colorado, when a young man in a booth selling cleaning products advertised as environmentally friendly asked me to take a look at them. When I said no thanks, he mumbled some insult suggesting that I didn't care about the environment. I walked on, dismayed.

In retrospect, I should have stopped to explain that my lack of interest in his products had everything to do with my environmental concern. I chose not to buy his line because at my house we do most of our cleaning with vinegar and baking soda. The vinegar comes in a glass container, which we recycle, and the baking soda comes in a box that is made of recycled paper. When the box is empty it goes in the compost bin, eventually to become organic soil supplement I add to my vegetable garden.

This incident underscored an often overlooked problem with green products: green consuming is still consuming. Dadd and Carothers note that individual action, when limited to the supermarket aisles, does little to advance the most fundamental of all changes needed to save the Earth—reducing our consumption, that is, learning to do less with less. The answer to the problems we face lies not only in consuming appropriately but also in consuming less.

In many ways, green products are akin to end-of-pipe pollution control strategies, say Dadd and Carothers. They put a dent in the pollution problem, but they don't solve it. One of the keys to protecting the planet is prevention, and in the consumer arena that means becoming a conscientious consumer—buying what you need, and only what you need.

Nonetheless, green products are an important step along the road to sustainability. They are a signal of a social need to live with less impact, and a signal that businesses are developing an environmental ethic. Ultimately, sustainability requires that virtually all products be green.

Greening the Corporation

Earth Day 1990, the twentieth anniversary of the original celebration, enlisted the enthusiasm and support of a wide range of groups, many of which had historically shown little interest in environmental issues. The newcomers included some of America's businesses. All of a sudden, banks were offering environmental tips to their customers and grocery stores were selling cloth bags as an alternative to paper and plastic. Even the Council of Chemical Association Executives, whose members include the National Agricultural Chemicals Association, the Society of the Plastics Industry, and the U.S. Chamber of Commerce, got into the act by publishing a booklet entitled "101 Ideas for Earth Day," which listed members' efforts in such areas as waste reduction and recycling.

INSPIRING CORPORATE RESPONSIBILITY

The challenge Earth Day 1990 posed to industry, however, runs much deeper than the high-profile events many companies sponsored, wrote Ken Sternberg in an article in *Chemicalweek* magazine.[13] "After all the trout are released and trees planted, industry will have the tougher job of transferring environmental piety to corporate philosophy in daily operating procedures," he added. Robert D. Kennedy, chairman of Union Carbide and the Chemical Manufacturer's Association, believes that the time is right for companies to reconsider their behavior and to think about the consequences of industrial processes. It's time for companies to consider how their products are used and disposed of—and to take action.

Kennedy notes that responsible leaders in industry feel that it is their Earth, too. They recognize that industry is largely responsible for the condition of the planet and, as such, that it holds many of the solutions.

One improvement in recent years is the routine performance of issue audits among some major corporations. Issue audits allow companies an opportunity to examine the ways they deal with issues of concern to the general public, including environmental issues. Besides raising corporate consciousness, this exercise helps foster corporate responsibility and action.

Greening the corporation requires more than audits, a few green products, and environmental evaluations, however. In an interview David Brower, former executive director of the Sierra Club, offers three suggestions.[14] First, corporate CEOs should be allowed to bypass economically profitable business opportunities without being sued by shareholders. Currently, he says, CEOs work under the subtle but constant threat of shareholder lawsuit. If a project is environmentally unacceptable, a CEO should be free to refrain without threat of lawsuit.

Second, Brower asserts that all investment offerings should come with an environmental impact statement. For example, each prospectus issued by a company for a stock offering should include a brief synopsis of the environmental and social impact of the company and its products. Independent analysts would write impact statements to prevent fudging. As a result, individual investment decisions could be based on profitability and environmental considerations. A sustainability index might even be included, helping investors decide whether a product helped or hindered efforts to attain a sustainable economy.

Third, Brower contends, environmental impact statements should be required for all takeovers. Although the corporate takeover frenzy has calmed somewhat in recent years, it remains a popular business option. Unfortunately, takeovers are often environmentally destructive. One noteworthy example is the Pacific Lumber Company takeover.

Before 1986, Pacific Lumber managed its redwood forests sustainably, removing trees at a rate equal to their regeneration—a remarkable feat considering that redwoods live 1,000 years and more. This changed in January 1986, when Charles E. Hurwitz, a wealthy Texas businessman, purchased the company. He and his co-owners financed the buyout by issuing high-yield, high-risk bonds commonly referred to as junk bonds. In 1989, the interest on the bonds came to $83 million, and to meet their payments the new owners abandoned sustainable harvesting practices and began cutting at a frantic pace. One Pacific Lumber worker said, "They're just leveling everything. . . . They're destroying the future, leaving nothing for the next generation."

An impact statement on takeovers might have averted this or at least alerted investors of the potential environmental disaster about to unfold.

THE VALDEZ PRINCIPLES

In September 1989, the Coalition for Environmentally Responsible Economies (CERES) drafted a series of guidelines for corporate conduct dubbed the Valdez Principles.[15] CERES consists of a number of environmental groups and several managers of major pension funds in the United States.[16] The Valdez Principles call on companies to

1. protect the biosphere by reducing and eliminating pollution;[17]
2. promote the sustainable use of natural resources by ensuring the sustainable use of land, water, and forests;
3. reduce the production and disposal of waste by recycling and other measures, and to employ safe disposal methods for wastes that cannot be handled otherwise;
4. employ safe and sustainable energy sources and use energy efficiently;
5. reduce risk to the environment and to workers;
6. market safe products and services—those that have minimal environmental impact—and inform consumers of the impact of the products and services a company offers;
7. restore previous environmental damage and provide compensation to persons who have been adversely affected by company actions;
8. disclose accidents and hazards and protect employees who report them;
9. employ environmental directors with at least one member of the board of directors qualified to represent environmental interests, and employ environmental managers with a senior executive responsible for environmental affairs; and
10. assess and audit progress in implementing the Valdez Principles.

Proponents of the Valdez Principles hope that they will eventually lead to responsible policy and action on the part of all businesses, here and abroad.

In addition to producing green products, there are signs that corporations are taking their environmental responsibility more seriously. IBM, for example, recently appointed a vice president of environmental health and safety with a staff of approximately 30 people to ensure that corporate environmental policy is carried out. The staff has been given greater power and broader authority to minimize pollution and environmental damage from production.

Environmental auditing is becoming more widespread as well. In Ciba-Geigy Corporation's Ardsley, New York, headquarters, for example, environmental auditors were placed in a stand-alone group that report directly to the CEO. Like financial auditors, environmental auditors must function autonomously, operating in a manner as free of corporate politics as possible. At the Ciba-Geigy plant, this system appears to be working. At one facility, for example, plant managers, lawyers, and engineers all agreed that a particular solvent was safe to use, but the environmental auditors disagreed. The people at the plant backed down, reasoning that if the internal auditors weren't satisfied, external auditors probably wouldn't be persuaded, nor would the CEO.

The success of these programs depends on leadership from above. One word from the CEO or president, in fact, can make or break a company's environmental policy. Bruce Karrh, DuPont's long-standing vice president of safety, health, and environmental affairs, noted that in the past plant managers often balked when he advised them to commit resources to environmental projects. He spent many hours convincing them of the merits of environmental protection. Then in May 1989 DuPont's chairman, Edgar S. Woolard, Jr., proclaimed a policy of "corporate environmentalism." All of a sudden, says Karrh, plant people were begging for environmental advice. Suddenly "it wasn't just me trying to get the organization to do things, it was Ed."

Another positive step in the greening of America's business community comes from the National Wildlife Federation and some of America's leading universities. In 1989 the NWF's corporate conservation council, working with three universities, designed a course for business students that teaches environmental policy and management. NWF reports success for the three-year-old program. Courses have been overbooked, and one of the professors received the highest course evaluation he has gotten in over a decade of classroom teaching. Another faculty member, instrumental in designing and testing the program, expects the curriculum to be in place in 25 U.S. business schools by 1992; an additional 15 schools may elect to teach modules on business and the environment. In 1991, the NWF published *Managing Environmental Issues* containing over a dozen case studies that will help students think through various business situations. The changes already under way in industry, government, and academia reflect a growing realization that profound change is required if industrial societies are to endure.

The Industrial Ecosystem

In a 1989 article in *Scientific American* entitled "Strategies for Manufacturing," Robert Frosch and Nicholas Gallopoulos argued against the traditional model of industrial activity by which individual manufacturers take in raw materials and generate products to be sold and waste to be discarded. This outmoded way of business, they said, should be transformed into a more integrated model, the "industrial ecosystem."

"The industrial ecosystem would function as an analogue of biological ecosystems," wrote Frosch and Gallopoulos. In such a system, producers of goods comply with the biological principles of sustainability. Conservation (efficiency), recycling, renewable resources, and restoration become the cornerstone of all manufacturing facilities. Like natural ecosystems, the use of energy and materials is optimized. Waste and pollution are minimized. There is an economically viable role for every product of manufacturing.

USING RESOURCES MORE EFFICIENTLY AND REDUCING DEMAND

The new industrialism requires extreme efficiency—that is, using energy, raw materials, and even recycled stock much more frugally. Over the past 20 years, some leaders in this movement have found ways to increase the efficiency with which they use resources. One dramatic example is cogeneration, a process in which waste heat is captured and put to use. For example, Dow Chemical, Scott Paper, and other companies generate their own electricity at many plants and use what had previously been waste heat to warm their factories.

Cogeneration schemes such as this can also be profitable on a much smaller scale. A McDonalds restaurant in Chula Vista, California, for example, is using natural gas to heat its water and generate electricity. This system produces electricity more efficiently than the utility company and at a lower cost. Moreover, the combustion of natural gas produces less carbon dioxide than coal and therefore contributes less to the greenhouse effect.[18] Similar systems could be installed in grocery stores, shopping malls, hospitals, airports, schools, factories, and government buildings. Unless utilities learn to increase their efficiency, small-scale units such as these may become part of a climate-safe sustainable energy strategy.

The conservation strategy also calls on producers to use less material, a measure called dematerialization. For instance, since 1975 the mass of a typical automobile has declined nearly 1,000 pounds, with about one-fourth of the weight loss due to the substitution of aluminum and plastics for steel, the rest largely due to a reduction in the automobile's size.

Dematerialization in the automobile industry saves energy not only in manufacturing and distribution but also in the daily operation of a car. This strategy, while useful, is a mixed blessing because the light-weight composite plastics that have replaced steel are much more difficult (if not impossible) to recycle. The net result may be an immediate drop in fuel consumption, but an overall increase in the waste created.

To offset this problem, the government of Germany is considering legislation that will require automobile manufacturers to make their cars 100 percent recyclable. Thus, after a useful life span, an automobile would be disassembled and the parts recycled. Two German auto manufacturers are developing a tear-down technology that would facilitate this process. Mazda Motor Corporation, also working on this technology, has introduced a universal numerical coding for plastic automobile parts that could simplify their recycling efforts. By 1992, most new models will bear the recycling codes.

Recognizing the economic advantages of dematerialization, Japan reduced the energy and raw material content of an average unit of production by 40 percent between 1973 and 1984, according to a report by the Center for Neighborhood Technology entitled *Sustainable Manufacturing: Saving Jobs, Saving the Environment.* West Germany, Sweden, and other market leaders have achieved similar reductions.

REDUCING WASTE: THE REUSE AND RECYCLING STRATEGY

In an industrial ecosystem, the effluents of one process often become the raw materials for another, thus eliminating enormous amounts of waste. In its quest for better waste control, the chemical industry and many others have found themselves moving farther and farther up the process stream. This venture has led waste control engineers away from time-honored but ineffectual end-of-pipe controls (common in the 1970s and early 1980s) to a new strategy, pollution prevention, ways that eliminate toxic wastes and pollution from being produced in the first place.

Industry is replacing and augmenting pollution control devices with a host of relatively simple but highly effective measures that prevent toxic pollution from being generated.[19] These generally fall into two broad categories: process manipulation, and recycling and reuse.

Process manipulation involves a number of steps to alter equipment and change manufacturing processes in ways that cut down on waste. Interestingly, even minor changes in manufacturing processes can prevent the release of many thousands of tons of hazardous material each year. One prevalent method is substitution, the use of nontoxic or less toxic chemicals in place of toxic chemicals. A Chicago electroplating shop, for instance, recently switched from cyanide zinc to an alkaline-based zinc containing no cyanide. Even simpler changes are possible. For example, lengthening the time that freshly plated automobile parts are allowed to drain over a plating bath lowers the toxic content of the rinse water.

Companies are also recycling some hazardous materials, using them in other operations or selling them to other companies. In some cases, toxic chemicals once dumped into the environment need only a small amount of purification to be reused; in other cases, they need no purification whatsoever.

The indisputable world leader in waste reduction is the Minnesota-based 3M Corporation. While many companies are just now tapping waste minimization strategies, the 3M Corporation launched its Pollution Prevention Pays program in 1975. Through a variety of cost-effective measures, 3M has cut its pollution per unit of production in half and in the process saved $500 million in the past 15 years. The 3M program eliminates nearly 100,000 tons of air pollutants, reduces solid waste production by 275,000 tons, and eliminates 1.5 billion gallons of wastewater each year.

Inspired by the 3M example, Union Carbide reduced air emissions by 45 percent between 1985 and 1988 through pollution prevention measures. Monsanto has committed itself to reducing the emissions of toxic chemicals by 90 percent by 1992 and to reducing all waste by 70 percent by 1995. DuPont, which currently pays more than $100 million a year in waste management, plans to reduce hazardous waste through pollution prevention measures by approximately 70 percent by the year 2000.[20]

As the 3M example shows, preventing pollution is not just environmentally good, it can be extremely profitable. At ARCO's Los Angeles refinery, for example, the company made a series of relatively low-cost alterations, slashing hazardous waste production from 12,000 tons per year during the early 1980s to about 3,400 tons today. The relatively simple and inexpensive measures will save the company about two million dollars a year in disposal costs. Spurred by the success of this effort, ARCO decided to install a one-million-dollar recycling facility for oil spilled on site that is expected to reduce hazardous waste production by another 2,000 tons a year.

Stories such as these are becoming more and more common in the industrial world. As the word spreads, companies are seeing that waste reduction through process manipulation, recycling, and reuse is not a threat to their economic well-being but a bonanza. One of the most encouraging changes in recent years has been the shift in attitude among chemical engineers and industry's technical experts. Twenty years ago, these people were chiefly concerned with yield and product quality. Today, more and more of them are looking at waste as a key element of the design process, recognizing that industrial technologies that produce byproducts society cannot absorb are essentially failed technologies.

CHALLENGES TO A CLOSED-LOOP INDUSTRIAL ECOSYSTEM

In an ideal industrial ecosystem, the use of energy and materials is optimized, waste and pollution are minimized, and every product has a viable role in the economy. "The difficulties in implementing an industrial ecosystem are daunting," write Frosch and Gallopoulos in their *Scientific American* article on industrial ecosystems, "especially given the complexities involved in harmonizing the desires of global industrial development with the needs of environmental safety."

Although an ideal industrial ecosystem may never be attained in practice, manufacturers can find ways to apply the biological principles of sustainability to their activities, creating an efficient, closed-loop system.[21] Developing an industrial model more closely aligned with sustainable principles still poses a number of challenges. In the plastics industry, for example, recycling is hindered by variety. Currently, at least 45 different types of plastic are on the market, making collection and recovery extremely difficult. Making matters worse, some plastic products consist of two or more types of plastic. The squeezable ketchup bottle consists of five different types of plastic, each endowed with special properties. Mixtures such as this are virtually worthless as a raw material for manufacturing. Plastic numbering codes have alleviated the confusion somewhat, making recycling a little easier.

Another problem is health regulations that prohibit the use of recycled plastics in food containers. As a result, plastic containers that are recycled often make their way back into the market in the form of less essential products like jump ropes and plastic novelties. In a sense, then, much that passes as plastic recycling is not true recycling since new plastic must be produced for food containers. To overcome this barrier, policymakers need to explore the feasibility of using discarded plastic food containers for new food packaging, thus closing the loop.

Even when a particular type of plastic is recyclable in theory, there may be obstacles. PET plastic, for example, used to make beverage bottles, can be reconstituted into its original resin and used to produce a variety of products, including automobile parts, electronic devices, and polyester fiber for pillows, furniture, clothing, and carpeting. Currently, however, only about 20 percent is recycled. The reasons? First and foremost, few manufacturers purchase recycled PET plastic. Second, the major PET recycler is located on the East Coast, making it expensive to ship the plastic from the South, Midwest, and West. To increase the rate of recycling, there need to be local or regional manufacturers that use recycled PET plastic.[22] To improve the economics of recycling in general, recyclers and manufacturers of secondary materials must be situated as close to one another as possible.

Iron presents a different set of challenges. Although a relatively good infrastructure for collecting scrap iron exists, the demand for recycled iron is lackluster in the United States and elsewhere. This is largely the result of technological change—that is, the shift from open-hearth furnaces to basic oxygen furnaces. Open-hearth furnaces use equal amounts of scrap and pig iron to make steel, but today they account for only 3 percent of U.S. production. In the 1970s, steel manufacturers looking for more energy-efficient and much cleaner ways of producing steel turned to the basic oxygen furnace, which uses half as much scrap steel. The more efficient and cleaner technology has dealt a severe blow to the recycling industry and clearly points out the importance of considering the total impact of any technological change.[23]

Some Thoughts on Systems Design

The goal of those who design industrial ecosystems is to imitate the best workings of biological ecosystems. This requires a whole-systems approach, that is, one in which individual manufacturing processes are considered as part of a larger whole. In an industrial ecosystem, decisions are based not simply on economic considerations but on ecological and social ones as well. For example, a manufacturer may design a process that produces very little hazardous waste, but if the waste is unusable this new process may be less desirable than one that produces relatively large quantities of waste that can be reused.

In an industrial ecosystem, the products themselves must be designed with recycling in mind. Composites and hard-to-recycle materials, for which there is no market, do not fit in an industrial ecosystem and an emerging sustainable economy.

In an industrial ecosystem, manufacturing processes and products are designed after thoughtful consideration of long-term resource supplies. Abundant, renewable supplies are selected over nonrenewables whose reserves are limited or could be used for more essential needs. A highly profitable venture that depletes the Earth of a vital resource is shunned.

While vital to efforts to create an industrial ecosystem, it is not enough for companies to develop recyclable products. Companies must also participate in the development of the infrastructure required for recycling them—that is, picking up their products and transporting them to remanufacturing plants. The codevelopment of markets and recycling infrastructures so foreign to industry may require cooperative ventures between competitive businesses. It may also require businesses to work with government to develop ways to minimize waste through recycling. Had the plastics industry created a distribution as well as a collection system at the outset, it would probably have met with much less community opposition to its products.

To avoid the problem of variety and mixture posed by plastics, manufacturers may need to reduce the variety of products they produce or, at the very least, develop ways to identify the composition of goods to facilitate recycling.

CHANGES IN CONSUMER DEMAND AND WASTE-DISPOSAL PRACTICES

Like all ecosystems, the industrial ecosystem consists of producers and consumers. Both play a key role in the workings of the network. Thus, the challenge of building an industrial ecosystem lies not just in the boardrooms of the world's corporations and in the minds of small businessmen and women—that is, the producers—but also in the minds of the consumers, people like you and me.

Consumers can participate in creating an industrial ecosystem by purchasing green products—that is, recycled, resource-efficient, and recyclable products. Consumers can boycott products like disposable razors, pens, and diapers, avoid cheap, poorly made ones, and choose durable items made with a minimum of material and sold with a minimum of packaging. Practiced widely, these efforts would send a powerful signal to manufacturers.

As noted above, the success of the industrial ecosystem depends in large part on the efforts of business to help codevelop markets and collection and recycling infrastructures. Consumers help to make these systems operate by seeing that recyclable and compostable materials are, in fact, recycled and composted.

Tom O'Leary, CEO of Burlington Resources, a Seattle energy resources firm, notes, "Firms that destroy the integrity of an ecological system are . . . the same . . . as individuals who make cash withdrawals from 7-Eleven with a shotgun."[24] Consumers who buy the products of these companies must be considered accomplices in the crime.

Businesses that protect the environment can make a healthy profit, says Worldwatch Institute's Cynthia Pollock Shea; environmentally sound business does not have to be an oxymoron.[25] Companies are learning that environmental protection is no longer an option, it is a precondition for success.

6 Third World Follies: Environmental Destruction in the Name of Progress

It is in exchanging the gifts of the Earth that you shall find abundance and be satisfied. Yet unless the exchange be in love and kindly justice, it will lead some to greed and others to hunger.

KAHLIL GIBRAN

THE THIRD WORLD is in a state of crisis. Despite billions of dollars in aid and loans, the economies of many Third World countries are in ruins. Making matters worse, the natural resources upon which these countries, their people, and their wildlife depend are rapidly being depleted.

The economic and environmental crisis gripping the Third World stems from a variety of factors. One of the most powerful and far-reaching is a continuation of the tradition of colonial exploitation by today's multinational corporations, which appropriate massive quantities of resources from the Third World to fuel the wasteful economies of many Western nations. Another, often overlooked, factor in the economic and environmental decay of the Third World is the generosity of the West. Ironically, well-intentioned but misguided food aid and development assistance of industrial nations lies at the root of much of the Third World's troubles. Rapid population growth, political tension, and a host of other problems contribute to the growing economic and environmental malaise. This chapter will focus on development follies and lay the groundwork for a discussion of sustainable economic development in the Third World, many lessons of which are applicable to the developed world as well.

The Impact of International Development

In an interview in *In Context,* Helena Norberg-Hodge, who has been working in a mountainous province of northern India for over a decade, says that development "initiated by government is pretty much the same everywhere in the world."[1] By that she means that most development efforts attempt to transplant the technology and infrastructure of the West into foreign cultures. Norberg-Hodge also notes that Western-style development tends to centralize wealth and power—that is, concentrate it in cities and in the hands of a few. Modern development strategies often do little or nothing to promote economic opportunity for rural residents, leaving many no choice but to leave homes where they lived sustainably for many years and move to cities where they enter the ranks of the unemployed and impoverished.

Two major players in Third World development are national development agencies such as the U.S. Agency for International Development and multilateral development banks (MDBs) like the World Bank. Over the years, these and other equally powerful organizations have paid little attention to the long-term economic and environmental impact of projects they have funded. Soil erosion, deforestation, species extinction, and other serious environmental problems are common consequences of many well-intentioned development projects, efforts that, in the final analysis, have actually worsened the lives of those they were designed to help.

In India, for example, numerous hydroelectric and irrigation projects have been built with financing from Western countries, private banks, and international lending institutions. Hydroelectricity is often considered one of the more environmentally benign Western technologies. In India, however, hydroelectric projects, which provide energy mainly to cities and towns, inundate highly productive farmland and displace thousands of rural villagers and native tribespeople. Ravi Sharma, editor of the international environmental magazine *Ecoforum,* argues that projects such as these are counterproductive, worsening the lives of many Third World residents.[2] The impact of such massive projects on wildlife is often equally devastating.

Compounding the damage, people displaced by dams and reservoirs are often relegated to marginal land that deteriorates with heavy use. Dam projects may also increase the prevalence of disease, as witnessed in Egypt when, soon after completion of the Aswan Dam, health officials noticed a marked increase in schistosomiasis. This debilitating, sometimes fatal disease was spread by snails that inhabited the irrigation ditches built to deliver water from Lake Nasser. In the Amazon river basin, where malaria is a significant problem, hydroelectric projects increase the number of suitable breeding sites for mosquitoes by hundreds of square miles.[3]

Dams also reduce the biological productivity of coastal wetlands and estuaries, because they trap nutrients that once nourished organisms at the base of the food chain. Reduced flow, moreover, makes estuarine water saltier, to the detriment of species uniquely adapted to a mixture of fresh and salt water characteristic of the estuarine zone.[4] The change in nutrient and salt levels can cause a sharp decline in commercially important fish species, many of which are dependent on estuaries and coastal wetlands during some part of their life cycle.

In Brazil and neighboring countries, massive hydroelectric projects funded by international lending agencies like the World Bank have flooded hundreds of thousands of acres of dense, virgin tropical rain forests, destroying countless species. Rather than clear-cut the land and salvage billions of feet of timber, developers simply flood massive areas. Inundated by warm water, the trees quickly begin to decompose, producing highly toxic hydrogen sulfide gas. In one project in Suriname, dam maintenance personnel were forced to wear gas masks for two years after the flooding was completed. Making matters worse, water in the reservoirs turns acidic from the rotting vegetation, and the acids corrode pipes and turbines, adding millions to the cost of these projects.

Not surprisingly, the cost of large-scale water projects often exceeds the direct economic benefit of irrigation and hydroelectric power. Walter Reid of the World Resources Institute in Washington, D.C., notes that in many cases dams operate only a fraction of the planned time because of the high rate of erosion in surrounding watersheds, land denuded by overgrazing, poor farming practices, and excessive timber harvesting. In the Philippines, for example, the

Magat reservoir and dam, which cost hundreds of millions of dollars, was designed to improve the economy of an entire region. Now, however, because of poor land management and soil erosion in the surrounding watershed, sediment is quickly filling the reservoir. The useful lifetime of the reservoir is expected to be cut by two-thirds.

India, observes Sharma, is a showcase of irrigation and hydroelectric projects in which the economic benefits promised to downstream users or to urban populations never materialized. A prime example is the Tawa River project, designed to provide irrigation water for farms and thus to increase regional food production. Unfortunately, the irrigation canals were constructed in highly porous soils. Water leaking from the canals flowed laterally into good farm soil during the rainy season, making the soil difficult to work and suffocating crops.[5] Farmers, who were supposed to benefit from this costly project and are now struggling under the burden of chronic waterlogging, have actually witnessed a decrease in agricultural production.

Developing countries are littered with the rusting good intentions of projects that failed socially and economically, concludes Walter Reid. For example, 40 percent of the productive capacity of Guatemala's land has been lost to erosion in large part because of ill-conceived Western-style development projects that sought to turn rain forest into farmland. The decline in productivity may be remedied by applying artificial fertilizer, but intensive fertilization is prohibitively expensive for most farmers in developing countries and is nothing more than a stopgap measure.[6] It's a little like pumping plasma into a person suffering from a hemorrhage: unless the bleeding is stopped, the patient will soon die.

The degradation of farmland could depress global food production by 15 to 30 percent from 1975 to the year 2000, predicts Reid. And soil erosion also increases pressure on forests and grasslands. Worldwide, in fact, more than half the forest cut down each year is cleared to replace degraded agricultural land, according to Reid, contributing to global warming and species extinction.

On still another front, a recent report by the U.S. Agency for International Development notes, Western-style development often fosters a crippling form of dependency—one of the many social impacts of development. In accepting Western assistance, Third World farmers inadvertently come to rely on high-yield crops, tractors, fuel, pesticides, fertilizer, and other Western products.[7] When a tractor breaks down, however, there is little or no money to fix it and there are few, if any, people trained to repair the equipment.

Pesticide use in the Third World, necessitated by the introduction of high-yield crops, increases dependency and rivals dams as the most extreme example of environmental abuse brought about by development funds. In fact, pesticide application in the Third World represents 10 to 25 percent of the global total, and it is growing very rapidly. In Central America, pesticide poisoning is one of the most pervasive health problems, according to some observers. Worldwide, approximately 500,000 (perhaps as many as a million) farmers and farm workers are poisoned each year by pesticides. About 5,000 to 10,000 die as a result.

Foreign aid can have an equally chilling effect on Third World cultures and economies. In 1954 the Farm Surplus Disposal Act, often known as the Food for Peace program, authorized shipments of surplus grain from the United States to hungry Third World nations.[8] This seemingly benevolent act has unfortunately devastated many Third World farmers. In Thailand, for example, commercial rice growers unable to compete with inexpensive, in some cases free, grain from the United States were forced to abandon their farms or begin growing more lucrative cash crops for export to the West. Instead of growing food for local consumption, Thai farmers began to produce an assortment of nonessential crops such as rubber, tea, and coffee.[9] In what must be one of the greatest ironies of our time, Thailand and other Third World countries have become increasingly dependent on the West not just for markets to sell their crops but for food to feed their people.

The shift to cash crops was hastened by another factor. Like other Third World countries in the 1970s and 1980s, Thailand went into debt to pay for massive development programs from the West. In an effort to pay their mounting debt, the government encouraged farmers to plant cash crops for export.

Another problem with Third World development is the introduction of Western technology that improves harvesting to the point of threatening resources. Consider the case of Thailand once again. Commercial fishing is one of its most important economic activities. In 1985, the sale of fish to countries in Asia, Europe, and North America earned Thailand $712 million in foreign exchange. Unfortunately, the long-term future of Thailand's fishing industry is in danger.[10] Before 1960, the industry consisted almost exclusively of small-scale operators, mostly families. Since then the introduction of trawl nets, coupled with a rise in the number of motorized vessels, has resulted in a dramatic increase in commercial fishing—so striking in fact that several natural fisheries may soon be depleted.[11] In their rush to increase yield, commercial fishing interests drag their nets along the bottom, near the shoreline, capturing young shrimp and fish and wreaking havoc on natural populations. Continuing this policy could bring ruin to the entire Thai fishing industry.

Governments and international development organizations also support a number of projects designed to move people out of cities to pursue economic opportunities in rural areas. In the Polonoroeste project in western Brazil, for example, Brazilians were encouraged to colonize the rain forests, cutting down the trees to plant crops and raise livestock. Settlers soon found that most tropical rain forest soil is unsuitable for grazing and farming; 80 percent of them abandoned their new homes within a few years, leaving in their wake a denuded, eroded landscape.

Large ranching projects have also been encouraged in tropical rain forests by government subsidies. Thankfully, in 1989 the government of Brazil ended its generous financial incentives that encouraged the development of farms and ranches in the Amazonian rain forest.[12] In other countries, however, similar projects are proceeding at full speed, their founders seemingly unaware of the history and the environmental consequences of earlier attempts.

On a final note, Norberg-Hodge believes that exposure to Western ways can cause serious cultural erosion in a society. In the area of northern India where she works, people once lived relatively well. They were psychologically healthy, endowed with a strong sense of identity and living in a close, nurturing environment. They ate locally grown food, and their clothes were made of local materials. The culture, says Norberg-Hodge, was shaped by a close and intimate relationship with natural surroundings, which she calls a "rooted" existence.

Today, however, after being exposed to Western ways through television and other sources, the people often compare themselves with opulent Westerners. In the process, they often reject their own culture. Lured by the seductive pull of Western lifestyles, they suffer social discontent.

Constant exposure to Western ideas in India and elsewhere creates a profound sense of inferiority. Norberg-Hodge tells the story of the head of one small country's power authority who, when asked about using small hydroelectric turbines to generate electricity, said, "If the small hydroelectric turbines are so good, why aren't they manufacturing them in the West?" If the characters on Dallas did their cooking with solar ovens, observes Norberg-Hodge, they might spread quickly through the Third World.

The exposure to U.S. and Western technologies, ideas, and lifestyles has left these people with two options. The first is an economy that was once self-reliant and sustainable; the second is the seductive, but clearly unsustainable culture of the West. Unfortunately, the deceptive glitter of Western ways often wins.

Rethinking Third World Development

The failure of economic development strategies and pressure from several environmental groups have forced the international development community to rethink its approach. The idea of sustainability, advanced by a publication from the World Commission on Environment and Development, *Our Common Future,* has pushed to the top of the international agenda. Today, in fact, many developers are rallying around the phrase *sustainable development.*[13] What exactly is it?

ECONOMIC DEVELOPMENT VS. ECONOMIC GROWTH

The World Commission on Environment and Development defines sustainable development as efforts that meet "the needs of the present without compromising the ability of future generations to meet their own needs." In a society based on ecological justice, sustainable development also requires that efforts to meet present human needs do not impair the survival of other species.

The steps required to build a sustainable economy differ from one nation to another, depending in large part on the state of the economy.

• *In industrial nations, the key to sustainability is development without continued growth.* In the developed world, sustainable economics stipulates that all human activity, especially economic enterprise, must take place and be maintained within environmental limits. Continued economic growth is dangerous, even suicidal. Ever-increasing production and consumption cannot continue if we are to live sustainably.

Michael Kinsley of the Rocky Mountain Institute points out that "human growth after maturity is cancer."[14] When a town or nation continues to grow after maturity, it becomes cancerous as well. Environmental degradation, resource depletion, spiteful controversy, and loss of a sense of community are four blatant symptoms of the cancer afflicting modern industrial nations.

Sustainable economics, however, does not mean stagnation. On the contrary, a sustainable economic system permits considerable opportunity for economic and social development. As Kinsley notes, "development is very different from growth. After reaching physical maturity, we humans can continue to develop in many beneficial and interesting new ways—learning new skills, gaining deeper wisdom and much more." Similarly, a nation or a community can develop without growth, creating jobs and expanding cultural and educational opportunities without cutting down every last tree in the wilderness and mining every last ounce of mineral.

For the developed world, then, sustainable development means striving for a higher quality of life without depleting resources or polluting the environment.

• *In the Third World, sustainability prescribes development and limited growth within ecological limits.* The doctrine of sustainable development holds that some reasonable economic growth is essential to raise the standard of living of the poor and to curb population growth. It is hoped that such growth, combined with sane development strategies, both of which seek to improve the lives of the world's people without requiring more resources, will help to end the cycle of poverty and environmental decay now threatening the world.

Specific strategies for sustainable Third World development are outlined in the next chapter. A few generalizations merit mention here. First, Trevor Burrowes, a community activist in East Palo Alto, California, argues that "instead of aid that supports industrialization, the West should be offering assistance that bolsters" sustainable lifestyles.[15] In areas where people live sustainably now, a hands-off policy may be required. If assistance is needed, it should seek to find ways to promote a currently sustainable economy and way of life.

Second, those involved in sustainable economic development must pay attention to the environmental foundations upon which a society is built.[16] Economics and environment must be given equal weight.

Like many other great ideas, sustainability poses a number of problems. Perhaps the most significant challenge lies in the precarious balancing act it requires—that is, efforts to balance people's current needs against the needs of future generations and other species. The greatest difficulties arise when people are starving. For example, a father and mother feeding a family of seven or eight children may act in ecologically harmful ways to feed their children, says Norman Myers, author of *The Sinking Ark*.[17] Their actions are based on immediate needs, not future needs, and few would deny they should act otherwise. This thought-stopper silences many a debate on what to do for the poor countries of the world.

ENVIRONMENTAL PROTECTION IS NOT A LUXURY

The notion that environmental protection is a luxury pervades the thinking of many people. The reason for this logic is simple and extremely convincing: as noted above, such protection cannot be a high priority among poor people because the meager resources they possess must be spent for survival.[18]

Let's look at an example that suggests otherwise. The village of Fre Charles lies in northwest Haiti. The region was once rich and heavily vegetated; today, its soil is barren. No trees, or shrubs, or grass—not even weeds—grow in the parched dirt around the village. Only the stumps of trees remain as a solemn reminder of nature's once-luxuriant growth. For all intents and purposes, the land is dead. Over the years, villagers chopped down trees to make charcoal, which was sold to urban residents to generate local income. Widespread deforestation in turn created severe erosion in the barren hills around Fre Charles.

The problem is aggravated by overpopulation, farming, and poor land management. In Fre Charles, virtually every square foot of land has been cleared to grow food. Every slope, no matter how steep, is planted, but when the rains come the topsoil washes away. Because of growing pressure to produce more food, time-honored practices of soil conservation have been gradually discarded. Most peasant farmers work small plots and do not practice crop rotation.

Sir Edmund Hillary once said that environmental problems are really social problems.[19] They begin with people as the cause and end with people as the chief victims. As the land erodes, so does the future of the people. Today, many in Fre Charles who once lived on one meal a day now subsist on one meal every other day.

Haiti is the poorest country in the western hemisphere. Today, one-third of its land is seriously eroded, and 30 to 40 percent of the people are malnourished. To many observers, the island nation is a living example of what happens when a natural system collapses around the humans who abuse it.[20] To others, it is an example of the need for a marriage between environmental protection and sane development strategies. It demonstrates that environmental protection is not a luxury but rather a precondition for survival. Clearly, Third World countries cannot afford to treat the environment with disregard. Their well-being—indeed, their survival—depends on the health of the ecosystem.

Efforts are now under way to reforest the island nation of Haiti, but they're not enough. The U.S. Agency for International Development currently distributes about 7.5 million tree seedlings each year to Haitian peasants, of which only half survive. Meanwhile, about 30 million trees a year will be cut down just for charcoal production. Making matters worse, Haiti's population is expected to double in the next 25 years, adding 10 to 12 million people to the already crowded island.

Examples such as this point out the absurdity of the view that environmental protection is an indulgence of the wealthy. Thankfully, this dangerous notion is beginning to be questioned, and many leaders in Third World countries now realize that environmental protection is vital. They also realize that the problem of poverty cannot be solved in isolation from the problem of the environment. Sustainable economic development in the Third World must link the two issues (and several others as well).

EFFICIENCY IS NOT A LUXURY

Efficiency is a key to sustainable economic development strategies. Like environmental protection, it too is a necessity, not a luxury. Developing countries with low incomes, for example, currently spend nearly two-thirds of their export earnings on oil from other countries. By introducing affordable, energy-efficient technologies that use oil much more efficiently, Third World nations could actively reduce the trade deficits that currently impair their economic health.

Energy efficiency not only saves money but can improve the lot of those far less fortunate than Westerners. In India, for example, the average citizen uses about 2 percent as much electricity as the average American. Despite this rate of consumption, Indians suffer from a growing shortage of electrical power, says M. Anjali Sastry, a researcher from the Rocky Mountain Institute.[21] As India's population grows, just maintaining the already inadequate state of affairs in the next 10 years will require a 90 percent increase in generating capacity, a goal that is unlikely to be met. "Difficult days are ahead," admits one Indian power minister, predicting summer power cuts of five to six hours daily in West Bengal. "Be prepared to read by candlelight," warns a newspaper advertisement by Maharashtra State Electricity Board, one of India's major utilities.

India's power system is chronically overloaded and riddled with inefficiencies. Approximately one-fourth of all electricity generated by power plants gets lost in the transmission lines. Blackouts and brown-outs are so common, in fact, that many wealthy Indians have generators in their own homes.

A number of obstacles stand in the way of efficiency today. One of the most obvious is that utility companies in India are not generally permitted to sell electricity to one another. In the United States and other countries, surplus electricity can be transferred from one company to another via interconnected electrical grids, making electrical supply more efficient and less costly.

A second obstacle is that many energy-efficient technologies that could help India use electricity more efficiently are not produced in the country. Making matters worse, the notoriously protectionist Indian government levies substantial duties on imports. Compact fluorescent light bulbs, for example, are subject to a 270 percent duty.

Another problem, says Sastry, is the knowledge gulf. Few Indians—even in the utility companies—have information about efficiency. But the single largest constraint on energy efficiency is inadequate capital. New power plants required in India over the next five years will consume 30 percent of the investment capital, leaving little money to build factories to produce energy-efficient light bulbs and other products. Even with this new construction, shortages are projected to be worse than they are today.

Instead of looking at efficiency as a relatively fast and inexpensive way to provide electricity to more consumers, many Indian decision makers see it as a luxury, something that they can pursue once more pressing problems are solved. A study by Sastry and several Indian researchers, however, shows that importing duty-free compact fluorescent bulbs would actually be seven times cheaper than building new power plants. Compact light bulbs provide as much light from 15 watts as incandescents do from 60. If India replaced just 20 percent of its incandescent bulbs over the next 20 years with compact fluorescent bulbs, says a team of American and Brazilian researchers, the country could avoid building 8,000 megawatts of new generating capacity—or eight large power plants at a cost of $500 to $1,000 million each.[22] India would save $4 to $8 billion. Even if the country paid $15 for each light bulb, that option would only cost about $0.9 billion.

As this example points out, energy efficiency is not a luxury; it is a prerequisite for sustainable economic development in the Third World. Without it, Third World countries will repeat the mistakes of the West, and as this chapter has pointed out, too many mistakes have already been made in the name of economic progress.

7 A Prescription for Humane, Sustainable Third World Development

It is in the knowledge of his follies that man shows his superior wisdom.
FRENCH PROVERB

IN THE MAJJIA VALLEY OF NIGER the wind whipped across farm fields, stripping the topsoil and causing a decline in crop yields. This, in turn, threatened the food supply of local villages. Instead of introducing fertilizer or other Western solutions to offset the steady decline in productivity, local villagers decided to strike at the root of the problem—wind erosion—by taking a relatively simple approach requiring only a few shovels and some tree seedlings. Planted along the perimeter of the fields, the trees have thwarted the erosive force of the wind and reduced the loss of soil moisture. In addition, the new windbreaks provide a sustainable supply of building material and fuel for heating and cooking.

Another example of sustainable economic development occurred near the village of Sukhomajri in India, where livestock overgrazing had reduced vegetation by 95 percent, resulting in serious soil erosion. To combat these problems, small earthen dams were built to capture water from rain, providing a relatively inexpensive source of irrigation water. Community members also agreed to restrict grazing and thereby help to break the seemingly uncontrollable cycle of destruction. Today, the land is on the mend.

These and dozens of other examples represent the new wave of development in the Third World, efforts aimed at ending the environmental and social destruction that frequently accompany traditional development efforts. Deceivingly simple and inexpensive, projects such as these help to foster sustainable economics by increasing self-reliance. While providing humans with basic goods and services—that is, the necessities for a good life—sustainable development projects also tend to preserve and enhance the biological capital upon which people depend.

In the words of the authors of *Our Common Future,* these projects are part of "a new development path" that "sustains human progress not just in a few places for a few years, but for the entire planet into the distant future." This chapter describes that path more fully, outlining strategies of sustainable economic development—efforts that promote self-reliance, meet human needs, and preserve the ecosystem upon which all life depends.

Making Use of Appropriate, Energy-Efficient Technologies

Ideally, sustainable Third World development should be a kind of demonstration project that introduces information, methods, and technologies to Third World nations, rather than an effort to impose Western ways on other people. That is, instead of transplanting Western ideas and technologies wholesale, much of the work should focus on gathering appropriate information and technologies from the industrial world and bringing them to bear on decisions and actions in developing countries.

"Appropriate technology" is a term popularized by the late E. F. Schumacher in his book *Small Is Beautiful: Economics as if People Mattered.* It refers to methods and machines that rely on local resources and local labor. Besides using resources efficiently and producing minimal waste, appropriate technologies tend to be labor- rather than capital-intensive. Because most Third World countries have an abundance of people who can be employed on farms and in factories, it makes sense to provide them with employment; in these countries, highly automated factories that use fewer people to produce goods waste this valuable local resource.

Gandhi summed up the needs of populous Third World nations when he said that the poor of the world cannot be helped by mass production, only by production of the masses. In Asia, Latin America, and Africa, small factories that produce well-designed metal plows from local resources with local labor, for instance, are far more appropriate than automated factories that produce tractors with a minimum number of workers. The products of the labor-intensive factory and the automated factory differ considerably. A plow drawn by oxen, for instance, may be easily repaired and fuel for the oxen readily available at the local level. A tractor, in contrast, may increase production but ultimately put farm workers out of work. These people often migrate to already overpopulated cities in search of employment, worsening already serious problems there. Furthermore, the cost of tractors, of their repair, and of the fuel they need is often prohibitive.

Besides promoting regional self-sufficiency, appropriate technologies are nature-compatible, making them doubly important to sustainable development. For examples we turn to some sustainable energy technologies.[1] Biomass currently accounts for nearly 40 percent of the energy used in developing countries, with wood the predominant form in most rural areas. Used for heating homes and cooking, biomass, like cattle dung, is frequently burned in inefficient cooking stoves. More efficient stoves could cut demand for fuel and greatly decrease deforestation around villages, bringing many long-term benefits to villagers, wildlife, and the planet.

Another inexpensive sustainable technology is the solar-powered cooking stove. Made from aluminum foil, glass, and cardboard boxes, solar "box cookers" perform admirably in sunny regions such as northern Pakistan, Nepal, and parts of Africa where firewood is scarce. Like more efficient cooking stoves, solar box cookers reduce the demand for wood and slow down deforestation, saving women enormous amounts of time each week. Solar box cookers also greatly reduce health problems resulting from the inhalation of wood smoke.

Another example of an appropriate technology is the photovoltaic cell, thin silicon wafers that produce an electrical current when exposed to sunlight.[2] In rural parts of the Third World, installing photovoltaics is much cheaper than building centralized coal-fired power plants and an interconnected web of transmission lines. The technology can be used to power refrigerators and freezers in remote areas and to power small pumps that provide water for drinking, bathing, cooking, and irrigating.

Despite the obvious benefits of such appropriate technologies, less than 1 percent of international aid is earmarked for efficiency measures in the Third World, observes the World Resource Institute's Walter Reid. Increasing expenditures on energy-efficient and renewable-energy technologies is vital to sustainable economic development.

MAKING USE OF LOCAL KNOWLEDGE AND SKILLS

Sustainable economic development, observes Helena Norberg-Hodge, needs to occur from the bottom up—that is, it needs to be grass roots or community based to tap local talent and knowledge. Successful development lies not in the far-flung, energy-intensive, and environmentally destructive projects of the West, she says, but in the wisdom and skills of local people.

Despite what "experts" in Third World development might think, local farmers often know better than anyone the farming methods best suited to local climate and soil conditions. For one reason or another, though, many local farmers have abandoned sustainable farming practices. One sustainable farming practice resurrected in recent years is agroforestry, the age-old practice of growing crops between rows of trees. Trees provide shade for certain crops, reduce erosion, and also provide nutrients for the soil from their leaves.[3] Many Third World farmers abandoned agroforestry as a result of inappropriate land tenure. Thankfully, the knowledge to make this system work is currently available in many Third World nations and could be used to help put an end to declining food supplies and deteriorating soil. Frankly, it is a solution that Western agricultural experts would have probably never discovered on their own.

In Mexico, the Lancandons, a group descended from the Myans, once farmed sustainably in the tropical rain forests, growing as many as 80 crops a year. They have an extraordinary knowledge of the rain forest and can grow crops year after year in the abysmally poor soil.[4] As is the case in other parts of the world, this sustainable culture is systematically being destroyed by the Mexican government, which has opened up their lands to development. Forced to move to villages far from their fields, these people have abandoned many of their proven farming practices. Fortunately, the knowledge is still alive.

Another group still practicing sustainable farming in tropical rain forests is the Kayapo people of Brazil. Relying on traditional methods of soil enrichment and cropping, they clear small plots that they farm for 11 years, followed by a five-year fallow period.

To stop the destruction of forests, soils, and waterways, it is imperative to introduce—sometimes reintroduce—practices such as those described above that enhance productivity and ensure the health of the soil and the surrounding ecosystem. These and other improvements could help many Third World countries to regain the ability to feed their people, so vital to the task of building a sustainable world.

Encouraging Public Participation

Successful development requires not just local knowledge and skills but also input from local residents. Multilateral development banks (MDBs), bilateral aid agencies, and national governments, however, often take a paternalistic and counterproductive approach to development. Instead of trying to tell people what they need, outsiders are advised to work closely with local residents and with knowledgeable nongovernment organizations from start to finish.

Public participation has both moral and practical implications. As a rule, projects are more likely to succeed if they seek input from local residents at the outset. In fact, many a project has failed because it tried to solve problems that were critical in the minds of the planners but not in the minds of local people.

Weaving Development into the Local Culture

In 1983, anthropologist Margaret McMahon Ellis and her husband William Ellis visited an appropriate technology center in Papua, New Guinea.[5] The center had been successful in designing and promoting small-scale technologies throughout the country and boasted of success in developing cottage industries. Interestingly, though, when the Ellises arrived they found that the director of the center had departed quite unexpectedly to visit the jungle village where he was born and raised, a place where he had been actively promoting sustainable economic development. The quick departure was necessitated by the sudden and mysterious death of a number of the man's relatives. The Ellises soon discovered that the victims, all of whom had become successful entrepreneurs, were murdered by the witch doctor at the urging of the village elders. One of the men had launched a successful business selling shredded coconut. Another one had a small business making and selling cane furniture for export. The third victim had started a business selling solar-dried tropical fruits.

From the outside, the sustainable development projects seemed to be working, but the village elders saw things differently. To them, private entrepreneurship was not an achievement worthy of praise but rather a violation of the principle of community. As they saw it, small-scale businesses were spawning individualism and competition in a society, like many others in the Third World, that is based on the ideas of community and cooperation. The elders ordered the entrepreneurs killed because it was believed they were no longer contributing to the common good.

The Ellises point out that there is an important lesson here for Third World developers—that is, successful development must operate within the cultural framework. The rule of thumb in Third World development is not homogenization—transplanting Western technology wholesale to a developing country without regard for culture, environment, and other factors—but rather diversification, weaving nature-compatible ideas from other societies into the cultural fabric of the country.

For many years native cultures have been seen as an obstacle to development in the Third World. Western programs have therefore often unwittingly attempted to efface Third World culture. Today, however, it is becoming painfully evident the stumbling block is really Western arrogance and the imposition of untenable ideas on local cultures.

To be successful, economic development must emphasize ways that preserve cultural values. This idea does not always sit well with the hard-nosed practitioners of development.

Modifying the Production System to Fit the Environment

Cultural imposition is not the only mistake we have made in our zeal to help the Third World. Another equally damaging one is technological imposition—forcing our ways on nature.

To make nature do their bidding, developers often attempt to modify an environment to fit a production system. A brief glance at past and present development disasters, contends the World Resource Institute's Walter Reid, leads to an inescapable conclusion: such modification is less likely to succeed and be sustainable than the converse, modification of a production system to fit an environment.

Environmental manipulation of the kind once favored by many in the development community brings with it serious impacts like erosion and salinization of soil. Growing crops in small clearings in the tropical rain forest, for example, is a sustainable economic activity, whereas leveling huge expanses of forest to grow the same crops is not. Even more sustainable would be harvesting local rain forest products such as rubber and nuts, a practice that honors the constraints of nature while taking advantage of its opportunities.

Healthy sustainable development requires regionally sensitive, generally small-scale actions that pay for themselves and do not burden countries with debt. Unfortunately, the old ways endure: huge sums of money are still being invested in Western-style development projects.

Ensuring Flexibility

Obstacles often arise quite early in the course of a development project, frequently because it relies on one type of technology or approach. Those that fund and direct development projects, MDBs and government agencies, are often too inflexible to make midcourse corrections. Instead, they attempt to force unworkable solutions to work.

Because midcourse corrections are often needed, mechanisms are required to increase flexibility. One way is to involve local residents or private nongovernmental organizations (NGOs) in the planning and execution of all development projects. Some observers believe that money for many development projects should be channeled directly through these groups, thus keeping the MDBs and other large and intransigent bureaucracies out of project management.

Being smaller and closer to projects, NGOs have the flexibility to permit changes in design that can lead to successful outcomes. In addition, there is less red tape and bureaucratic resistance to change. Several recent projects using private volunteer organizations have been remarkably successful.

Another way of building flexibility into development efforts is to spend proportionately more money on pilot projects. A pilot project permits people to work out the bugs and provides an opportunity to study the proposed project's impact and benefits before enormous amounts of money are committed.

Fortunately, MDBs appear to be opening the doors to more contact with NGOs. While these changes are encouraging, more efforts are needed to make Third World development a community-based endeavor.

INTEGRATING THIRD WORLD DEVELOPMENT EFFORTS

African economic development is currently served by 82 international donors and more than 1,700 private organizations. Although the World Bank is the major player, the sheer number of others who take part in the process suggests the need to coordinate efforts. Agreement on a common goal of sustainability would help to ensure that all parties are playing by the same rules.

PRESERVING BIODIVERSITY

In years past, economic development was commonly viewed as an activity that is incompatible with the preservation of species diversity, generally referred to as biodiversity. This need not be the case. Today, for example, more than one million people live in the Amazon Basin of Brazil, meeting their needs for food and commodities through small-scale agriculture, hunting, fishing, rubber tapping, and nut gathering. These people live and work in a relatively undisturbed ecosystem without destroying the breathtaking biodiversity that makes tropical rain forest the crown jewel in the Earth's terrestrial biomes.

Interestingly, research on the Brazilian rain forest shows that the income from rubber, fruits, nuts, and other products sustainably harvested from it actually exceeds the revenues generated from agriculture, grazing, and lumber on the same land. These findings have not escaped the attention of the development community. Officials in charge of a project funded by the Agency for International Development in Niger, for example, recently reversed their course, letting a natural rain forest regrow after discovering the economic and social benefits of this course of action. Sustainable harvest of the forest is expected to provide a 48 percent annual return on investment—six times greater than that of a typical plantation in the region.

Similarly, the gathering of wild fruits and rubber and other products from the Amazon rain forest could generate six times as much cash income as logging. With fish and other renewable resources such as caiman skins factored in, the economic benefits are even greater.

This knowledge, combined with pressure from local rubber tappers and some environmental groups, convinced the government of Brazil to set aside a large tract of Amazon land in the state of Acre for sustainable harvest of forest products in 1989. Known as an extractive reserve, this tract of undisturbed forest will protect biodiversity and safeguard human inhabitants, many of whom have reaped the bounty of the forest for decades without harming it.

Extractive reserves contrast sharply with commercial logging and cattle ranching, which are generally short-term endeavors that leave in their wake a denuded, eroding landscape. What is more, research suggests that tropical rain forests may offer many additional products in the years to come. Al Gentry, a botanist with the Missouri Botanical Garden, for example, recently discovered a tropical vine that produces an oil suitable for a variety of uses. According to his estimate, this plant growing in the forest could produce more oil per acre than the most productive oil-seed plantations anywhere in the world. Moreover, says Gentry, this economic bonanza would be achieved without destroying species diversity.

Recognizing the value of forestland and indigenous people, the government of Colombia has recently begun to return much of its forest to native tribes. To date, 45 million acres of Colombian rain forest—an area three-fourths the size of Great Britain—have been ceded to tribal peoples. These lands cannot be sold without approval from three-quarters of the adults in the community.

Robert Goodland, chief of the environmental division of the World Bank's Latin American and Caribbean regional office, and George Ledec, a consultant to the World Bank's Office of Environmental Affairs, argue that many other wildlands besides rain forests can sustain significant harvests of natural resources while providing environmental services and without threatening species diversity. Mangrove swamps, for instance, are a nursery ground for commercially important fish and shrimp; they also reduce coastal flood and storm damage and help filter sediment from waterways. If properly managed, mangroves can be a source of timber for construction, pulp for paper, and charcoal for energy. Mangrove swamps also provide food for livestock, shellfish for human consumption, and a number of other products—all sustainably.

In Matang, Malaysia, well-managed mangroves produce fish and wood products worth more than $400 an acre per year. One job is generated for every seven and a half acres. To give you an idea of the economic potential of such sustainable activities: if all of Southeast Asia's roughly 200,000 square kilometers of mangrove were managed sustainably, they would pump about $25 billion annually into the region's economy and provide as many as eight million new jobs.[6]

Do no harm. Most money for Third World development comes from four MDBs: the World Bank, the Inter-American Development Bank, the Asian Development Bank, and the African Development Bank. As noted above, the World Bank contributes the lion's share, making about 70 percent of the loans to Third World countries.

In years past, development projects funded by the World Bank and others often encouraged the conversion of relatively untouched wilderness to human use, in large part because planners had no idea how important wildlands were for sustainable development and long-term human well-being.[7] Today efforts are under way to stop the unnecessary destruction of natural habitats. In addition, more and more lending institutions and development agencies have begun to recognize that wildlands offer direct economic benefit to local residents, who can be employed as managers, guards, wardens, and guides needed to support a thriving (potentially sustainable) tourist industry.

Protecting wildlands requires efforts on several levels. First and foremost, it is important that developers, working with local leaders and citizens, examine the environmental services provided by a region under consideration. In many cases, they will find that these services are more important to the community than the proposed project. Replacing lost benefits may be exceedingly expensive. Corrective measures, in fact, may necessitate massive outlays for reforestation, erosion control, levees, dredging, water purification, and so on, diverting scarce economic resources from economically productive ventures to remediation—that is, repairing past messes. Failure to protect wildlands that offer vital services to the present generation also tends to increase the capital cost of economic development for future generations. Thus, the short- and long-term success of national economies depends in large part on their ability to improve the economy without destroying nature's capital. The first rule of a development project should be, First, do no harm.

Lending institutions see the light. In the Third World, good intentions and money are the root of much evil. Fortunately, MDBs and bilateral aid agencies such as the U.S. Agency for International Development have begun to recognize that business as usual is a near-guarantee of ecological backlash. Adopting the concept of sustainable development, the international lending agencies are now changing their practices. Nowhere is this more evident than in the World Bank under the leadership of a former congressman from New York, Barber Conable. Thanks to pressure from environmentalists and responsible individuals within the banking and the development community, the bank has adopted a broad policy to protect wildlands. Several key provisions of this policy are worth noting.

First, World Bank policy denies financial support for projects that will destroy "wildlands of special concern"—for example, wetlands and estuaries—even if the conversion was in progress before the bank had been asked to consider financing.

Second, the bank gives preferential support to projects on land that has already been cleared, cultivated, and logged.

Third, when development of wildlands is justified, the bank favors projects on less valuable land, then calls on participants to offset losses by improving wildlife management in ecologically similar areas.

Fourth, the World Bank requires that development projects include measures to protect surrounding regions. Dams built to generate electricity or provide irrigation water, for instance, require well-vegetated watersheds to minimize erosion and sedimentation, so the success of many projects hinges on measures that safeguard watersheds.

To cite an example, in 1980 the World Bank financed the construction of a major dam in northern Sulawesi, an island in Indonesia. To ensure a reliable supply of water and to minimize sediment deposition in the reservoir, the program included provisions that protect the vegetation in the watershed. One measure of extreme importance was the establishment of the 3,000-square kilometer Dumoga-Bone National Park, within the reservoir's watershed. Off-limits to logging and other human activities that could reduce vegetative cover and increase erosion, the park serves as a kind of insurance policy, protecting the watershed and providing an abundant supply of clean water for the reservoir and for farmers. The park also helps to preserve native plant and animal life, much of which is unique to the island. The cost of establishing the Dumoga-Bone National Park was $1.1 million—only about 2 percent of the irrigation project's overall price tag of $53 million.[8]

One of the most significant threats to wildlands and species diversity in the Third World is roads that penetrate remote areas. Roads bring people into unsettled areas. Soon after a road is completed, settlers pour into the wilderness in search of home sites. In this newly opened territory, they hunt for wildlife and cut down forests to make room for farms and small cattle ranches. The result is often biological impoverishment, severe erosion, and soil degradation in areas long protected by natural vegetation. Even paving or improving an existing road can have a detrimental effect, because it improves access to outside markets.

The World Bank's policy for road development reflects a concern for the damage caused not only by the structure itself but also by the settlement that follows. Its policy stipulates that roads should bypass the most important wildlands, like wetlands. If a road is intended to facilitate the settlement of new lands, the bank's policy requires the establishment of "compensatory wildlife management areas" to off-set damage. If a road is not intended to facilitate settlement or conversion, a guard station or some other measure must be set up to restrict immigration.

As a lending institution, say Robert Goodland and George Ledec, the World Bank is neither able nor willing to coerce governments to protect or better manage their environment. However, it can dramatically influence development in Third World nations through the specific conditions attached to its loans. And because wildland management must continue beyond the life of any development project, the World Bank also insists that loan agreements specify long-term measures that the borrower agrees to implement.

IMPROVING THE PRODUCTIVITY OF EXISTING LANDS

The provisions outlined above help to protect land from unnecessary destruction and improve land management on contiguous property. Another related effort, often overlooked in the quest to develop the Third World, is the protection and enhancement of land already under use. The erosion control project in Niger and the irrigation project in India mentioned at the beginning of the chapter are good examples of improvements in the interests of long-term, sustainable production.

By protecting land already under cultivation from erosion, over-grazing, and other destructive forces, developers can lessen the conversion of forests and other habitats to farmland carried out to make up for agricultural land lost to erosion. Enhancing productivity requires efforts that build soil fertility—for example, crop rotation, organic fertilizer, terracing, windbreaks, and small-scale irrigation projects.

As noted earlier, livestock production also impacts wildlands in a profound way. In the tropics, for example, huge forests are cut and bulldozed to make room for cattle pastures, which all too often succumb to erosion, compaction by hooves, and nutrient depletion. Clearing also paves the way for noxious, unpalatable plants unsuitable for cattle and other livestock. In Costa Rica, for example, approximately one-third of the rain forest has been cut for cattle grazing. Today, much of this land is choked with a thick, noxious weed unsuitable for grazing. Few cattle can be seen on the verdant hills and only patches of forests remain, hinting at the splendor that once existed throughout this country. Instead of supporting such projects, then, development efforts should be channeled into improving cattle ranching on existing range- and pastureland. Improvements in pasture management and animal husbandry are possible and would, like other measures that raise the productivity of land under use, eliminate the need to expand into wildlands.

One innovative way of protecting pasture- and rangeland is the use of native grazers, wild animals that are well adapted to the environment. In Africa, for example, indigenous species like gazelles, antelopes, and others fare much better than introduced cattle and do far less damage.

Overcoming Economic Obstacles

Currently, the developed world spends about $35 billion a year in assistance to Third World nations. While this may seem like a great sum of money, it is small in comparison with Third World debt— presently estimated at about $1,000 billion annually. The interest on this debt is about $60 billion a year.

As noted in the previous chapter, debt contributes significantly to environmental deterioration in many Third World countries for a variety of reasons. One of the most important is that it fosters unsustainable harvest practices aimed at increasing export earnings to service loans. Another problem with the massive debt is that many countries must devote inordinate portions of their national budget to paying interest, which leaves little money to finance important activities such as education, health care, family planning, and conservation projects.

Clearly, solving the Third World economic/environmental dilemma requires debt relief. One way, albeit minor, is the debt-for-nature swap.

DEBT-FOR-NATURE SWAPS

Debt-for-nature swaps, the brainchild of Dr. Thomas Lovejoy, are three-way deals involving countries in debt, the banks to which they owe money, and interested third parties such as international environmental groups. A typical swap works as follows. First, a third party like the Nature Conservancy purchases part of a nation's debt from the lender. This purchase is usually discounted—for example, a lender might sell a million dollars of debt (money owed to it by a Third World country) for $500,000. Next, the conservation organization that purchased the debt agrees to forgive the loan in return for a concession on the part of the debtor nation. In some cases, the latter agrees to set aside large tracts of land as nature preserves. In others, the debtor nation agrees to invest in educational programs or conservation.

The incentives for this kind of transaction are many. Banks that lend the money in the first place may receive tax breaks for a charitable donation to an environmental group. In addition, they recover some part of their loan, which might otherwise have remained unpaid. Conservation groups that purchase the debt benefit because they gain concessions from the debtor nation in the form, for example, of land set aside to protect wildlife. Debtor nations benefit because they end up paying much less for loans.

Several debt-for-nature swaps have already taken place among private commercial banks, environmental groups, and various nations. Encouraged by success, some international environmental groups are attempting to convince the U.S. Congress and the Bush administration to forge similar agreements with nations now in debt to the United States. According to the proposals, debtor nations would invest money they owe the U.S. government in local conservation projects.

A closely related concept is the debt-for-development swap, a two-way deal in which debt owed to a nation is forgiven if the money that would have been paid to the creditor is used to support development projects in the debtor nation. These moneys could support rural health clinics, agroforestry demonstration projects, family planning programs, appropriate technology, energy efficiency technology, and education.

DEBT RELIEF AND OTHER ECONOMIC MEASURES

Debt-for-nature and debt-for-development swaps, though promising, are not without their problems. One of the most significant is followup, that is, ensuring that once a debt is forgiven, the debtor nation will make good on its promises. In addition, swaps make only a dent in the gargantuan Third World debt. Relieving that debt requires several additional steps.

One important action is outright debt relief—forgiving a portion of a nation's debt with no tradeoff at all. Additionally, lending agencies and national governments can renegotiate interest rates on loans, since many loans now crippling the Third World were made in the 1970s when Third World economies were in better shape than they are today. Interest rates then were often quite high; simple reductions would make it easier for Third World countries to pay back their loans and reallocate money for education, environment, health, and other areas.

Reductions in tariffs (import fees) in industrial nations, which prohibit trade with Third World nations, could also help countries extract themselves from burdensome debt.

William D. Ruckelshaus, former administrator of the Environmental Protection Agency, argues that substantial amounts of foreign aid should also be given to Third World nations to improve the status of their environmental ministries.[9] As it is now, these ministries are chronically understaffed and underbudgeted, particularly in comparison with economic development and military ministries. The result is lopsided government emphasis on military buildup and Western-style development.

Industrialized nations might help Third World nations by voting to increase the budget of the UN's environment program, which operates with a paltry $30 million a year budget. If the world's nations are really serious about achieving sustainability, funding and staffing will have to be increased substantially (more on this in chapter 9).

Still another economic measure for fostering sustainable development is the microenterprise loan, money lent directly to individuals for starting up or improving existing businesses in a country. Microenterprise loans were pioneered by Mohammad Yunus in Bangladesh, who offered low-interest loans to small businesses and farmers. Many projects proved remarkably successful. By encouraging the spread of wealth laterally rather than having it concentrated in the hands of a few, microenterprise loans promote development that actually helps people.

Controlling Population Growth and Ending Hunger

No discussion of Third World development would be complete without a few words on population growth, a topic discussed in greater length in chapter 12. With world population projected to increase by five billion people in the next 40 years and 90 percent of that increase taking place in the Third World, controlling growth—preferably stopping it for the time being—is essential. Numerous books and articles on the topic suggest a variety of ways to make population control a reality, but without political will and a sizable investment in time, energy, and money, little progress toward a solution can be expected.

Another item high on the list and discussed in more depth in chapter 12 is ending hunger. Carla Cole, former director of the Campaign to End Hunger, argues that awareness of hunger is widespread, but the call to feed everyone has to be translated into policies, programs, and practices that allow people to feed themselves sustainably.[10] Many of the recommendations made in this chapter seek this end.

Learning from Third World Cultures

In the classes I teach on sustainability, many students remark that the guidelines for sustainable development in the Third World also apply to the industrial world. That is, by following the advice we give to them, we can protect environmental resources vital to our mental and physical health. Another point that comes up from time to time is that Third World development is riddled with a subtle bias, an implied belief that Western ideas, lifestyles, technologies, and indeed entire Western culture is superior to anything the Third World has to offer. This unsettling attitude leads many to believe that information must flow from west to east, north to south.

Just as a good teacher gains from the insight and experience of his or her students, so the West stands to learn a great deal from the Third World. It is conceivable that lessons from the Third World could profoundly influence cultural evolution in the West.[11]

Modern writers like Alvin Toffler, Hazel Henderson, Lester Milbrath, Robert Gilman, and the late E. F. Schumacher champion a new world view that might reshape human behavior, institutions, and economies. Calling for a shift in outlook that is more cooperative, anticipatory, participatory, and holistic, this group of visionaries is advancing an ideology and a way of life that is already in place in many parts of the world.[12]

On this matter, Margaret and William Ellis write, "Studies of other cultures could open our eyes to the options for a more positive future." Native cultures have much to teach us about living peacefully with the natural environment and forging a system of commerce mindful of ecological imperatives. Consider the Australian aborigines. With no concept of land ownership, they see themselves as part of the land and cannot conceive of being separated from it. In the African nation of Ghana, most natives give with no mind to getting something in return. These people offer philosophical guidance desperately needed in the West. More practical guidance may come from the indigenous farmers of the Third World, whose primitive farming practices have, in many cases, persisted for thousands of years. Operating in harmony with the environment, these people have an extraordinary knowledge of plants and animals and have skills far exceeding those of modern farmers, who rely less on knowledge and skills than on elaborate and costly tools.

Community and cooperation are two features characteristic of many Third World nations and are, quite interestingly, two of the

central goals of the visionaries. The Ellises point out numerous examples in the Third World that provide a model for the West. In a
village they visited in Fiji, for example, the community harvests,
dries, and exports sea cucumbers to Japan. The proceeds from this
cooperative venture go to the village elders to support community
projects. In Papua, New Guinea, roads are maintained by "youth
clubs" formed by young men who have reached puberty and are not
yet married. Payment for road work does not go to individuals but
to the common house in which they live.

Few scholars have explored the concept of community and cooperation in indigenous cultures to see what we can learn from them. In
Cultural Transition, published in 1986, Richard Katz compares the
"synergistic economy" of the African !Kung with the "scarcity economy" of Westerners. Functioning as guardians, not owners, of resources, the !Kung are motivated by the notion of service to others.
Rather than assuming that resources are scarce and that individuals
must compete for them, the !Kung believe that collaboration makes
more available to all.

In sharp contrast, the industrial world operates largely on the notion of the sovereignty of nation states and the principle of economic
competition. While sovereignty and competition have their merits,
they are the source of many world problems—poverty, pollution,
war, hunger.

Other cultures have a lot to teach us. Say the Ellises, "There are
new future concepts already conceived and still practiced by various
people around the world that we need to understand, adapt, and
adopt." Intercultural understanding provides a platform from which
we can see ourselves and adapt, creating a vibrant mix of cultures
living sustainably on this small, endangered planet.

8 Government of the People, by the People, and for the Planet

One generation passeth away, and another generation cometh, but the Earth abideth for ever.

ECCLESIASTES 1:4

In 1988, THE CANADIAN GOVERNMENT voted to approve a free trade agreement with the United States. Developed by U.S. and Canadian government economists, the agreement is aimed in part at removing crucial trade barriers that have hindered U.S. multinational corporations from operating in Canada. Toppling these barriers, the Canadian government hopes, will increase the export of Canada's natural resources—resources like oil, water, timber, and natural gas—thereby boosting the nation's economy.[1]

Not all Canadians view this decision as a step forward. Among other things, they say that the agreement undermines domestic energy policies to improve efficiency and reduce energy demand, efforts that could help protect Canada's natural resources and ensure a steady supply for many years to come. Today, Canadian citizens have remarkably little input into resource management policy. Opening the country to U.S. companies, say some critics, will render Canadian citizens even more impotent in determining their own future.

Some critics believe that the agreement will also discourage energy conservation in the United States. Why should the United States implement energy efficiency policies when Canada's resources are freely available? Furthermore, the agreement has no regulations that would allow for the return of wealth (via user fees, for example) to areas from which resources are extracted; as a result, it may encourage exploitation at the expense of future generations as well as Canada's environment. Toby Vigod, of the Canadian Environmental Law Association, characterizes this decision as "a resource grab with devastating environmental implications."

Some Canadians fear that they are giving up control over their own natural resources. The trade agreement says, for instance, that their government cannot deny water to the United States even if Canada is suffering from drought. The agreement also calls for a harmonization of pesticide regulations. Thus, say some critics, Canada's more stringent pesticide guidelines could be weakened to correspond more closely with those in the United States.

As an example of what might come in the name of free trade, President George Bush recently complained to Canadian officials that a government-sponsored tree planting program represented an unfair subsidy to Canada's timber industry. Canadian officials buckled under the pressure, ending a program to restore a heavily timbered region.

The U.S.-Canadian free trade agreement is not an isolated case. U.S. government negotiators are actively pursuing a worldwide campaign to make trade freer, an effort that could have potentially devastating international environmental implications. Under direction from the Bush administration, negotiators are attempting to persuade 98 nations that have signed the General Agreement on Tariffs and Trade (GATT) to accept a plan that would give multinational corporations even freer access to resources.[2]

GATT, writes Robert Schaeffer in *Greenpeace* magazine, has governed international trade since 1948 and is a rule book that establishes something of an international code of business ethics. In 1986, the United States began to urge a revision of the rules that would permit international corporations to set up operations in any corner of the world with minimal government interference. What this means is that multinational corporations could exploit the natural resources of a host country while remaining more or less immune to its environmental laws. Critics suggest that liberalizing GATT will translate into fewer regulations and limited compliance with emissions standards. Any country that imposes restraints, say the opponents, might be accused of restraint of trade.

The implications of such a move are frightening. Efforts to protect the environment would be set back decades, perhaps permanently. No step could more seriously jeopardize efforts to build a sustainable society.

Free-trade agreements and countless other decisions made by all levels of government throughout the world are part of a body of public policy that is shortsighted, wasteful of resources, and exploitive of nature. Unsustainable government policies almost always place immediate human needs above long-term environmental considerations. Such policies reflect an obsession with growth and economic and resource interdependence rather than self-sufficiency.

Since government plays a pivotal role in the economic life of a nation, the "flaws" in government are not unlike those observed in the economic system discussed in chapter 4. The flaws of economics and government ultimately reflect the "flaws" in human thinking and human ethics outlined in chapter 2. Making our society sustainable requires a transformation of ethics on various levels: individual, business, and government. The lattermost challenge is the focus of this chapter.

Building a Sustainable Government

Building a sustainable society requires a realignment of government priorities to include something larger than defense systems, economies, education, and welfare. It requires a dramatic shift in policy and action to protect the Earth. It requires that sustainability become a filter through which all decisions pass.

GOVERNMENT WITH VISION

Henry Kissinger once said that in government the urgent often displaces the important. This, in turn, leads to crisis politics, policies and actions that address immediate problems while ignoring long-term trends that have not yet reached crisis stage. A government practicing crisis politics is not unlike a damaged ship whose captain and crew work frantically to plug up leaks while the ship herself drifts toward a rocky coast.

Kenneth Hunter, a senior official in the General Accounting Office, notes that "America's political institutions have great difficulty dealing with issues that are long-term, global, or cross-cutting"[3] (cross-cutting refers to problems requiring action by two or more divisions of government). Politicians, he argues, seek marginal adjustments and quick fixes in the hope that problems will go away. Lest we forget, politicians operate with a public mandate, and the public is usually unable or unwilling to come to grips with unrealized crises. Frontierist beliefs are particularly influential in this matter, creating a kind of optimism that leads to denial.

In crisis politics there is little room for planning, much less for acting, in thoughtful ways. However, it is precisely under these conditions, says Burt Nanus, professor of management at UCLA, that long-range thinking becomes most necessary. Why?

In a society operating in the crisis mode, years of neglect or marginal attention result in a metamorphosis of small problems into intractable nightmares. A good example is the U.S. savings and loan debacle. When the S&L problem was first pointed out, Hunter asserts, no one responded. It was not until the problem had reached a crescendo that action was taken, and then it was too late to do much of anything except bail out the failed institutions and increase an already mammoth budget deficit.

Inattention to the long-term, growing problems of a nation sets up a vicious cycle. Governments find they must devote large amounts of money to problems that could have been corrected more cheaply in the past. In the meantime, the public grows increasingly intolerant of investment in the future when today's needs are not being met. So says Richard J. Gross, legal counsel and director of policy for Governor George Sinner of North Dakota.[4]

Ironically, crisis politics and management pervade our most progressive and visionary environmental institutions. Take, for example, the U.S. Environmental Protection Agency, founded in the 1970s in part to perform long-term studies of the health of ecosystems in face of growing pollution. In 1988, an independent science advisory board reported that research carried out by the EPA was largely shortsighted and thus failed to live up to its original raison d'être.

In *Beyond the Fray: Reshaping America's Environmental Response,* I argue that many environmental organizations are also enmeshed in crisis politics. Busily putting out brush fires, they have failed to establish a vision of where they are heading.[5] For years, many environmentalists (myself included) have assumed that new laws and tighter regulations would be sufficient to put out the bigger fire that was burning at the heart of the nation. As a result, the formal environmental movement with many noteworthy achievements is sometimes a knee-jerk reaction to modern society's transgressions. Most environmentalists, says author Bill Devall, rarely question basic social and philosophical assumptions of modern industrial societies.[6] They favor government intervention to regulate business, and they seem to stay within the parameters of established philosophy, politics, and social action. Devall notes, "Many leaders of mainstream environmental groups in the United States espouse a political agenda that is not based on a new philosophy of nature, nor on the premise that radical changes in politics and culture are necessary to solve the problems of this civilization."

Political leaders also rarely question the basic assumptions of our society and, consequently, the debate over solutions has been superficial. Now, more than ever, it is time to go beyond the immediacy of partisan politics and engage in a systemic rethinking of government. Without a fundamental overhaul of the notions that drive politics and economics, without a fundamental restructuring of government and our way of life, efforts to build a sustainable society will likely wither and die—the demands of the immediate are bound to prevail, and the urgent will negate the important long-term changes we need until crisis envelopes us.

Critical Trends Assessment Act. In 1985, in an effort to encourage more far-range thinking in the U.S. government, Senator Albert Gore of Tennessee introduced federal legislation known as the Critical Trends Assessment Act. The purpose was twofold: to help the federal government gather information about economic and environmental trends in our society and throughout the world, and to apply that information in public policymaking.[7] The Critical Trends Assessment Act did not survive the rigors of American politics in 1985, but it was resurrected by Senator Gore and reintroduced in the 101st Congress.

If passed, Gore's act would establish an Office of Critical Trends Analysis (OCTA) in the executive branch of government to assess critical trends, not just environmental but also economic, political, and social. The OCTA would advise the president on the potential effect of current government policies on various trends and produce a report every four years that would identify and analyze the trends, as well as outline alternative futures for the next 20 years.

The information feeding this process would come from the gold mine of underutilized data available from the Census Bureau, Social Security Administration, Department of Energy, Department of Agriculture, EPA, and other government agencies. Much of this information is currently gathering dust on shelves or locked away in computer memory where it is, for all intents and purposes, useless to public policymaking.

To alleviate this problem, the OTCA would serve as a repository for trend data. The staff would review it and translate it into meaningful terms for the president, the general public, and our legislators, in hopes of encouraging debate—not just in government but in the private sector as well—over future policies. The OCTA would focus attention beyond immediate concerns to help us "futurize" the U.S. government and thus better shape the world that lies ahead.

State governments could begin their own offices to examine long-term trends. Like Gore's proposed OCTA, state offices might examine state, national, and even international trends in a variety of areas: population, resource supplies, pollution, employment, economics, technology, and capital for investment. Based on critical analysis of the information, state OCTA's would make recommendations to an audience ranging from the governor to legislators to business owners to citizens on changes in policy and actions to help build a sustainable future. State offices would therefore help the government and the private sector formulate policy with an eye toward the future and would encourage the inclusion of additional viewpoints in state decision making.

To begin the process, state offices must explore the economic, social, political, and environmental requirements of a sustainable future in conjunction with citizens, environmentalists, educators, business leaders, and government officials. This would help ensure that critical trends were analyzed through the lens of sustainability.

To keep reports from gathering dust, the offices would need to devote considerable resources to the dissemination of their findings. The four- or five-year reports they issued, for example, might be drafted in a language accessible to the general public and sold in bookstores. Summaries of the report could be disseminated to universities, media, legislators, government agencies, businesses, and citizens. The offices could also sponsor press conferences and workshops to present their findings. Direct consultation with interested parties would be an additional avenue.

Futurizing Government, Futurizing the People. One of the challenges in futurizing the U.S. government or any government is the unwillingness on the part of many people to believe that human beings can actually destroy the Earth's rich biosphere. For them, it seems unimaginable and completely at odds with common sense. The OCTA might convince influential policymakers that we are indeed making global changes of profound influence.

The basic questions in leadership and government, says Burt Nanus, professor of management at UCLA, are this: Will the future be created carefully and well, and with due attention to the impacts of our choices? Or will the future happen by default and the consequences be dealt with after the fact, as has been the case for the last several hundred years, perhaps for all of human history? Given the built-in flaws of governments and economies, it is unlikely that a desirable (sustainable) future can evolve by default. Long-term planning and action are needed, and the first step is enlightening the people who are, after all, the roots of democratic government.

William E. Halal, professor of management science at George Washington University, says that "a new planning system [like the OCTA] is fine, but we need to plan a new system."[8] A new system requires fundamental statutory change.

Offices of critical trends analysis at the state and national level could also review key economic and environmental laws, then make recommendations for statutory changes or new laws that promote sustainability. One of the first orders of business would be the repeal of the Employment Act of 1946, which declares that it is the continuing policy and responsibility of the federal government to "promote maximum employment, production and purchasing power."[9] In the niche created by its dissolution, there would be room for a sustainable futures act that declared it the continuing policy and responsibility of the federal government to promote a society that lives within the limits posed by nature—a society that conserves resources, recycles as much as possible, relies heavily on renewable resources, restores damaged ecosystems, and controls population growth at home and abroad. A sustainable futures act would provide impetus to eliminate laws and policies that waste resources, pollute the environment, and destroy the habitat of other species. If nothing else, it might encourage congressional debate on the underlying causes of our environmental problems and focus attention on the need for root-level solutions. Rather than proffering more stopgap measures, Congress might just turn its attention to systemic solutions, escaping the grip of crisis politics long enough to do the rethinking that's essential to a sustainable future.

Expanding the role of state OCTAs further, staff members could review pending legislation before it is voted on by the legislature, preparing briefs that outline the pros and cons of each piece of legislation with respect to sustainability.

Futurizing government will also require efforts to promote the study of the future in schools and universities. High-school and college students, for example, might be required to take an introductory course on the future. This course could help sensitize students to the needs of future generations and to other species by showing how current policies and actions affect the future, both positively and negatively. Courses on the future could be included in secondary education programs as well, thus ensuring a broader audience.

Thanks to the efforts over the last two decades of Edward Cornish and his colleagues at the World Future Society, the study of the future has emerged as a legitimate academic endeavor. Its adherents typically transcend well-defined academic boundaries, looking at political, economic, and environmental factors, among many others.

Despite these pioneering efforts, considerably more formal research in universities and private think tanks is needed. In addition, improved mechanisms are required to disseminate the knowledge gleaned from such studies.

Election Reform. Establishing an Office of Critical Trends Analysis, passing a sustainable future act, and increasing education and research on the future would broaden the planning horizon of government. The limited planning horizon might also be pushed back by increasing the length of office key officials hold. A president's first term becomes a kind of juggling act. He (and someday maybe she) is kept from making hard decisions that might prove unpopular and damage prospects for reelection. One measure that could help avoid the problem would be to elect our presidents to one nonrenewable six-year term. This would permit presidents to concentrate on decisions and policies necessary to untangle the wide array of domestic and international problems currently addressed with quick fixes. Likewise, U.S. House members, who currently serve two-year terms, could be shifted to four-year stints, allowing them to spend more time studying issues and solving problems—and more time in their seats while Congress is in session—and less time producing TV advertisements for reelection campaigns.[10] Limiting the number of terms legislators serve might also compel leaders to lead—that is, to make the hard but necessary decisions required if we are to build a sustainable society.

Fed up with politics, citizens of Colorado, California, and Oklahoma have passed referenda that limit the terms of state legislators. The Colorado referendum puts an eight-year cap on terms of office for state legislators and is unique in setting a limit for U.S. legislators at twelve years.[11]

Although radio and television stations and advertising agencies might object, legislating shorter election campaigns would permit leaders to spend more time doing what is necessary and less time strutting their political feathers. In Great Britain, campaigning begins six weeks before a general election. In the United States, it's not uncommon for a campaign to begin a year or so before an election.

CREATING A NONEXPLOITIVE GOVERNMENT

Making people and governments more farseeing and proactive can reduce the exploitive nature of human society. However, if governments and the economic systems they support are to become even less exploitive, numerous changes in policy and management are also required.

Before we look at measures to reduce the exploitation of nature and of people, a few comments on political systems are in order. First, it is important to point out that exploitation is not unique to democratic governments. Democratic, socialist, and totalitarian nations all tend to operate under the belief that nature is a resource base for human exploitation. They all seek to maximize economic productivity and wealth. Until recently, little concern was given to the long-term environmental impact of various governments' actions.

Another unifying characteristic of these systems is that they don't take resource limits very seriously; most societies view growth as an unquestioned good. In all these systems, a minority of the population generally holds most of the wealth, and this group has a disproportionate influence on public policy. As a result, the economic well-being of a few takes precedence over the health of the planet and its less fortunate people.

A good example of the influence of wealth and power is the Clean Air Act of 1970, one of the most expensive and far-reaching pieces of legislation in U.S. history. According to former EPA administrator William Ruckelshaus, important sections of the Clean Air Act were designed not so much to clean up the air but to protect the jobs of coal miners and the income of owners of coal mining companies in the eastern and midwestern states that produce high-sulfur coal. These provisions, says Ruckelshaus, impede the shift to low-sulfur coal from the West to meet regulatory demands for reduced sulfur-dioxide emissions. Instead, utilities were forced to install expensive smokestack scrubbers.[12] Low-sulfur coal would have eliminated or reduced the need for smokestack scrubbers and toxic ash disposal resulting from the use of this device.

Another example is the Alternative Motor Fuels Act (AMFA). Ostensibly designed to stimulate research and development on alternative liquid fuels to promote U.S. energy independence, this law really is not much more than a shot in the arm for the coal industry. Of all of the alternative fuels available, the AMFA preferentially supports methanol from coal (a nonrenewable fuel). It pays lip service to ethanol production from crops, a potentially renewable source of liquid fuel that could replace oil. When burned, methanol adds to the carbon-dioxide in the atmosphere, whereas ethanol combustion produces no net carbon dioxide because it is produced from plants that absorb that compound from the atmosphere.[13] Sustainably produced, ethanol would help us reduce global warming, acid deposition, urban air pollution, and other problems. Methanol is merely an alternative fossil fuel that does little to solve the fundamental environmental problems we face.

In industrial democracies, making government policy less exploitive requires efforts that prevent, even reverse, the concentration of power in the hands of a few. In 1988, an estimated 23,000 lobbyists wandered the halls of Congress peddling their influence. In Harry Truman's time there were only 450 lobbyists. Today's massive army of lobbyists comes largely from the business community, whose influence on public policy has helped to create a government that caters to wealth and power at the expense of the ecosystem, future generations, and other species.

Another sign of the influence of power and money: in 1988 4,500 political action committees operated in the United States, many of them representing big business. The PACs donated approximately $140 million to reelect sympathetic members of the House and Senate. In 1974, there were only 600 political action committees, which contributed about $8 million to political campaigns. Today, when PAC members speak, congressional representatives listen.

Reducing the exploitive policies of the wealthy may require limitations on business contributions to PACs and even regulations to reduce the influence of lobbyists. These measures have the potential to increase the voice of the public.

Creating Offices of Sustainable Economic Development. Reducing exploitation also requires a shift in business practices as outlined in chapters 4 and 5. You may recall that this involves efforts to use resources more efficiently and to tap hidden opportunities. State governments can be catalysts in the change through offices of sustainable economic development (OSEDs), which would function in two broad ways: assisting existing businesses and promoting environmentally responsible new businesses. Offices of Sustainable Economic Development would replace Offices of Economic Development, found in all state governments. By changing the emphasis from business development to sustainable business development, OSEDs would contribute to two mutually supportive goals: building a sustainable society and helping to create strong, stable, and regionally self-sufficient economies.

OSEDs might begin by establishing advisory committees with representatives from business, government, and environmental organizations to explore with staff the requirements of a sustainable economy and to develop a set of criteria for sustainable commerce. These guidelines could form the foundation of statewide campaigns to convert existing businesses to sustainable businesses—for example, by encouraging efficiency, the use of renewable resources, recycling, the restoration of damaged lands, and waste minimization. The staff of the offices of sustainable economic development might offer seminars, technical expertise, videos, and printed information outlining the requirements of sustainable economics and featuring case studies showing the economic and environmental benefits of sustainable business practices.

A second priority of the OSEDs would be to help find hidden opportunities, for example, ways to develop new businesses using local labor and resources like recyclable waste. Hidden opportunities might also include ways to start businesses that promote energy efficiency, sustainable agriculture, renewable resource use, or the restoration of damaged ecosystems for long-term, sustainable harvests in the future.

On a final note, OSEDs could also advise government officials on the types of business, if any, they should recruit into the state. By establishing criteria for environmentally sustainable business, OSEDs could filter out undesirable companies such as heavy polluters.

Transforming existing state offices of economic development to

OSEDs will require time and strong leadership. The support of governors is as essential as support from CEOs is in corporate changes. Citizens and environmental groups could join forces to lobby their governors—or form a coalition with business, academicians, and governmental representatives to make a formal recommendation to their governors—to change the mandate of the office of economic development. The latter approach, though requiring a lot of work, would be a consensual process; the more players who bought into the idea, the more likely it would fly.

Pollution Prevention and Demand-Side Management: A Kinder, Gentler Nation. Changes are under way in the U.S. government that could help to reduce exploitation by business. Two of the most noteworthy are the shift to pollution prevention and demand-side management. Pollution prevention offers many economic and environmental benefits. As an example, Martin Marietta's astronautics group in Denver, Colorado, recently embarked on a number of projects to prevent pollution through process manipulation. The company used to clean the aluminum panels of its Titan missiles with an ozone-depleting compound, TCA (1,1,1-trichloroethane), but today it uses a nontoxic, biodegradable, recyclable cleaner. According to Dave Weiland, manager of environmental communications, this switch cost the company $70,000 for research and development and approximately $200,000 for new plumbing. Although the costs to make the switch were impressive, the savings were even greater. Reduced material costs will net Martin Marietta about $100,000 per year, and reduced maintenance costs will make them another $50,000 a year. This change will also save the company about $400,000 between 1991 and 1995 in taxes imposed on TCA by the new Clean Air Act regulations. This relatively simple switch to a nontoxic degreaser has reduced the release of TCA by 375,000 pounds a year. Much to the delight of company officials, the new cleaning process seems to work better and poses a much lower risk to workers.

Through various other measures, Martin Marietta cut hazardous waste production by 82 percent from 1987 to 1990; the company's goal is to reduce it by 87 percent by 1992.

Another pollution prevention strategy is recycling hazardous waste. In some cases, hazardous waste produced in one process can be reused in other industrial processes with little, if any, purification.

A few state governments currently support innovative waste management. The state of California, for example, publishes a catalogue that lists waste generators and waste buyers, that is, manufacturers that will purchase materials that might otherwise be disposed of. In 1987, about a half a million tons of hazardous waste that would have gone to landfills was recycled in California. A dozen other state, provincial, and regional waste exchanges are now operating in the United States and Canada. In other encouraging news, the EPA recently agreed to alter its research emphasis from pollution control to pollution prevention, a step that should accelerate this already popular approach.

As noted above, pollution prevention also involves efforts to reduce demand—that is, measures that promote demand-side management. Reducing demand means that fewer resources are needed and less pollution is generated. Government can promote pollution prevention and demand-side management through conferences and information sharing jointly sponsored by businesses already engaged in these practices. In Colorado, for example, Martin Marietta helped to organize the Pollution Prevention Partnership, a group of industries, public interest groups, and government agencies that promote statewide hazardous waste minimization through seminars and conferences. Although the economic benefits of pollution prevention and demand-side management can be enormous, governments might facilitate the shift by small tax incentives or medium-interest loans, especially for smaller companies that would like to realize the profits of retooling but can't put up the money.

GOVERNMENT THAT PROMOTES ECONOMIC HEALTH AND SELF-RELIANCE

In chapter 4 we discussed economic measures that temper the industrial world's obsession with growth and encourage self-reliance in communities, states, and nations. Here we reexamine these strategies to see how governments can facilitate their adoption. We will begin with the growth orientation.

As noted earlier, futurist Hazel Henderson is currently promoting an alternative multidimensional measure of economic health that would replace the GNP as an indicator of economic success. Some governments are looking at broader indices that encompass quality of life, not just the traditional economic measures. Also noted earlier, the Chamber of Commerce for the city of Jacksonville, Florida, publishes an annual report entitled "Quality Indicators for Progress" that includes statistics in nine general categories, including public safety, health, education, environmental quality, recreation, and culture.[14] Jacksonville could serve as a model to other cities, towns, states, and even nations.

Employing an alternative measure of progress is one of the most important steps that governments can take at this time. Legislators can aid in this process by introducing legislation that would fund staff to gather the data needed. Staff could be housed in OSEDs or offices of critical trends analysis (in state and federal government). In the absence of such legislation, existing health departments and departments of natural resources could appoint a multidisciplinary working group to gather data and present an annual report on social, economic, and environmental progress. In the absence of state action, environmental groups could develop their own indices, calling on expertise from academia, business, and government for balance. Citizens can assist by writing legislators and discussing the need for alternative indicators of economic health.

Governments can boost economic health and self-reliance by supporting legislation and regulations aimed at increasing recycling. In 1991, Senators Tim Wirth and the late John Heinz introduced two amendments to the Solid Waste Disposal Act that would require producers and importers of tires and newsprint to recycle a certain percentage of scrap tires and newsprint each year. Several states have already taken action to stimulate recycling by requiring newspaper and book publishers to use a small, but gradually increasing, amount of recycled paper each year. Similar legislation would promote remanufacturing of other secondary materials such as glass, cardboard, and plastic.

Governments can set an example by adopting procurement policies that require their own agencies and departments to purchase recycled products. Collectively, local, state, and national governments account for about 20 percent of the total U.S. GNP. Government procurement programs aimed at buying recycled goods would therefore be a powerful shot in the arm for the recycling industry. Many states and some cities have already instituted procurement programs. New York and California, for example, permit the purchase of recycled products if the cost is no more than 5 to 10 percent above the cost of virgin materials.

Unknown to many, the 1976 Resource Conservation and Recovery Act allows federal agencies and departments to purchase numerous recycled products *if* they are reasonably priced. Unfortunately, the "reasonable cost" language of RCRA is often translated to mean "lowest cost." Changes in this language could create one of the largest markets in the world for recycled products, giving the recycling industry a much-needed boost.

To encourage recycling and slow the growth in the demand for raw materials, governments can also eliminate economic, legal, and regulatory barriers to recycling, such as the preferential freight rate that permits carriers to charge less for the transport of virgin materials than of recycled scrap.[15] Another barrier to recycling is the depletion allowance, a tax credit given to mining companies as they deplete their resources. Intended to free up capital for mining companies to develop additional resources, depletion allowances give the extraction industry an economic advantage over the generally unsubsidized or poorly subsidized recycling industry. Creating a freer free market by eliminating depletion allowances and preferential freight rates would clearly make the recycling industry more cost-competitive.

The quest for self-reliance must involve government efforts to promote the sustainable use of renewable resources by supporting research programs aimed at reducing the cost of photovoltaics and other renewable-energy technologies. Government-sponsored public education programs are needed to encourage builders and homeowners to install cost-efficient technologies, such as passive solar heating. A series of television advertisements and statewide conferences cosponsored by solar builders could help raise public awareness and knowledge. Government contracts for photovoltaic cells could stimulate mass production, a step almost everyone agrees is necessary to make them affordable.

Creating a self-reliant economy would require additional action on the part of governments to prevent urban sprawl, to save farmland and open space, and to make cities more amenable to mass transit. And finally, regional self-reliance must entail efforts to stabilize human population growth, nationally and internationally.

A GOVERNMENT THAT FOSTERS COOPERATION

Besides the measures mentioned above, government can help to build a sustainable society by fostering cooperation among the segments of society, especially among government, citizens, and business. Cooperation also requires ways of collaborating with nature, or weaving the human economy back into the economy of nature. Consider an example of social synergy first, one that attempts to foster cooperation between government and citizens for a better environment.

People and Policy: Better Air a Better Way. In 1984, the Colorado Department of Health proposed a revolutionary plan to help the city of Denver and its suburbs reduce urban pollution. Among other solutions, the Health Department suggested a voluntary no-drive program during the winter months, when Denver's air pollution is the worst.[16] Denverites would be asked to leave their cars at home one day a week during the high-pollution months. Commuters would be asked to seek alternative means of transportation—carpooling, walking, or riding the bus. Some might even work at home.[17] After much skepticism on the part of the EPA and local media, the program was approved for trial.

Unlike typical government programs, which depend on laws and regulations to impose restraint on the public, this plan was entirely voluntary and required an entirely new approach. The Department of Health began by hiring an advertising agency to come up with a catchy name, the Better Air Campaign. The agency then devised a series of engaging radio, television, and newspaper ads extolling the virtues of clean air and individual action. "You hold the key" to better air, one ad proclaimed. In the second year of the campaign, the Better Air Campaign used Paul Simon's hit song, "Fifty Ways to Leave Your Lover," in its advertisements. The song encouraged people: "Drop off the keys, Lee," and "Hop on the bus, Gus."

The goal of the Better Air Campaign was not to force people to seek alternative transportation but to inform the citizenry about the problems and solutions and then encourage them to take action. There were no penalties for failing to observe one's no-drive day. No police officers lurked under highway bridges in hopes of catching violators. Indeed, the program relied on positive encouragement and public attention on individual responsibility and action. One of the most important features of the advertising campaign was that it offered a laundry list of ideas on ways individuals could contribute. If you had to drive to work, the ads said, find some other way to clean up the air.

Better Air Campaign officials stirred public imagination when they began to report the successes of the program—a decrease in carbon-monoxide levels during the high-pollution winter months. Although later statistics would show that there was no statistically discernible reduction in driving, the program has to be counted as a major success. Why?

First of all, surveys of the public showed that many individuals continued the activities they had begun during the program. One survey conducted after the 1988–89 campaign, for instance, showed that 13 percent of the people who had participated in the voluntary no-drive day continued riding the bus or carpooling. Another survey of 2,000 Denver-area citizens indicated that over one-third had continued some kind of gas-conserving activity—not necessarily carpooling or riding the bus, but consolidating trips or other such actions. Another measure of success: in November and December 1988, bus ridership statistics showed an additional 116,000 boardings, suggesting that Denverites were indeed leaving their cars at home.

The program was also instrumental in changing the public's attitude about individual action. Before the program began, a survey had shown that most people were skeptical about the significance of individual action on a problem so large and complex as air pollution.

Follow-up surveys, however, measured a dramatic turnaround in attitude. People quickly realized that individual effort could be brought to bear on important environmental problems.

The program also inspired businesses to participate. After the 1987–88 air pollution season, a survey indicated that only 8 percent of the businesses in the Denver metropolitan area were actively promoting better air. The next year, that number had climbed to 30 percent.

The Better Air Campaign illustrates a way in which government can work without fines or legal retribution. It shows that government can be an agent of social change through partnership with people. In short, people and their government can work together, rather than at odds. This model could be brought to bear on a great many issues facing the world. Governments would be well advised to find ways to build more creative and cooperative partnerships.

Business and Government Working Together. The Better Air Campaign brought businesses as well into a cooperative relationship with government. During the 1988–89 high-pollution season, for instance, the Better Air Campaign offered an award to the business that contributed the most to help clean up the air. To the surprise of many, the prize went to the Total Petroleum Company, which owns and operates Vickers gas stations throughout Colorado.

During the high-pollution season, Vickers gas stations handed out bus passes to area residents who came in for a fill-up. Over 200,000 bus passes were given out in the 1988/89 pollution season, of which 125,000 were used. The company also sponsored employee programs to reduce driving, and over half of its workers participated.

Largely because of its inability to produce a statistically significant reduction in vehicle miles traveled, the Better Air Campaign changed its name to Clean Air Colorado and shifted its focus from the general public to Colorado businesses. Gone are the catchy radio and television advertisements encouraging area residents to leave their cars at home and seek alternative means of transportation. In their place, however, is an ambitious program aimed at encouraging Colorado businesses to reduce pollution—not just carbon monoxide, but acid precursors, ozone-depleting chemicals, and carbon dioxide, a major contributor of global warming. This statewide program has come to symbolize the "think globally and act locally" strategy vital to the sustainable revolution.

Toward this end, Clean Air Colorado has devised a computer program to determine the amount of pollution businesses generate from all of their operations—from electric lights, heating systems, manufacturing facilities, cars and trucks used by company officials, and workers who commute. Armed with an estimate of the total environmental pollution for which they're responsible, companies work in partnership with Clean Air Colorado to plot a strategy to cut emissions. This may require installation of high-efficiency light bulbs, starting an office recycling program, or encouraging workers to carpool or take the bus. It may mean finding ways to better insulate office space or factories or finding ways to make industrial processes more efficient. The options are many. The coordinator of the program, Anne Grady, says, "I want to be able to give . . . businesses a sense that not only do they contribute to the problem, but they can materially contribute to the solution."

In 1989–90, Clean Air Colorado selected 14 public and private organizations—large businesses, small businesses, schools, and state and city agencies—to participate in a pilot program aimed at reducing air pollution. The goal, says Grady, was first to document successes and then to market them to other organizations.

To cite some examples, the Marriott Hotel, one of the 14 participants, converted from electrical heat to steam heat and began an office recycling program. The Public Service Company, Colorado's leading utility, instituted a wide range of programs. For example, it's finding ways to reduce commuting by employees, paying them a dollar a day to use an alternative (nonpolluting) form of transportation. The company is also converting some of its fleet vehicles to compressed natural gas. YLS Computer Systems Consultants started a telecommuting program that allows over half of its employees to work at home. The city and county of Denver developed a model program to introduce telecommuting in city offices.

Businesses and government, like citizens and government, can work in partnership rather than opposition. The goal of partnership is to establish ownership of the problem and avoid recrimination and bad feeling. By recognizing the true dimensions of a problem, government, business, and the individual can work jointly to solve it. Widely adopted by governments throughout the world, efforts such as these might allow society to direct its intellectual, financial, and technical resources to solving problems rather than doing battle over them. Cooperative alliances are only a part of the solution to creating systemic change in society, but they're an important one.

Uniting Warring Factions. State, national, and even local governments should consider the possibility of forging coalitions among disparate members of their constituencies to bring about constructive change. In the Pacific Northwest, acrimony has been at the heart of forest management for many years.[18] Timber companies, environmentalists, anglers, and Indian tribes have waged numerous battles over the best way to harvest timber without damaging other resources, such as recreation and wildlife.

In 1986, representatives from the Indian tribes and the timber industry decided to devise a creative, noncombative solution to several key resource management issues over which they had strong disagreements. The thorniest issue was timber cutting and road building near lakes and streams. Both practices result in excessive soil erosion, which destroys spawning beds and reduces salmon populations, already endangered by a century of human disregard.[19]

At the time it was approached by these factions, the state of Washington's Forest Practices Board (in the Department of Natural Resources) was drafting some management recommendations for timber harvesting. The commissioner of public lands, however, liked what he heard so much that he decided to suspend the board's activities, giving the factions some time to work out an agreement.

The first step in the process was for them to sit down together and discuss their interests. Representatives from Indian tribes, environmental groups, and timber companies met with foresters and researchers from the state government. To help the process along, several ground rules were established. First, there would be no votes; all decisions would be achieved by consensus. The group would focus on solutions that pleased everyone. Second, each group would have all the time it needed to present its case. Third, as a condition for participation, groups were forbidden to posture and advocate.

One surprising result was that traditional enemies found they actually agreed on many issues. Within six months, the unlikely alliance had developed a fairly comprehensive document called the Timber, Fish, and Wildlife Agreement, which outlines acceptable forestry practices. Two of the most important achievements were the establishment of procedures for making site-by-site determinations on timber-cutting permits and on-site reviews for areas of special sensitivity. This so delighted the Forest Practices Board that it scrapped its recommendations and adopted the regulations recommended by TFW participants. The state legislature appropriated $4.5 million to implement the agreement, which became effective January 1, 1988. When the program began, 1.5 million acres of commercial forestland were managed according to the TFW agreement. Today, 4 million acres are under the TFW program.

This sort of consensual policymaking exemplifies the way that cooperation profits people and the planet. During the TFW process new working relationships formed, uniting traditional foes around a common good—environmental protection—and reducing costly litigation. Those who participated in the project believe that the process worked because of a willingness on the part of the participants to go beyond confrontation—to cooperate.

The TFW Agreement is a model for reaching creative solutions to a wide variety of economic, social, and environmental problems. With the insights and experience gained from the TFW experiment, governments could sponsor similar programs to address pressing economic and environmental issues.

Adaptive Management Fosters Cooperation. One of the reasons the TFW Agreement succeeded was that it called for the establishment of a new kind of management. Known as adaptive management, this revolutionary process provides land managers an opportunity to monitor on-going activities and alter them as needed. Modifications are based on scientific data from field studies aimed at assessing the effectiveness of current management practices.

Adaptive management is based on a simple but elegant idea: if human understanding of nature is imperfect, then human interaction with nature should be experimental, according to Professor of Political Science and Environmental Studies Kai Lee of the University of Washington.[20] If resource management is considered from the outset as an experiment, surprises become opportunities to learn rather than failures to predict. In the TFW experiment, information gained from monitoring management practices is evaluated and reviewed by a multidisciplinary policy group. If management measures prove inadequate, this group suggests changes in the regulations that would improve forest management and protect the environment.

Besides improving resource management, adaptive management is useful in building cooperation among disparate factions. For example, environmentalists often fear that rules and regulations, once established, will be nearly impossible to change, but adaptive management views them as hypotheses—testable assumptions about management. The process is open to discovery and adds an element of flexibility in government decision making. Flexible rule making has an interesting effect on participants' willingness to reach agreement. If environmentalists believe that rules can be changed if they prove inadequate, they are more likely to agree to them.

Adaptive management not only permits us to learn from experience and to change policy as needed, it gives us a mechanism to develop insights into the process of nature and how humans can most effectively interact with nature. Unfortunately, says Lee, problems arise because bureaucracies don't have much tolerance for trial and error. Although virtually all policy designs take into account feedback from action, the idea of using a deliberately experimental design is almost unheard of.

To be successful, adaptive management requires extensive interaction between government agencies charged with managing resources in a region, observes Lee. For example, it calls for tremendous sharing of information, cooperation, and compromise for the benefit of the resource. As it stands, government agencies frequently work at cross-purposes.

While cooperation is the cornerstone of successful adaptive management, implementing such a plan may depend on the decentralization of activities and the participation of a great many different individuals. That, says Lee, is because activities are generally carried out by agencies whose responsibilities are rather narrow. He points out that consensus by negotiation tends to link the common goals of a project to decentralized action, thus enabling the parts to work together.

Flexible Policy Options. For nearly 200 years, Americans have solved their differences by the double-L approach—the legal and legislative approach. To end environmentally destructive practices, for example, environmentalists have usually either sued offenders or rushed to government to convince officials to pass new laws. Legislation often resulted in strict government rules and regulations. Federal pollution control laws are a good example. This system of broad legislative mandates manifest through detailed regulations drawn up by government agencies has many deficiencies, note the authors of *An Environmental Agenda for the Future*. It can be inflexible. It is complex. It is difficult to administer and enforce, and it is difficult for businesses to comply with.[21] The EPA, for example, currently regulates chemical pollution under nine different statutes. Regulations aimed at controlling exposure to toxic chemicals require the EPA to protect Americans from minute quantities of a large number of chemicals present in many media (air, water, and land) over long periods.

Rules and regulations breed contempt and resistance. In addition, most government regulations require companies to control pollutants at the effluent pipe, a regulatory bias that diverts attention from inexpensive and effective measures that prevent pollution in the first place. Regulatory compliance, important as it is, may actually thwart the implementation of creative, cost-effective solutions.

To build a cooperative relationship with business that improves environmental protection, government rules and regulations could be made more flexible. Instead of stipulating end-of-pipe solutions or specific technologies to reduce pollution, government regulations could set overall performance goals, for example, a 50 percent reduction in carbon-dioxide emissions or a 75 percent reduction in hazardous and solid waste by certain dates. Companies would be permitted to reach these goals themselves through creative means. Technical assistance and oversight from the government would move the process along.

Efforts such as these would save money and reduce antagonism, speeding up the transition to a sustainable way of life. Government regulation to control the emission of pollutants will undoubtedly continue to play a role in the coming decades, but flexible rules that encourage alternative processes, substitution, and other innovative methods of complying with the law might be a welcome change to mainstream government policy.

Increasing Cooperation and Coordination within Government. One hindrance to building a sustainable society, alluded to above, is institutional contradiction—government agencies whose policies and practices are at odds with one another. Overcoming this barrier requires efforts to unify government agencies and departments under a common goal, sustainability.

At the highest level of government, the president could assemble the cabinet and department heads for a weekend retreat to explore ways of collaboratively implementing sustainable practices. The overarching message would be that environmental protection is the responsibility of all, not just the EPA. Governors and mayors could hold similar meetings with their staff and department heads.

Ultimately, efforts to align government policies with the tenets of sustainability require that all decisions pass through a sustainability filter. This, in turn, may help agencies transcend traditional boundaries and look beyond narrow, short-term solutions. It should help them develop strategies that compliment, rather than contradict, one another.

Cooperation is also needed among agencies and departments at different levels of government—between national and state agencies, between state and local agencies, and so on. If that means bringing on additional bureaucrats to network with other agencies, then it's a sacrifice worth considering.

Funding Environmental Protection. Globally, nations spend about one trillion dollars—or $1,000 billion—a year for national defense. The

United States spends nearly $300 billion, about a third of its annual budget, for defense (the Defense Department recently requested $1.6 billion simply to air-condition the hangars of the Stealth bomber). In comparison, environmental protection receives a paltry $5.6 billion. Surprisingly, two-thirds of the 1990 EPA budget is earmarked for two programs, construction grants for wastewater treatment and Superfund cleanup, leaving little for other essential programs.[22]

The authors of *An Environmental Agenda for the Future* argue that one of the reasons Americans have failed to achieve the environmental goals set out nearly two decades ago is that there has been a terrible mismatch between the work required by the EPA and the agency's funding. From 1975 to 1985, the agency's operating budget steadily declined in real dollars while its workload doubled. Although funding has been increased somewhat, the EPA is still underfunded and understaffed.

Environmental agencies the world over are short of money and staff. As a result, they remain powerless to reverse the steady decline of the environment. Increasing funds for these agencies is essential if humans are to make significant inroads into environmental decay. In an era of fiscal shortages, increasing funding for the environment may be difficult. However, if environmental agencies can find ways to work with business to prevent pollution and use resources more efficiently, it is possible that resistance to requests for additional funding may diminish.

An example of cooperation is the EPA's Green Lights program, begun in January 1991 to convince America's 1,000 largest corporations to reduce pollution and increase profits by installing energy-efficient lighting. The EPA is recommending installation of compact fluorescent light bulbs; improved fluorescent tubes; new electronic ballasts, which use half the energy of conventional ballasts and also eliminate the flicker and hum typical of fluorescent lights; and special control devices that turn lights off when a room is vacant or that adjust interior light according to window light. EPA officials estimate that these steps would reduce U.S. electrical demand by 11 percent per year, cut sulfur-dioxide emissions by 7 percent, and save businesses $18.6 billion a year. If the EPA captured some of the savings, it would be able to promote additional programs aimed at making business and society more efficient and economical.

Government Policies to Promote Cooperation with Nature. Lest we forget, building a sustainable society requires another form of collaboration: the fundamental realignment of the world's economies and governments with the forces of nature. Two examples illustrate this point and suggest some policy changes.

The first involves efforts to control flooding and ensure adequate supplies of municipal water in two different parts of the United States: Boston, Massachusetts, and Woodlands, Texas.[23] Both regions have made important decisions in land-use planning that will save millions of dollars and help to protect the environment. Let's begin with Boston.

Boston has a beautiful city park system that stretches from the center of the city into the outlying suburbs. Some consider it a landmark of park planning. But few people realize this system with its meandering stream was constructed to absorb flood waters and reduce flooding and property damage, saving millions of dollars.

In recent years, Boston city officials added an 8,500-acre wetland to their park. This parcel, once slated for development, not only provides additional habitat for fish and wildlife but greatly augments flood control at one-tenth the cost of a dam.

The second example hails from Texas. In the 1970s, oilman George Mitchell set out to build a new town he called Woodlands on a 20,000-acre site north of Houston. Unlike most developers, who tear down trees and then name the streets after them, Mitchell envisioned a community that would exist in harmony with nature and set out to build it. By preserving the existing natural drainage as open space, which could carry water away more effectively than an elaborate storm sewer system, Mitchell saved $14 million. In 1979 heavy rains hit the area, causing flooding in neighboring communities built the old way. In Woodlands, streams swelled by 55 percent, but there was no damage.

Woodlands is a model of the concept of designing with nature. Most of the original trees still stand, and the open spaces set aside for natural drainage harbor numerous birds and mammals, including bobcats and white-tailed deer. To protect groundwater supplies of nearby Houston, the planners decided to build roads and houses in the subdevelopment on high ground, out of the way of aquifer-recharge zones.

Clearly, designing with nature requires wisdom and foresight. It is an approach to development in which nature calls some of the shots.

These two examples bring to mind some words of Montaigne, the French essayist and philosopher: "Let nature have her way, she understands her business better than we do." Using eco-logic, human thinking consonant with the laws of nature, humankind can learn to live peacefully with the birds and the insects and the rocks and the trees.

State and local governments could stimulate eco-logical solutions to environmental problems by mandating least-impact analyses for all housing developments, shopping malls, new factories, and so on. This novel idea would require developers to first examine a range of options, then choose the least-damaging one. Least-impact analysis would differ sharply from the environmental impact statements currently required in the United States in at least two significant ways. First, instead of studying the impact of one project, then offering a few token options, the least-impact analysis would call for a careful study of all options. Each option would be considered equally and the developer would be required by law to choose the least-damaging one. Second, least-cost analysis would apply to all projects that could result in significant damage to the environment, not just to federally funded projects or to projects on federal land.

Making Unsustainable Systems Sustainable

Politicians of all affiliations frequently espouse ever more growth to solve the problems facing the world. In so doing, they overlook a simple fact: the optimum size of an economy is not necessarily its maximum size.[24] "Unfortunately," says the Worldwatch Institute's Sandra Postel, "decision makers have not yet grasped that at some point growth begins to cost more than it is worth." Continued growth could, in fact, cost us a planet, and lest we forget, good planets are hard to come by.

The challenge, says Robert Gilman, a leading proponent of sustainability and founder of the Context Institute, is to "set our own limits or have limits disastrously imposed on us."[25] If we choose to set our own limits, we must first establish a new definition of humankind, one that permits us to match the scale of human endeavor with the scale of nature, refitting the human economy to the economy of nature. Such a definition will, ultimately, redirect future activities. We might, for example, choose energy efficiency over plans to drill oil wells in the Arctic National Wildlife Refuge. Or we might elect to recycle paper rather than continue expanding timber cutting. In the words of Harry A. Merlo, chairman and president of Louisiana-Pacific Corporation, one of America's largest timber companies, wastepaper "is the largest remaining forest." It has "no owls or woodpeckers, and you don't even need a chain saw."

In an article in *Environment Magazine,* University of Washington's Kai N. Lee outlines efforts to achieve a more sustainable relationship with nature in the Columbia River basin.[26] Over time, he notes, the Columbia River basin has been grossly altered by human activity. Today, 19 major dams and five dozen smaller hydroelectric projects exist in the basin. The governing principle behind the many functions of the river, says Lee, has been to maximize economic return. The river's uses have been ranked accordingly: power, urban and industrial activities, agriculture, flood control, navigation, recreation, and lastly, fish and wildlife.

The priority given fish and wildlife is evident in the dramatic decline in the salmon population. In the pre-industrial era, the basin supported and produced an estimated 10 to 16 million salmon a year; by the late 1970s, the number had fallen to about 2.5 million. Recent estimates put the number far lower.

Sustainable management in the Columbia River basin began in 1980 with the passage of the U.S. Northwest Power Act. A monument to sustainable development, the act was designed to mitigate the effects of more than 50 years of hydroelectric power development in the basin. The Northwest Power Act gave birth to the Northwest Power Planning Council (NPPC), an agency charged with formulating a long-term power plan for the region and developing a program to rebuild fish and wildlife populations.

In 1982, the NPPC adopted an ambitious fish and wildlife program that called for a wide range of activities, including major changes in river operations to provide "equitable treatment" for fish. The result, says Lee, is an effort to rehabilitate fish and wildlife on an economic scale unheard of in natural resource management. Sustainable economic development of the Columbia River basin requires managing an ecosystem the size of France. If there is to be a sustainable Columbia, it will be governed by the rules of nature. It will be a place where human, economic objectives are deliberately balanced against natural boundaries and biological rhythms.

The work in progress is quite remarkable. For example, the harvest of Pacific salmon is being regulated by states and tribes in the Pacific Northwest and by the Canadian and U.S. governments to rebuild fish stocks while ensuring a fair apportionment of the catch. Efforts are also underway to increase fish populations by protecting streams, improving natural spawning grounds, and building fish hatcheries.[27] Currently, over 100 hatcheries are producing fish that are released into protected spawning grounds in the basin. Government officials hope that these fish will imprint on their adopted waters and will return to spawn as adults, helping to reestablish the "wild" population of salmon.

Natural spawning habitats are being improved by reopening fish passages, and rebuilding inadequate fish ladders near dams. The NPPC has also put 40,000 miles of stream off-limits to small hydroelectric projects in order to protect fish spawning and migration. Officials are also installing screens on dams to deflect young fish on their migration to the sea from power turbines.

In addition, and perhaps most ambitious of all, the river's flow has been altered for the benefit of fish migration at an annual cost of more than $40 million in lost power revenue. The program recreates the spring snow melt to flush migrating juveniles to the sea. Without it, many migrating juveniles would get lost along the way.

The cost of the council's fish and wildlife programs in 1990 is about 1.5 percent of the Bonneville Power Administration's annual budget of $2.7 billion. Thus, the NPPC can search for sustainability under conditions where budgetary limitations are only a secondary consideration, says Lee.

Achieving a more sustainable relationship is a colossal challenge, given the institutional and economic interests that evolve in an area. The goal, says Lee, is to find some kind of a workable compromise that is perhaps neither wilderness, or in this example, power plant, in those regions already severely affected by human activities: "To achieve sustainability, humans must somehow pick a path between preservation and profit maximization." This is not to imply that sustainability is a midpoint between preservation and the maximization of profit. Sustainability, says Lee, is a departure in a new direction.

Sustainability, which must be a product of political choice, is a stimulus for tremendous institutional reform. But for sustainability to work, the choices must become part of government policy. The Columbia River basin project can be a model to the world, showing how systems that are out of balance and out of scale with nature's economy can be brought more in line. If the human activity in the river basin is to become sustainable, observes Lee, it will have to be managed with an awareness of biology rare in human affairs. The same can be said about virtually all human activity throughout the world.

9 Making Peace with the Planet: Some Thoughts on Global Environmental Protection

Nothing can survive on the planet unless it is a cooperative part of a larger, global life.

BARRY COMMONER

BANGLADESH IS A COUNTRY UNDER SIEGE. About the size of Wisconsin, Bangladesh is home to over 118 million people (almost half the U.S. population), most of whom live in abject poverty, eking out a living from the tired landscape.[1] The signs of environmental decay are ubiquitous. Sediment-choked streams, denuded land, and treeless forests tell the story of a people living well beyond the carrying capacity of their environment. Overpopulation and poverty, added to environmental decay, threaten the country's future. But the dangers do not end here. Outside the country's borders, a host of problems mount, putting additional pressure on Bangladesh. One of the most significant is global warming.

If computer models are correct and the sea level rises two to three feet by 2050, 17 percent of Bangladesh's land area will be reclaimed by water, destroying much of the nation's coastal farmland. In a starving nation, any loss of productive farmland is a tragedy. Although levees could be built to combat rising seas, Bangladesh lacks the financial resources for such an undertaking. In the absence of massive aid from other countries, global warming would likely have a devastating effect on this already-desperate nation.

Bangladesh will bear the brunt of several other environmental transgressions wrought outside its borders. One of the most notice-able is deforestation in the Himalayas, now occurring in neighboring China, India, and Nepal. Excessive timber harvesting in these coun-tries, assert Bangladeshi government officials, has greatly increased the occurrence and severity of flooding in Bangladesh since the 1950s. In 1988, one flood left 25 million Bangladeshis—nearly one-fifth of the entire population—temporarily homeless.

Bangladesh, like dozens of other countries, is endangered by a complex mix of internal and external forces that, until recently, have received little international recognition.

Redefining National Security

Slowly but surely, most of the world's nations are recognizing the importance of a healthy environment to their social, economic, and political futures. As a result, nations are beginning to rethink out-dated notions of national security, which generally equate military strength with security.[2] True national security, they're saying, in-volves efforts to protect the ecosystem not just within the confines of a nation's boundaries but globally. National security also involves freedom from hunger, poverty, and disease.

Achieving Global Environmental Protection

The new national security hinges on changes in ethics, economics, business, and government, topics discussed in previous chapters. Be-cause of the transnational scope of the environmental crisis, it also requires changes in the way nations interact. More than anything, national security necessitates cooperation among nations on a scale unheard of in human history. International cooperation to eliminate pollution and to end the rampant exploitation of natural resources is the focus of this chapter.

Unfortunately, some observers note, widely shared environmental problems do not necessarily guarantee cooperation and common policy. One of the reasons is that national priorities differ; environmental protection may be high on the agenda of Sweden, but barely rate in a nation hard-pressed by poverty, food shortages, overpopulation, and civil strife. In Eastern Europe, for example, poor economic conditions have over the years relegated the environment to the bottom of the list of priorities. Compounding the problem, countries with heavy debt often exploit their natural resources to ease the crippling burden. As mentioned previously, however, it is becoming increasingly obvious that environmental protection is not a luxury, a matter a nation can attend to when it has more time and money.

Distrust also stymies cooperation. For example, exhortations to halt environmental destruction and reduce pollution in Third World countries are often seen by these countries as a deliberate effort on the part of the West to deny economic opportunities it already enjoys.

Finally, international cooperation is thwarted by a reluctance on the part of governments to relinquish sovereign rights for the sake of the whole. As they see it, international accords to control pollution or reduce environmental destruction give outsiders an unprecedented say in internal government policy, obstructing the right to self rule. While most of us recognize that giving up a little control to save the planet is a small price to pay for our common future, not all countries agree. In the face of these very real obstacles, how do nations that recognize the need for global cooperation foster the kind of working relationships needed to confront global environmental problems?

A Source of Inspiration and Guidance: Unilateral Action

What the Earth needs most is a variety of useful models, says Karl-Henrik Robert, a leading cancer researcher in Sweden.[3] By that he means model homes, buildings, companies, communities, and, indeed, countries that demonstrate how to live and work sustainably on the planet—examples that can become powerful stimuli for change.

A stellar example is Sweden. Already divesting itself of nuclear power and seeking to make up the loss by simply using energy more efficiently, Sweden is a world leader in sustainability. In a remarkable effort to transform his country into an even better model for the world, Robert recently set out on an ambitious project to change the thinking of the entire nation. Convinced that the root of the environmental crisis is modern society's dependence on linear systems and linear ways of thinking, Robert decided to build a national consensus on the need for recycling all waste—not just municipal solid waste but hazardous industrial waste as well. To do this, he met with influential scientists, musicians, artists, politicians, educators, and even the king of Sweden to share his ideas.

The success of his approach lay in working on root causes and refusing to get bogged down in the scientific uncertainty, where much of the debate over environmental issues still lies. After reaching agreement with a wide number of influential people, Robert and his new-found colleagues began issuing "consensus reports" on the condition of the environment and on root-level strategies needed to reverse the deterioration. Through booklets and audio cassettes sent to all of Sweden's schools and households, seminars for members of Parliament, television programs, and journal articles, they spread the word deep and wide. This unprecedented and ambitious effort to reshape the thinking of a people should have profound effects on the way the people of Sweden live and work.

Other nations may follow suit. And fortunately, says Robert, it appears as if there is "a growing core of thoughtful decision-makers who understand that the time to act is now. Whether we want to help others or ourselves, to conduct our affairs ethically or compete in tomorrow's markets, the possibility of success rides on the shoulders of well-informed business and political leaders who are supported in their efforts to base the foundations of society on natural laws."

Robert also points out that despite all the quibbling over peripheral issues, there is already enough of a scientific consensus to get on with the necessary work. In most cases, more research is not needed. Furthermore, since environmentally sound technology is already available, the pace of transition to cyclic processes is limited only by our willingness to act. The longer we delay, the more painful the sacrifices will be down the road.

The Netherlands and Norway are likewise becoming models of thoughtful, environmentally responsible living. For example, to curb global warming both have unilaterally adopted policies to either freeze or cut their carbon-dioxide emissions. Although these steps will probably have little effect on climate, given the massive production of pollutants by the United States, Europe, and the former Soviet Union, they may inspire other countries to follow suit.

Model countries provide inspiration and also experience that can steepen the learning curve in countries that choose to follow suit. Moreover, model countries are positioning themselves to become innovators and exporters of technological know-how for which the rest of the world may soon be clamoring. Those countries that insist on quibbling over global warming, say some critics, may be losing an opportunity to become leaders in resource-efficient technology and other areas vital to building a sustainable world.

FORGING ENVIRONMENTAL ALLIANCES

Another force transforming the world is the environmental alliance, pacts made by countries that share environmental problems. In 1984, for example, nine European nations and Canada, which together produce 30 percent of global sulfur dioxide, agreed to reduce sulfur-dioxide emissions by 30 percent by 1993. Nineteen other countries have since joined in. A similar pledge to cut nitrogen oxides by 30 percent by 1998 was made in 1988 by 12 European nations.

Another sign of the growing willingness of nations to cooperate was the 1988 Montreal Protocol, an agreement to halve ozone-depleting chemicals by 1999. Sponsored by the UN Environment Program (UNEP), the Montreal Protocol was ratified by 24 nations. In June 1990, signatories of the protocol amended the agreement, calling for a complete phaseout of all chlorofluorocarbons (CFCs) and halons by the year 2000.

Critics argue that the complete phaseout is vital but that it should be made more swiftly. One group, the Natural Resources Defense Council, is currently pressuring the U.S. government to establish a shorter time line for eliminating CFCs and is putting pressure on industry to accelerate the development and implementation of alternatives to ozone-depleting chemicals.

Nonetheless, the Montreal Protocol remains a landmark agreement marking a turning point in the history of international environmental cooperation. In February 1991, scientists and government officials from 130 countries gathered for what would be the first of five conferences to forge a world response to global warming, slated to be signed in Rio de Janeiro in June 1992.

Experience with the Montreal Protocol could be extremely valuable in reaching agreement on climate change. Most important of all, participants can benefit from issues raised by Third World nations being asked by the protocol to limit CFC production. China, for example, was reluctant to go along with plans to phase out CFCs by the year 2000, because it was just gearing up to produce CFCs on a massive scale as part of a nationwide effort to put a refrigerator in every home. Technical and financial assistance from the West convinced the Chinese government to sign on.

The International Whaling Commission (IWC) is another encouraging example of international environmental cooperation. Composed of members from the whaling nations, the IWC has set quotas on kills to protect whale populations. In 1983, IWC members reached an unprecedented agreement to halt all commercial whaling starting in 1986.[4] Even though the IWC has no enforcement power and must rely on the cooperation of governments, it has proved to be an effective force in saving the whales.

Clearly, international alliances are vital to solving global environmental problems, but issues that affect narrower regions are best addressed by smaller-scale cooperation. Two notable examples are regional environmental alliances formed by countries bordering the North and Baltic seas, which are badly polluted by industrial and domestic waste. In 1987, eight countries on the North Sea reached an agreement to halve their discharge of nutrient pollutants (nitrogen and phosphate) and toxic chemicals by 1995. A similar agreement was signed by seven Baltic nations.

Lending a Hand: Innovative Financial Arrangements

In the late 1970s, the U.S. EPA pioneered an idea in pollution control called the emissions offset policy aimed at preventing regional air pollution in the United States from worsening as new businesses open up.[5] Under this policy, a company that is interested in expanding its operations or opening a new facility in a region that fails to comply with federal air-quality standards can do so only if it offsets its predicted pollution output—by paying a company already in operation to cut back further. If company A wants to operate in an area and is going to produce 10,000 tons of air pollution a year, it must pay company B, already in business in the region, to reduce its emissions by at least 10,000 tons a year. By cutting back on pollution from existing sources, new companies make room for the air pollution they will produce. Air quality also can be improved in a region by forcing larger cutbacks. Company A, for example, might be required to pay for pollution controls on company B that would eliminate 15,000 tons a year, even though company A was only going to produce 10,000 tons a year.[6]

Emissions offsetting has not escaped international notice. A number of countries, in fact, have entered into financial agreements to offset emissions in neighboring nations. In other cases, they merely offer technical assistance for pollution control. Former West Germany, for example, paid for some smokestack scrubbers on Czechoslovakian power plants in an effort to reduce air pollution drifting across the border and devastating German forests. At this writing, Sweden is considering a measure to finance pollution control measures in Poland.

Emissions offsetting is an example of a win–win–win strategy. That is, it helps producers of pollution that may not be able to afford pollution control, it helps "victim nations" suffering under the burden of pollution from afar, and, of course, it helps the environment.

Pollution prevention strategies are even better because they often cost less than pollution control devices. Besides costing less, pollution prevention strategies eliminate hazardous wastes often generated by pollution control technologies and therefore eliminate many potential environmental problems in "host" countries.

Rethinking International Governance

Twenty years ago, the economist Barbara Ward argued that the biosphere of our inheritance and the technosphere of our creation are out of balance: "The door of the future is opening onto a crisis more

172 LESSONS FROM NATURE

sudden, more global, more inescapable, more bewildering, than any
ever encountered by the human species. And one which will take
decisive shape within the life span of the children who are already
born. . . ."[7]

Harlan Cleveland, a professor at the University of Minnesota's Hubert H. Humphrey Institute of Public Affairs, writes that "Everything that has happened since those words were written reinforces
their prescient wisdom." Truly, our problems have become international and inescapable. In order to solve them, some observers believe
that we must go beyond cooperative alliances and find more effective
ways to govern the world's nations.

In 1986, scholars at the Hubert H. Humphrey Institute of Public
Affairs at the University of Minnesota launched a project to encourage a rethinking of international governance. They assembled an international body of "rethinkers" to sketch a credible, workable system of peaceful change.[8] The group began by looking at international
systems and institutions that already work to see what can be learned
from them. One example is the multinational corporations that,
while tending to be exploitive of people and environments, operate
across national boundaries much more easily than governments.[9] Regional cooperation coordinated by UNEP is another fairly successful
example. International civil aviation is yet another.

After examining why these organizations work, the participants
turned their attention to an analysis of the areas that require cooperation. Two prime candidates, they concluded, were global environmental protection and global military security. International governance, they concluded, should concentrate on those areas to limit
infringements of national sovereignty.

While most people can agree with the need for global environmental protection and military security, opinions differ on ways to
achieve these goals. Some observers believe that it's enough to simply
find ways to build more cooperative systems—that is, to support regional alliances and international coalitions. One way of creating alliances is to expand the funding base of UNEP, which has been an
important catalyst in previous agreements like the Montreal Protocol. Others believe that international governance requires efforts to

create a more powerful institution that could help govern the world from existing international organizations like the UN.

BUILDING ON EXISTING STRUCTURES: THE UN ENVIRONMENTAL SECURITY COUNCIL

In 1988 Edvard Shevardnadze, then foreign minister of the Soviet Union, made a stirring speech to the UN General Assembly. He said what humanity was doing to the Earth was an aggression against nature and spoke of the need to rethink the way humans use the Earth's resources. Although he argued that the human species has grown in its ability to solve problems of planetary scale, he questioned whether the existing institutions that deal with the environment were adequate to the task. He concluded by calling for the creation of a UN ecological council on a par with the General Assembly or the Security Council.

Noel Brown, director of UNEP, argues that we cannot dally on this matter. Creating an ecological council or better yet an environmental security council is "not only timely," he says, "but necessary, and anyone who would challenge this in terms of legal niceties would be stupid or inattentive."

Headquartered in Nairobi, Kenya, UNEP currently employs 340 people and has a $40 million annual budget. Although UNEP has made a substantial impact on global environmental protection, its efforts fall short of the task at hand. At the very least, UNEP needs additional funding and staff to improve four areas: data gathering, dissemination of information on environmental trends, dissemination of ideas on practical sustainable solutions, and expansion of efforts to promote alliances around key issues such as overpopulation, deforestation, acid deposition, and desertification. These efforts would encourage nations to take a long-term view and make changes in policy and management strategies necessary to ensure the long-term habitability of the Earth.

Although some would not like it, an environmental security council could take on a more prominent role, for example, condemning nations that continue environmentally irresponsible behavior. Japan might be condemned for the continued slaughter of whales under the guise of scientific research or for its participation in tropical deforestation. The United States and Canada might be condemned for cutting their old-growth forests and using energy inefficiently, thus contributing to global warming and acid deposition. Member nations of an environmental security council might pass resolutions that encourage, even compel, other nations to behave more responsibly in the world community.

DO WE NEED A WORLD PARLIAMENT?

Still others think that the seriousness of international social, economic, and environmental problems points to the need for more powerful forms of international governance, for instance, a democratic world parliament.[10] Efforts to begin a world parliament began in the late 1950s by a loosely knit coalition of people from a handful of nations. In the early 1970s they drafted a world constitution, which was mailed to all national governments in 1978. In the early 1980s they set up a provisional world parliament, the first session of which was held in Brighton, England, in September 1982. During that meeting five legislative acts were adopted, including one to outlaw nuclear weapons and establish a world disarmament agency. In 1985, the world provisional government adopted the Emergency Earth Rescue Administration to stop global warming.

Under its constitution the world parliament would have three houses: a house of peoples, consisting of 1,000 representatives elected by the people of the world; a house of counsellors, nominated by universities and colleges; and a house of nations, whose representatives would be appointed or elected by the nations of the world.

Lack of interest has frustrated efforts to build a world government. For many countries, the UN is sufficient, and in some cases may be too much. They see additional efforts to form a world government as a threat to national sovereignty. Proponents of world government, however, believe that the global environmental crisis requires nothing short of world government. According to the World Constitution and Parliament Association, "World Government is, in fact, the first practical requirement for survival and progress. . . ."

A World with Nobody in Charge

The challenge of governing the world today is very similar to the challenge faced by Thomas Jefferson, James Madison, Alexander Hamilton, and others when they sat down to write the U.S. Constitution 200 years ago, says Harlan Cleveland of the Hubert H. Humphrey Institute of Public Affairs. The U.S. Constitution was written to govern a large, diverse, developing nation through institutions designed so that no one arm of government was in command of the whole. A constitutional separation of powers and a system of checks and balances would be vital to the success of a world government.

World governance therefore poses the challenge of developing a global system of management amidst pluralism. No nation, creed, race, or ideology would be in charge, says Cleveland. That does not mean it would be a leaderless world, rather that decisions would be made jointly. Powerful governments of leading nations would exercise restraint, refraining from threatening, pressuring, or invading countries with which they do not agree. What is required is a coherent multilateral, consultative, and consensual process.

For many of us it is clear that something bigger, more powerful, and more unifying than UNEP is needed. Whether it is a UN environmental security council or a world government remains to be seen. Given the time it would take to set up a global government and the urgency of environmental problems, the best hope may lie in transforming UNEP into an environmental security council with political muscle and a budget commensurate with the task ahead.

A New World Leadership

William Ruckelshaus, former administrator of the U.S. EPA, points out that most industrialized nations have environmental laws and policies that to some extent reflect values consistent with sustainability. Laws that promote recycling and the development of renewable resources are examples. There is even a small number of international agreements such as the Montreal Protocol that reflect sustainable thinking. Unfortunately, these laws and alliances are rare threads in the larger fabric of unsustainable public policy. The tens of thousands of laws and policies that underlie an unsustainable world outweigh the impact of a few threads of sanity.

Sustainable policies are, however, a point of departure in the course of human cultural evolution. They provide a model for revising laws and regulations. Changing the fabric of public policy so dramatically, however, will require a new leadership—progressive, farseeing "evolutionaries."

LEADERS WHO LEAD

Despite their good intentions, many world leaders conduct public affairs with their ears to the ground, listening for the sound of footsteps. Focusing chiefly on internal affairs, they miss the truly important "external affairs"—outside influences that often have profound long-term effects on a nation.

If the world is to reach a sustainable state, leaders must learn to pay attention to the future. This, of course, requires people who can mobilize and inspire others to think and act anew.

MOBILIZING PEOPLE

David Gershon, who organized the First Earth Run, believes that the challenge of building a sustainable society is not just coming up with solutions.[11] There are many good solutions. The challenge, he says, is mobilizing people to believe that they can actually make change.

That requires individuals who understand the course of human civilization is unsustainable. It also requires individuals with a vision of a sustainable future, people with courage to step out in bold new directions for the sake of our common future.

Inspiring people to re-prioritize their lives on behalf of something larger than themselves—building a sustainable relationship with the planet—is no easy task. Only when people see where we are heading and what is possible through individual action will success be possible. To paraphrase Robert Gilman of the Context Institute, individuals need to see that their drops can actually fill up the bucket.

Overcoming the myths of modern society. To create a new generation of leaders, David Gershon has started the Gaia Leadership Training Program. One of the purposes of this project is to teach future and present leaders to overcome the crippling beliefs that prevent people from taking action. In the United States, at least three myths of modern society stand in the way of individual action.

The first myth is that individual actions don't matter—that what we do as individuals has little bearing on the problems we face. Many among us are paralyzed by the paradox of inconsequence, convinced that our actions are meaningless either in creating problems or solving them. The truth is, individual actions do add up. Many environmental problems are the composite of individual decisions and actions, each seemingly inconsequential. Together, individual actions spawn massive problems like solid waste, traffic congestion, and urban air pollution. Just as our problems are created by the sum of individual acts, so they can be solved by individual acts times many. In fact, effective solutions must involve individual responsibility and action.[12]

The second myth is that people don't care. That is, we are too self-centered and money oriented to do anything to help solve the problems we face. Government, we think, must force us to do good things because we will not do them on our own.

The third myth is that acts of kindness to the Earth are forms of sacrifice. In other words, individual actions for the benefit of the whole will lower the quality of our lives. Conservation, says solar electric expert Joel Davidson, does not mean doing with less; it means using what you have more wisely.

Leaders can dispel these myths rather than perpetuate them by showing people that what they do individually has broad consequences. Again, this is not to say that individual actions are the only answer, just that they are an integral part of any solution and must be paralleled by change in corporate and government action.

Leaders can also show that people do care for one another and for the planet. Deep inside, most of us want to leave a better world for our children and most of us are kind and generous, although it may take a tornado or an earthquake for the kindness and generosity to manifest itself. The new breed of leaders would nudge us along.

Finally leaders, both spiritual and political, must demonstrate that conservation and other acts of kindness in the name of the Earth are not sacrifices. As the root of the word *sacrifice*—"to make sacred"— implies, conservation is humanity caring for the future. Instead of giving up, we are giving *to*. The generous self is an idea powerfully articulated by John F. Kennedy so many years ago in his famous but often-ignored plea, "Ask not what your country can do for you, but what you can do for your country." As Alan AtKisson of the Context Institute notes, "Leaders must show that what feels like sacrifices to most people is necessary and prevents sacrifice in the long run."

Focusing on solutions. Besides helping to overcome crippling beliefs that hamper progress toward a cooperative society, leaders can change the focus of public attention from what isn't working to what could work. Says Gershon, we need "to find new models, new systems, new approaches—drawing upon the old ones . . . but looking at what we want as opposed to what we don't want in our lives, our communities, or the world at large."

Leaders as a source of cooperation. Many business people, farmers, environmentalists, and lawmakers share a concern for the deterioration of the environment and the survival of life on Earth. However, their views often differ when it comes to the seriousness of the problem and the solutions required. Leaders with vision are needed who can bridge the differences among the various factions and convert similarities and differences into strong working relationships.

Although leaders talk about the need for cooperation, few know how to go about creating it. True cooperation, says David Gershon, requires an alignment of people, vision, and projects so people and nations work together rather than at cross-purposes. Better training is necessary to create a cooperative leadership base in the world community.

Helping people believe in themselves and in the possibilities of the future. John W. Gardner, former secretary of the U.S. Department of Health, Education, and Welfare, currently teaches in the graduate school of business at Stanford University. In an article in *The Futurist* he writes, "Sooner or later, all leaders find themselves trying to build confidence."[13] This requires a positive attitude about the future and what individuals can accomplish.

Confidence has a subtle but powerful effect in shaping the future of a nation. The settlement of the West, for example, was marked by a positive belief in the future, says Gardner. Settlers felt they were a part of an immensely exciting drama about to unfold.

Most political leaders (and their speech writers) understand the necessity of instilling hope and reassurance in people. Ronald Reagan and his speech writers were masters at conveying the hope of prosperity and growth. But like many others today Reagan was living in a dream world, promising a new future based on an impossible extrapolation from the ways of the past. He promised more growth, more wealth, and more prosperity. What he and others forget is that you cannot plan the future by the past. Reckless optimism makes for good speeches but is a disservice to the public.

We need a future we can believe in, a future that's attainable and, more important, desirable—economically, socially, and environmentally. And we need a sense of confidence that we can achieve our goals.

Gardner tells a story about a conversation he had with Martin Luther King, Jr., at a seminar on education. A black woman leading the seminar had entitled her talk, "First, Teach Them to Read." Martin Luther King leaned over to Gardner and said, "First, teach them to believe in themselves." In his book *No Easy Victories,* Gardner writes that "the first and last task of a leader is to keep hope alive." As a rule, he says, fatalists have little impact on events. The future is shaped by people who believe in the future and in themselves, who "help people believe they can be effective, that their goals can be accomplished, that there is a better future that they can move toward through their own efforts."

Leaders should also seek to correct the circumstances producing negative attitudes. In the transition to a sustainable state, that means working diligently to confront the root causes of human unsustainability and finding ways to alter individual, corporate, and government behavior so that it complies with the biological principles of sustainability.

Effective solutions also depend on leaders and governments giving feedback to people to demonstrate the tangible success of individual effort. Others can contribute to the feedback process. Already, environmental groups are demonstrating how individuals can have an impact. In its magazine *National Wildlife,* the National Wildlife Federation regularly features articles on individuals who make a difference.

Another encouraging development in the feedback process is the Global File, a project of the Elmwood Institute.[14] The Elmwood Institute of Berkeley, California, was founded by one of America's leading rethinkers, Fritof Capra, author of *The Turning Point* and other books. Designed to promote sustainability, the Elmwood Institute's Global File records successful ecological practices in business and government throughout the world. This information is distributed worldwide to empower corporations and businesses to develop sustainable policies.

Achieving the goals of sustainability requires hard work. Gardner, therefore, suggests the need for tough-minded, optimistic leaders— people who can instill optimism tempered with a measure of realism.

Leadership from Below

Modern society operates with a rather narrow definition of leadership. For most of us, the word *leader* brings to mind mayors, governors, presidents, and congressional representatives. But these make up just a small and slow-moving segment of the leadership pool; behind them is a silent army of leaders, mothers and fathers who set examples for their children, students who become models for their classmates, workers whose actions inspire others to take action, and so on.

Leaders in the family, community, and workplace are sources of inspiration and direction, models of human behavior for those fortunate enough to live within their sphere of influence. Indeed, community leadership is as important as government leadership in building a sustainable future, perhaps even more; most people agree that if we have to wait for our elected officials to act, we're in big trouble.

The successful transition to a sustainable society requires people who will follow as well. "It is not enough for a nation to have a handful of heroes. What we need are generations of responsible people," writes Richard D. Lamm, former governor of the state of Colorado and a leading rethinker of American government policy.[15] Thus, in building a sustainable society, success depends on the ability of our leaders to establish a base of responsible citizens. Nurturing effective "followership" means overturning the idea that leaders do all of the thinking and followers merely carry out the commands.[16]

Thousands of pages have been written about leaders in business and government, but very little has been said about responsible citizenry. Of the many leadership training programs set up by companies, for example, only a handful address the problem of responsible followership. As a result of this cultural oversight, citizens (followers) are treated as if they were unimportant and, not surprisingly, often act the part. Can there be any doubt why people sit back and wait for their leaders to act?

If we are to create a responsible citizenry, we need leaders who respect and inspire their followers. And we need schools to teach students not just about the rights they are entitled to in a democratic society but also about their obligations to the system—in particular, how they can be active participants in the democratic process. We need education on the issues and an understanding of the ways individual actions contribute to solving the problems we face. In the words of H. G. Wells, our future is becoming "more and more a race between education and catastrophe." Leaders can be a part of education.

The world is rife with conflict over resources, land, and ideology; it is torn by vast inequalities of power and wealth. International environmental problems can function as an adhesive that helps humanity to overcome its differences, or they can compound the strife. The choice is ours and the time is now.

10 The Re-Evolution of Human Habitat: Building Sustainable Cities and Towns

We should seek the atmosphere and the surroundings which call forth the best that is in us.

COUNCILLOR

THE MODERN CITY AND SUBURB are the product of abundance. Cheap oil and ample supplies of timber and other natural resources have permitted this unwieldy form of human habitation to evolve and thrive, if only for a while.

From a biological perspective, modern cities and suburbs resemble the noisy, crowded bird colonies scattered on offshore islands and rocky coastlines across the globe. In the animal kingdom, colonies are a fairly sustainable way of life, providing two basic conditions are met. First, colonies can persist, even thrive, *if* the demand for resources by the inhabitants does not exceed the supply readily available from surrounding areas. Second, colonies can be sustained *if* the waste they produce does not poison its inhabitants.

Like bird colonies, cities and suburbs draw heavily on the resources of the surrounding environment. What was once a relatively small stream of resources flowing into early cities, however, has in this century become a deluge. To satisfy resource-hungry human colonies, land is often stripped bare or trampled or overgrazed, soil is subjected to erosion, and farmland is transformed into desert. Cities and suburbs also produce sizable amounts of waste. Air pollution, hazardous waste, sewage sludge, garbage, and other wastes pour out of our cities, far in excess of the environment's ability to assimilate them, threatening not only the health of urban inhabitants but the health of the entire biosphere.

The problem with human colonies is that they violate the conditions required for sustainability. Metropolitan areas are out of balance with the environment upon which they depend. According to Lester Brown and Jodi Jacobsen of the Worldwatch Institute, the number of people living in cities has increased from 600 million in 1950 to over 2 billion in 1986.[1] If this growth continues, they say, more than half of humanity will reside in urban areas by the turn of the century. The ever-persistent spread of cities will continue to devour valuable farmland, forests, and pasture. Gobbling up land and polluting the water and air upon which all life depends, our cities are on a collision course with the future.

Ironically, like many human inventions, cities and suburbs have come to victimize the people they were designed to serve. The cities themselves have become centers of work and commerce, the suburbs a place in which to live and play thanks to cheap oil, expensive highways, and the automobile. This schism of our two worlds results in inordinate amounts of energy consumption—fossil fuels burned to shuttle us back and forth between work and home. Today, in the United States, many Americans spend one to three hours a day traveling to and from work, and according to national figures, the average suburbanite makes 13 automobile trips a day just to run errands. Peter Calthorpe summed it up best when he said, "People moved to the suburbs for mobility and privacy. What they got was gridlock and isolation."[2]

Building a sustainable society means altering cities and suburbs to reflect ecological limits. This chapter examines several key steps for transforming the urban environment into a sustainable colony. We begin with some novel ideas on growth management, then focus on specific changes in transportation, waste, and housing—three areas critical to sustainability.

Containing and Modifying Growth

Just as resource abundance led to the evolution of the unsustainable city-suburb, resource depletion is likely to be the principal driving force in the dramatic re-evolution of the city-suburb. Shortages of oil, water, and minerals will generate much of the change, but public concern for environmental destruction, traffic congestion, and pollution and crime in urban centers will inevitably play an important role as well.

The first step in building a sustainable habitat is to slow, perhaps stop, the outward migration of cities and towns to minimize the loss of farmland, forests, and other natural resources that could, if managed properly, sustain humanity. Thwarting the geographic expansion would also help to protect native species that live a precarious existence on the fringes of human territory. One strategy that can help contain the outward expansion of human population is land-use planning.

LAND-USE PLANNING

Land-use planning is a means by which governments put land to its best use, dividing it up into zones each with a specific function, such as agriculture, industrial activity, and residential living.[3] Land-use regulations determine where people can live and where they can locate their businesses. Land-use planning determines the best location for pipelines, electrical lines, roads, and shopping malls. Historically, environmental considerations have played a minor role in planning. The marketplace has generally had a greater influence on the allocation of land use and other resources. Unfortunately for people and the environment, the market usually seeks immediate gain at the expense of the future.

By elevating the importance of environmental considerations, land-use planning can become an implement of sustainability. If this process can be made to fully incorporate sustainability, it could be transformed from an exercise in fitting human activities within a limited area to a way of accommodating the mutual needs of humans and nature.

As the example of Woodlands, Texas, cited in chapter 8 suggests, sustainable land-use planning takes into account a variety of considerations such as the slope of the land, soil quality, aquifer recharge zones, natural drainage, wildlife, and trees. Making best use of the land, therefore, means designing human habitation with nature, rather than attempting to redesign nature.

Nationwide land-use planning is a necessity because it eliminates the emergence of hundreds of local plans with conflicting goals and standards. Japan's nationwide program, started in 1968, is a good model. By designating land for urban, agricultural, and other end uses, the Japanese protect their nation from the abuses of the market system.

Many European nations have similar programs. In the 1960s, Belgium, France, the Netherlands, and West Germany adopted national guidelines for land-use planning. Administered by local governments, these programs seek to protect farmland by reducing urban sprawl and to protect open space by establishing greenbelts, undeveloped areas in or around cities and towns. The Netherlands has perhaps the best program of all, for it also sets guidelines for water and energy use.

In the United States, land-use planning at the national level is minimal. Besides establishing national parks, wilderness areas, national forests, and wildlife preserves, the federal government has done little to protect the nation's vanishing farmland, pastures, and open space. Most zoning, in fact, occurs on the community level, and current systems are generally not designed for sustainability. On the local level, planners primarily concern themselves with restrictions on land use for commercial purposes, for example, housing and industrial development. Regrettably, local zoning ordinances that govern such development are often waived to accommodate powerful economic interests.

As a result of community-level planning, states have become a patchwork quilt of conflicting rules and regulations. Statewide land-use planning could bring a degree of order to the chaos, but it is an idea slow in coming.

A leader in sustainable policy, the state of Oregon introduced the urban-growth boundary concept in the 1970s in an effort to better manage its growth. By law, each city and town is required to create a zone in which growth will be restricted. State law permits city officials to plan for a 2 percent annual growth in population over 20 years. When the 20 years are up, they can reassess the boundaries and consider expanding them.

Urban-growth boundaries in Oregon, now going on their second decade, have reduced leapfrogging subdevelopments, a leading cause of the destruction of open space and farmland. As many city officials will attest, urban sprawl usually increases the cost of services, roads, electric lines, water, and sewer lines. In Oregon, urban-growth boundaries have reduced taxes and held down utility costs.

Land-use planning within urban-growth zones in and around Portland has provided a wide range of housing opportunities. The result is smaller lots but generally more affordable housing than in unregulated regions.

By concentrating growth within a confined region, urban-growth boundaries make mass transit more feasible. In Portland, a light-rail system currently serves residents on the east end of town. Another such system is being built to serve the southern part of the metropolitan area, and a third is being sought for the west end of town.

The success of this containment strategy is evident when one compares Portland to its demographic cousin, Denver. Although these metropolitan areas have approximately the same population, Portland occupies only 350 square miles. The Denver metro area—without growth boundaries of any sort—sprawls over 500 square miles. While the city of Portland has contained 95 percent of growth within the boundary since the early 1970s, Denver continues to spread outward like many other metropolitan regions and is expected to cover 1,000 square miles by the year 2010.

Urban-growth boundaries or similar measures exist in Maine, New Jersey, Florida, Vermont, Washington, and Hawaii. Several other states are considering statutes to contain urban sprawl.

Growth Pays Its Own Way

Another innovative idea for checking urban sprawl is the "growth pays its own way" concept, which requires developers and businesses to pay the cost of any new infrastructure—schools, roads, sewer lines, water lines, and the like—required by the construction of homes and businesses or additions to existing businesses. The principle behind this idea is that those who make the money pay the bills.

According to a 1987 report by Population-Environment Balance, several studies have shown that the cost of new schools, roads, police and fire protection, water and sewer lines, and other services required by residential development and indirectly by new businesses and business expansion generally exceeds the tax revenues new construction generates.[4] For example, in Loudoun County, Virginia, a suburb of Washington, D.C., a new house generates tax revenues that cover only 70 percent of the cost of services provided to its occupants by the county. The remaining portion, says the report, is paid by county residents.

The report also notes that to offset tax drains from housing development, commercial and industrial development is encouraged because they presumably generate substantial tax revenue without as much infrastructure. The Population Environment report notes, "In isolation this is a valid argument, but new commercial and industrial development tends to attract new residential development," creating a self-perpetuating cycle. As a result, commercial development is likely to result in a net loss to the county and thus require additional taxpayer subsidies.

Under the growth-pays-its-own-way strategy, city or county officials calculate the projected cost of new schools, roads, and other services required by growth, then assess a "development fee" to all new housing, new business, and business expansion. The development fee, in turn, must be paid before a certificate of occupancy is issued.

By requiring business and developers to pay the full cost of additional services such as roads and sewer lines, development fees would encourage builders to locate new housing projects closer to existing roads, schools, fire stations, and so on, thus reducing urban sprawl and its economic and environmental consequences. Fees might also inspire developers and new businesses to install water-efficient fixtures in their buildings or, better yet, to pay for water-efficient fixtures in existing facilities, thus preventing an increase in water demand. Offsetting measures similar to those discussed in chapter 9 might save a builder thousands of dollars in water development fees and reduce environmental damage from new projects.

ZONING AND TAX INCENTIVES

As noted earlier, the main tool of land-use planning for years has been zoning, or classifying land according to use. In cities, zoning helps to separate potentially noisy, smelly, or hazardous activities from residential areas. In some cases, zoning laws have been modified to protect farmland and other undeveloped land from urban encroachment. In rural Black Hawk County, Iowa, for instance, zoning laws allow permits for well-conceived housing developments on farmland with lower productivity but restrict development from prime farmland.

Differential tax assessment laws also are being used to protect farmland. Under these laws, agricultural land is assessed according to its value for farming, not for housing development or other purposes. Agricultural designation is guaranteed, and city officials are not permitted to change zoning on farmland to raise taxes and force farmers to sell their land.[5] Currently, most states have laws that permit differential taxation.

Another measure that helps protect farmland is the purchase of development rights by state or local governments. A development right is the difference between the price of a piece of property as farmland and the price for other uses, such as housing. For example, a given piece might be worth $500 per acre as farmland. A developer, however, might be willing to buy it for $1,000 or $2,000 an acre. States or local governments can buy the development rights from the farmer, then hold them in perpetuity. No matter how many times the land changes hands, it must be used for farming.

The myths of growth management. Several public myths have stymied growth management in the United States. The first is that growth management programs cause land prices to escalate.[6] Overregulation, say opponents, adds significantly to the cost of housing. Population-Environment Balance points out, however, that most growth-management programs streamline the permitting process by centralizing all of the agencies with which a developer must deal. In addition, well-devised growth-management programs generally stabilize land prices by eliminating land speculation, a driving force behind escalating development costs in most urban regions.

The second myth is that growth management will increase the cost of public services such as water and sewer lines. Population-Environment Balance argues that all evidence is to the contrary. Without growth management, sprawl and strip development invariably increase demand for a new infrastructure and new taxes to build it. In contrast, programs that channel growth into areas with established public services can be extremely cost effective.

The third myth about growth management is that it is elitist—that is, it excludes low-income families. As noted earlier, modern growth-management programs such as Oregon's provide for a mix of housing, including apartments, condominiums, and single-family units of varying expense, thus permitting a wide range of family incomes.

The fourth myth is that if every community in the United States adopted a growth-management plan, a housing shortage would emerge. Population-Environment Balance points out that "The fear of a housing shortage . . . is unfounded and results from a mischaracterization of modern land-use planning as being anti-growth." Growth-management programs contain and modify growth, they do not put an end to it.

Land-use planning and land reform are needed in the Third World. Land-use planning is equally important in nonindustrial or developing nations, where urbanization is a major problem. Each year, millions of acres of farmland fall to the bulldozer as cities devour land that once sustained people and wildlife. Like their industrial counterparts, Third World cities are destroying the sustainable resource base upon which they depend.

In some areas land reform is badly needed. Wealthy landowners in Latin America tend to, for example, graze their cattle in rich valleys while peasants scratch out a living on erodible hillsides. Hilly terrain that should be protected from erosion is being torn up by plows and eroded by rain. Sensible land use in the Third World hinges on major reforms in feudal landholding patterns, says Lester Brown, president of the Worldwatch Institute.

ENDING THE HEMORRHAGE

Containing cities and suburbs also requires an end to the hemorrhage of pollutants from urban centers. As noted earlier, two of the best strategies are pollution prevention and demand-side management.

Containing the city and suburb also means ending the steady stream of municipal solid waste through conservation and recycling. This can be achieved by legal mandate or cooperative programs between government and citizens. Containment calls for individual action based on a new way of thinking. Parents, teachers, religious leaders, and politicians can teach a sustainable Earth ethic to stimulate a sense of individual responsibility and action.

The measures discussed in this chapter will not convert cities and suburbs into self-contained sustainable units. Cities, suburbs, and towns will always rely on the surrounding countryside for food, water, and other resources, that is, they will always be colonies of sorts. Making them sustainable requires the adoption of sustainable practices within the boundaries of metropolitan areas but also outside urban centers where resources lie. With these thoughts in mind, we turn to three areas critical to sustainable human habitation: transportation, housing, and waste.

The Shift to a Sustainable Transportation System

Residents of the industrial countries of the world are engaged in a dangerous and unsustainable love affair with the automobile. At least three convergent forces spell doom for our *affair de coeur:* urban air pollution, declining oil supplies, and congestion on urban highways.[7]

IMPROVING AUTOMOBILE EFFICIENCY AND INCREASING MASS TRANSIT

Today, nearly one-third of the energy consumed in the United States is for transportation, and much of it for America's 170 million automobiles—approximately one car for every two people. The American passion for automobiles has spread throughout the world. Since 1950, the number of cars in use worldwide has climbed from 50 million to over 400 million.[8] By the year 2025, it is expected to reach 700 million. Automobile travel accounts for 90 percent of motorized passenger transport in the United States and 78 percent in Europe. Each year, Americans travel nearly 2,000 billion miles in their automobiles, equivalent to more than ten round trips to the sun, which is 93 million miles away.

Declining oil supplies, the accompanying rise in gasoline prices, and regulatory changes mandated by urban pollution and traffic congestion will likely put the automobile craze into reverse gear. Although liquid fuels from coal, oil shale, and fuel farms might provide a temporary remedy, it's doubtful that modern society can maintain such an energy-intensive activity in the long run. Not even hydrogen, an abundant source of energy, will save the auto from obsolescence in the coming decades.

Changes in the transportation system of industrial countries probably will occur in increments in response to resource shortages, economic pressures, deteriorating environmental conditions, and public concern. Within the next decade or two as demand for fuel outstrips supplies, gasoline prices will begin a dangerous upward spiral. High-efficiency automobiles already in production will become more commonplace.

The rise in fuel prices and increasing regulatory pressure may also inspire businesses to promote employee carpooling and "vanpooling." Still providing the door-to-door convenience many of us are accustomed to, vanpools and carpools use about one-third as much energy as private automobiles carrying one passenger. To promote carpooling, cities and businesses will offer free parking or other financial incentives to workers, as some are doing now. Businesses may supply vehicles to employees who participate in vanpooling, and cities will open more lanes for multiple-occupancy vehicles during the morning and evening rush hours, making the carpool and vanpool a speedy alternative to the single-occupant automobile.

As the energy crunch deepens, ultra-high-efficiency vehicles will make their debut. Mass transit options will expand, and more and more people will take the bus or light-rail systems, selling their second and third cars.

The shift toward efficiency will likely result in a combination of energy-efficient options—fuel-efficient automobiles, buses, and carpooling. Important as it is, this shift will only be the first stage on the road to a sustainable system of transportation in the developed world.

EXPANDING MASS TRANSIT

As oil prices continue to climb, nations may be forced to ration oil, gasoline, and diesel fuel, diverting supplies for essential needs such as home heating, agriculture, food transport, and mass transit. Should rationing become a reality, automobile transportation will decline sharply. Even without rationing, rising fuel costs could lead to a phasing out of the auto. Either way, buses and trains are likely to emerge as the dominant form of transportation within cities and suburbs. Fuel-inefficient jet travel will give way to more efficient forms of transportation as well, especially high-speed trains.

The shift from automobiles to trains and buses makes sense from an evolutionary perspective because even the most efficient cars compare poorly to buses and trains for energy efficiency. In urban centers, for example, buses and light-rail transport achieve a fuel efficiency of about 150 passenger miles per gallon of fuel, about seven times better than the average new car today. Not even a doubling of their gas mileage would give cars an advantage.

Automobile transportation is also an inefficient use of land. A far greater number of people can be moved on railways and bus lines than on highways jammed with cars. According to the American Public Transit Association, a single bus displaces about 40 to 60 cars on the highway, and every full rail car is the equivalent of 75 to 125 single-passenger automobiles.[9]

As the demand for mass transit increases, many cities will begin to look favorably on high-speed rail systems, which can be constructed on the median strips of existing highways. In some cities, declining automobile traffic may lead city officials to turn highway lanes over to light rail. Rail lines could shuttle commuters back and forth from work to home. Since the cost of upgrading and rehabilitating old tracks is only about one-tenth the cost of building a new system, cities could take advantage of existing rail lines and decommissioned passenger trains.

Unfortunately, the economics of mass transit is currently skewed by massive subsidies for oil and automobiles. Consider oil first. Although prices at the pump do not reflect this fact, gasoline really costs Americans about $5 to $10 a gallon because of generous subsidies granted to oil companies at taxpayers' expense. According to one calculation, if subsidies were stripped from the American oil industry, a barrel of oil would cost about $100 to $200—about five to ten times more than its current price tag. If you paid the price at the pump, you would be shelling out $5 to $10 a gallon. Oil from the Persian Gulf is even more expensive. Calculations from the Rocky Mountain Institute, for example, put the cost to American taxpayers of military escorts of oil tankers in the Gulf at about $50 billion a year. If that were added to the cost of oil, it would drive up the price to about $495 a barrel![10]

Automobiles also receive a generous subsidy at the expense of taxpayers. According to Stanley Hart, a transportation analyst for the Sierra Club, every automobile on the road in Pasadena, California, costs taxpayers about $2,500 a year. This includes expenses for such services as police protection, traffic control, and city-paid parking.[11] According to national statistics, the automobile is subsidized to the tune of about $260 billion a year—or about $1,500 per car.[12] Like solar energy and other sustainable strategies, mass transit has a hard time competing with the automobile because the playing field is terribly uneven, tilted, as it were, in favor of the automobile. Removing the hidden subsidies from oil and automobiles—or providing more support for mass transit—would allow mass transit to compete with the auto on even ground.

Signs of change. The evolution of a sustainable transportation system is already under way. In Sweden, for instance, the Office of Future Studies recently recommended that the private automobile be phased out in one major city. Recognizing the imminent shortage of oil and the environmental cost of automobile transportation, this organization suggests that the city expand existing mass transit systems and turn to the nation's fleet of rental vehicles to provide transportation for vacations or special occasions.

Another more dramatic example of the evolution is provided by the city of Los Angeles, currently undergoing dramatic changes in response to concerns over air pollution and traffic congestion.[13] Home to the nation's most polluted air, Los Angeles will soon be home to some of the cleanest cars in the world. Beginning in 1994, "ultra-clean" cars will begin to make their way onto L.A. freeways. The new generation of vehicles include electric cars and automobiles that run on a mixture of methanol and gasoline, cars with advanced catalytic converters, and cars that burn natural gas or propane. All new cars sold in Los Angeles must be ultra-clean by 2003.

California's pollution control program will also force changes in individual behavior. The plan calls on employers with 100 or more workers to devise a program to reduce the vehicle miles employees travel or risk a $25,000 per day fine. Companies can offer monthly bonuses to employees who join carpools or use mass transit. Employers may also permit workers to telecommute—that is, work at home, where they remained linked to the office by phone. Others may shift to four-day work weeks.

At this writing, the California state legislature is considering tax incentives to individuals who purchase energy-efficient automobiles and a tax on gas-guzzling automobiles. Also under consideration are a number of proposals that would change the state's land-use planning laws to allow higher densities along transit corridors, a step that could improve the economics of mass transit.

THE ROLE OF THE BICYCLE IN A SUSTAINABLE SOCIETY

For decades, the bicycle has been a major means of transportation in Europe and Asia. Some cities in the United States have followed the European model, laying out extensive bike paths for commuters. In Davis, California, for example, where there are 40 miles of bike lanes, one-fourth of all commuter transport occurs by bicycle. Some streets are actually closed to automobile traffic.

Few modes of transportation measure up to the bicycle in terms of fuel efficiency. Weighing only 20 to 30 pounds, a bicycle requires only 35 calories per mile, compared to the automobile, which burns about 2,000 calories of gasoline per mile.[14] Useful for short trips, the bicycle can move at the same speed as most urban traffic, and it has the added benefit of exercising the heart, lungs, and leg muscles. Quiet side streets and a growing system of convenient paths make it possible for many commuters to get to work faster by bike than by bus.

The bicycle may prove to be a valuable supplement to buses and high-speed trains in many regions of the world. We can expect cities and suburbs to increase efforts to promote bicycle commuting as gasoline prices rise. But because of vast differences in the climate, layout, and topography of cities, the bicycle won't find a place in all cities and towns. San Francisco's terrain is probably too steep for widespread bicycle commuting. In Los Angeles the terrain is flat, but the city is too expansive to make bicycling a viable option for many. Denver and other cities, however, offer great opportunities for bicycle commuting for people living within five to ten miles of the city center. Even in winter months, the bicycle can be used in Denver because snow there tends to melt quickly.

"DENSIFYING" BUSINESS DISTRICTS, SUBURBS, AND URBAN NEIGHBORHOODS

Redesigning transportation systems in cities and towns is one of the greatest challenges facing industrial nations. But redesigning transportation is not simply a matter of opening up bus lanes and providing additional buses or building high-speed rail lines. To be economically successful, all mass transit systems—especially light rail—require participation, and this is possible only if they link high-density suburban regions with high-density central business districts. To make light-rail systems work, then, cities will have to find ways to increase density at both ends.

How will cities "densify"? One possibility is to convert empty parking lots produced by the decline in automobile use to office buildings. Although costly, it would be possible to move streets underground, creating additional building space. More efficient use of existing office space could help. In many cities, builders could restore abandoned buildings and build on vacant lots that are surprisingly close to urban centers.

Efforts to increase population density in suburbs and even some urban neighborhoods are also essential to making large-scale mass transit work. One way is to change zoning regulations, allowing families to convert unused living space into apartments.

In the case of new developments, builders can maximize density by reducing street widths, building smaller homes, and reducing lawn size. Backyards might open onto common greens that provide communal playgrounds and a gathering place for adults. These steps would decrease the land required per family and could result in a substantial savings on home costs and lawn maintenance. Attached housing units would further reduce these factors, saving substantial amounts of timber and other resources. If adequate sound insulation were installed between the units, many of the disadvantages of condominium and apartment living would be eliminated.

New developments should be as self-contained as possible, with shops and stores within walking or biking distance. Special walkways or bikeways would connect homes and shops. Builders that concentrated development along major transportation routes—bus routes and new or planned light-rail systems—would make mass transit more convenient.

ECONOMIC OPPORTUNITIES WILL SHIFT

The shift to a more efficient transportation system is bound to cause a significant mutation in manufacturing in the United States and abroad, particularly in the automobile industry. Automobile manufacturing is the world's largest industry, and it supports many other industries such as rubber, glass, and steel.[15] As the shift to mass transit begins, employment in auto manufacturing is bound to decline. Many opportunities will open up for displaced autoworkers, for instance in bus and light-rail factories. Steelworkers will continue producing steel, but for buses and trains rather than cars. Automobile mechanics might find employment servicing buses, electric cars, or clean-burning hydrogen- and ethanol-powered cars.

The service sector will change as urban-suburban centers re-evolve. Gas stations, automobile dealerships, and repair services, for example, will begin to close their doors as the shift to more environmentally benign forms of mass transportation takes place. The car salesman may be a thing of the past! Restaurants and stores currently dotting the roadways that connect suburb to city will begin to disappear as automobile traffic declines, relocating near businesses, homes, and transit stations.

Shifting toward a sustainable transportation system is bound to change lifestyles built around the oil and automobile economy. The challenge today is to recognize the inevitability, perhaps even the desirability, of these changes and to take action now.

A Continuing Role for Automobiles?

In the scenario pictured above, the gasoline-powered automobile is slowly and inexorably phased out. However, it probably will not ever completely disappear from the roadways of the industrialized world. In fact, many families may well retain one energy-efficient car, a compact, durable vehicle incorporating the latest innovations in materials science, powered by renewable fuels such as ethanol, solar electricity, or hydrogen, and used for short vacations or errands.

Larger cars and trucks are likely to remain as well, but in greatly reduced numbers. Salespeople and service technicians who travel freely within a metropolitan region, for example, may own energy-efficient automobiles powered by sunlight, hydrogen, or ethanol. Construction workers who travel to and from scattered work sites may rely on energy-efficient light trucks powered by renewable fuels. Certainly, medium- and large-delivery trucks will stay with us, permitting industries to distribute their goods throughout metropolitan centers.

A healthy automobile and truck rental industry may spring up as private ownership declines. This service industry would provide rental vehicles to ensure maximum flexibility. A family living close to work, for example, may rent a van for a summer vacation. Throughout most of the rest of the year, they would rely on public transportation and their small, energy-efficient automobile.

WILL CHEAP ALTERNATIVE FUELS SAVE THE AUTOMOBILE?

During the evolution of an environmentally sustainable form of transportation, a number of alternative fuels are likely to emerge. Capable of powering a wide range of vehicles, these fuels—if renewable—could play a significant role in creating a sustainable system of transportation.

One of the most promising of the clean renewable fuels is ethanol. Ethanol can be made from carbohydrate-rich crops such as corn, sugarcane, and sugar beets. Blended with gasoline, it can be used in most cars on the road today. It can also burn by itself in specially modified engines.

During the transition to a sustainable transportation system, it is likely that more and more gasoline will contain ethanol, and automobile manufacturers will produce more vehicles powered exclusively by ethanol.

The shift to ethanol may have already begun. In Brazil, for example, ethanol from sugarcane fuels about half the country's cars and trucks. If, as is likely, other countries follow suit, food and fuel production will compete for vanishing farmland. The rising demand for liquid fuel from crops may well come at a time of rising demand for food. In Brazil, ethanol production from sugarcane currently requires about one-fourth of the nation's agricultural land. At the current rate of growth, world population will increase by five billion people in the next 40 years. If the worldwide destruction of farmland continues, fuel production may be forced to take a back seat to food production. If, however, countries can stop the rapid decline in farmland—from erosion, desertification, and other factors—and can restore land already lost, it may be possible for them to provide food *and* fuel from farmland.

Scientists at the Solar Energy Research Institute (SERI) in Golden, Colorado, recently announced the results of a study that could reduce the alcohol-fuel industry's dependence on farmland. Thanks to this and other research, the cost of ethanol produced from wood has dropped from $4 per gallon to approximately $1.35 per gallon in just 10 years.[16] The ultimate goal of SERI researchers is to reduce the cost to $.60 per gallon, low enough to compete with gasoline at current prices.

The SERI plan to produce ethanol from wood could help build a liquid-fuel industry that provides alternative employment for displaced oil workers. But with many of the world's forests stretched to their limit, further cutting for fuel could worsen global warming and destroy watersheds. To ensure the emergence of an ethanol industry that contributes to environmental sustainability, provisions are needed to ensure sustainable harvests, to protect watersheds, and to maintain healthy forest soils.

Ethanol can also be produced from a variety of wastes. By one estimate, 40 billion gallons' worth of ethanol could be produced each year from corn cobs and rice hulls alone, satisfying about one-fifth of the world demand for liquid fuel. Sawdust from lumber production could also be made into fuel.

Alternative fuels will not save the automobile; they will only delay its demise. Too many other factors are stacked against the two- and three-car family and the single-occupant commuter, not the least of which are urban congestion, pollution, and mineral shortages. Let me hasten to point out, though, that efforts to develop clean, renewable fuels are not meaningless. They are important to provide the sustainable energy source required by mass transit, rental cars, and the skeleton fleet of vehicles needed to service farmers, salespeople, construction workers, and so on.

Ending Our Wasteful Ways

David Morris notes that a city the size of San Francisco *annually* discards more aluminum than is extracted from a small bauxite mine. Each year, he says, a city this size throws away more copper than a medium-sized copper mine produces, and it discards more paper than is produced by a good-sized timber stand. From a resource perspective, cities and suburbs are really repositories of "urban ore." Unfortunately, the mountains of post-consumer scrap generated by cities and suburbs are often produced many miles from factories that could put them to use. To remedy the problem, manufacturing companies are already beginning to set up facilities in cities to gather recyclables, package them, and ship them to the factory. A change in freight rates to eliminate the most-favored status of virgin materials would spur this effort.

As resources become scarce, factories that manufacture goods from secondary materials may also begin to set up shop near cities and towns. These factories will probably be much smaller than present-day mills that rely on virgin steel, timber, and other such materials. Since the use of secondary (recycled) materials requires less energy and water, the new generation of minifactories will inevitably be much cleaner.

Following in the Footsteps of Japan and Other Countries

With its tiny land mass, high population density, scarce resources, and penchant for efficiency, Japan is a good model for sustainable waste management. The average Japanese citizen produces only about half as much waste as the average American. In addition, the Japanese discard only about 20 percent of their household waste; most of the rest is recycled or reused. Today, half of Japan's paper is recycled and 95 percent of the beer bottles sold in the country are reused an average of 20 times. In contrast, the United States recycles only about one-fourth of its paper and only 7 percent of its glass. Very few glass bottles are reused.

Much of what is not recycled in Japan is incinerated to produce energy. The Japanese, however, take stringent measures to reduce air emissions, and they properly dispose of toxic ash from incinerators to avoid polluting groundwater. In the United States, the EPA does not regulate the disposal of ash from solid-waste incinerators, which is currently being dumped in landfills.

Three Steps to a Resource-Efficient System

Ending the waste of valuable resources by cities and suburbs here and abroad requires efforts to transform the one-way production-consumption system into a cyclical system, a topic mentioned in earlier chapters. We will outline a three-step hierarchal approach to conversion. The first step, the input approach, includes efforts to reduce the amount of material entering the production-consumption cycle.

The input approach: reducing solid waste. The first step in reducing waste is to reduce consumption. In a society whose economy is based on runaway spending, however, reducing consumption is no easy task. Nonetheless, it has to be done.

Many efforts are needed to bring about necessary reductions in consumption. High on the list are voluntary measures by individuals who recognize the shortsightedness of the frontier mentality. The rising cost of energy, water, and other resources will no doubt play a major role in curbing consumption. Increasing landfill costs may play a part as will legislative mandate, such as limits on packaging. Statutory controls on packaging materials are especially important because bags, boxes, and other miscellaneous wrappings currently account for one-third of America's total municipal solid waste. Moreover, approximately 90 percent of the glass produced in the United States and about 50 percent of the paper consumed each year is used for packaging.[17] Packaging taxes applied to nonreturnable, nonrecyclable materials could prove to be a powerful economic disincentive for manufacturers. Tax credits or deductions for environmentally sound packaging might prove to be a more palatable incentive.[18] Another idea is an outright ban on environmentally unfriendly packaging. In 1988, for example, Suffolk County, New York, passed an ordinance that banned plastic grocery bags and many plastic food containers, including polystyrene (commonly called styrofoam) fast-food packaging. This ordinance started a wave of similar actions in California, Minnesota, New Jersey, and elsewhere.

In November 1990, Germany's minister for the environment issued a decree calling for an 80 percent reduction in the amount of packaging entering the waste stream. Retailers will soon be required to collect primary packaging and recycle it, a measure that is inevitably going to pressure manufacturers to reduce excess packaging wherever possible. To ensure consumer participation, the government will levy a deposit equivalent to about 30 cents in U.S. currency on virtually all liquid containers. Retailers can avoid the deposit and take-back requirements if industry establishes alternative collection and recycling systems that meet established goals.

Reducing waste also entails a phaseout of disposable goods. Each year, Americans discard approximately 18 billion disposable diapers, which, if linked end to end, would extend to the moon and back seven times. Approximately 95 percent of these diapers end up in landfills where they remain entombed for centuries. "What started out as a marketer's dream of dryer, happier, more comfortable babies," write Carl Lehrburger and Rachel Snyder in the *Whole Earth Review*, "has become a solid waste nightmare."[19] Besides wasting valuable materials, disposable diapers are a health hazard. Feces and urine leaching from landfills can seep into aquifers and pollute drinking water for generations to come.[20]

The disposable diaper is a product of the frontier mentality that sees the Earth as an unlimited supply of resources and a limitless repository for waste. With the huge profits disposable diapers bring in, manufacturers have a built-in incentive to produce them. Valued at more than $3 billion per year, disposable diapers are a boon to companies such as Procter and Gamble and Kimberley-Clark. A child uses an estimated 6,500 to 10,000 disposable diapers before toilet training. While ecologically more sound in many respects, the reusable cotton diaper accounts for only 10 percent of the U.S. diaper market.

Nationwide, disposable diapers constitute roughly 4 percent of the solid-waste stream. Although that may seem like an insignificant amount, disposable diaper production requires 100,000 tons of plastic and 800,000 tons of wood pulp each year. Disposal costs for the eighteen billion diapers Americans produce is approximately $350 million a year.[21]

One of the major obstacles to finding an alternative to the single-use diaper is the value Americans place on convenience. Conscientious diapering, like conscientious living, requires a deliberate decision to align individual actions with sustainable ethics.

Physicians, midwives, nurses, and hospital staff can play a significant role in promoting the shift from disposable diapers. Special taxes could be levied on disposable items to discourage their manufacture, and tax incentives of various sorts could be set up to encourage environmentally sound alternatives.

Another way to reduce consumption is increased product durability so that toys, tools, clothing, and so forth don't have to be replaced so often. Eco-labeling programs, discussed earlier, would encourage customers to purchase such items. Making products easier to repair could promote longevity. Another idea is dematerialization, the production of goods with less material. In the 1970s, Campbell Soup redesigned its cans to use 30 percent less steel. Dematerialization could be boosted by tax credits from the state and federal governments.

The throughput approach: composting and recycling. Yard waste currently accounts for about 19 percent of the municipal solid waste generated in the United States. At certain times of year, yard waste comprises up to 75 percent of the weight of the garbage streaming out of our cities to landfills. Composting organic waste rather than banishing it to landfills is tremendously beneficial.[22] Compost is a rich soil supplement useful for gardens, city parks, and as topsoil in landfills. Cities and states could use it to restore eroded soils on hillsides and along highways. Compost can also be used to rebuild unreclaimed strip mines, overgrazed fields, and depleted farm soil.

Composting is profitable in places where landfill costs are high. In New Jersey, for example, a nonprofit composting program in Morris County charges municipalities $16 to $32 per ton to compost leaves, a fraction of the current cost of landfilling, which exceeds $110 per ton. Collecting and composting leaves and yard waste in Minneapolis–St. Paul cost the city about $65 a ton, compared with landfilling at $90 a ton.

Several obstacles must be overcome if composting is to be successful. One of the biggest is location. Like landfills, large municipal composting facilities are rarely welcome neighbors. To reduce transportation costs, however, they must be located near sources. One excellent site is the existing landfill, which often lies on the city outskirts close to farms where compost is useful.

Municipal composting will not solve the world's solid-waste problems, but it will put a substantial dent in the waste stream. An even better strategy from the standpoint of resource use is backyard composting. Leaves, grass clippings, branches, and organic kitchen wastes can be deposited in small backyard bins where they decompose over time. Far less energy intensive than municipal composting programs, which often require weekly pickups and massive machinery to process the compost, a backyard compost bin takes very little effort on the part of the homeowner. Bacteria and other microorganisms do most of the work. An occasional application of water and a periodic turning of the pile is about all a homeowner need do to produce a rich organic soil supplement.

Another troublesome urban waste product is sewage sludge, solid organic material generated by sewage treatment plants. In most cities and towns sewage sludge is dried and dumped in landfills where valuable nutrients contained in human waste do no good.

One way to avoid wasting valuable nutrients is co-composting, a process in which dried sludge is mixed with municipal solid waste like leaves, paper, and grass clippings. Bacterial decay in this rich organic mixture creates temperatures sufficient to kill viruses and bacteria. The resulting product can be sold for use in gardens, lawns, and farms.

Co-composting municipal solid waste and sewage sludge is expected to become increasingly popular in the United States because it costs less and is more ecologically sound than landfills. An even better strategy is the use of artificial ponds and wetlands to "treat" sewage. Properly designed, such a system can purify sewage without elaborate engineering or expensive and potentially hazardous chemicals. In the northern California town of Arcata, sewage enters large settling ponds where bacteria in the water and on the bottom break down organic matter. The remaining liquid drains into another pond where bacteria continue the decomposition of organic chemicals. Nitrates and phosphates are consumed by algae and aquatic plants in the ponds. Eventually, the naturally treated water drains out of the artificial wetlands so pure and free of bacteria that it requires no chlorination.

Besides treating sewage inexpensively and without toxic chemicals, artificial wetlands provide wildlife habitat, reduce energy demand, and eliminate sludge disposal. Aquatic plants grown in and around ponds can be harvested for animal feed or feedstock for ethanol production.

To reduce the outflow of solid waste and its attendant problems, cities and states and nations must also recycle materials to the maximum extent possible. One of the most ambitious recycling programs in the United States is in the city of Seattle. Aimed at reducing trash by 60 percent, primarily through recycling and composting, this program was adopted in part because of citizen protest over plans to build a garbage incinerator. Economic studies showed that recycling was a better environmental choice, would avoid costly landfilling, and would be approximately ten times cheaper than incineration.[23] Seattle began its curbside recycling program in February 1988 and by the end of that year was recycling 28 percent of its municipal waste stream. In 1990, the amount climbed to 31 percent. To promote recycling, the city offers several economic incentives to homeowners. Residents who recycle, for example, pay $5 per month less if they fill only one trash can each week; "superrecyclers" get an even lower rate.[24]

The city of High Bridge, New Jersey, found another way to encourage its residents to recycle. At one time, the city charged an annual flat fee of $280 for garbage collection, which gave customers virtually unlimited trash pickup. Today, however, residents purchase stickers that they attach to every trash bag left by the curb. Fifty-two stickers cost $140. Additional stickers cost $1.25 each. Interestingly, since the pay-as-you-throw-away program began, waste output has dropped by 25 percent thanks in part to increased recycling and composting.

Recycling programs are cropping up everywhere in the United States. By 1989, more than 600 major cities had started some form of recycling. Like Seattle's program, cities and towns can realize substantial economic gains by reducing landfill costs.[25] A growing number of recycling programs are being run by private haulers.

Laws that require deposits on beverage containers, commonly referred to as bottle bills, are another way to increase recycling. Currently, nine U.S. states have bottle bills, as does the Netherlands, Scandinavia, the Soviet Union, Canada, Japan, parts of Australia, and many developing countries.

Jim Johnson, former director of Ecocycle, a nonprofit recycler in Boulder, Colorado, once quipped that recycling has become "the motherhood and apple pie issue of the 1990s." Still, there are several key obstacles to overcome. Two of the most significant are plastics and markets.

Plastic is the product that everyone loves to hate. Several features of plastic like durability and light weight that make it desirable for packaging also render it a public nuisance. Although most plastics are recyclable, U.S. plastic recycling amounts to 1 percent of the total production.

At least three factors, mentioned in chapter 5, hinder the recycling of plastic. First, over the past two decades plastics manufacturers have focused their efforts on developing markets and paid little attention to developing a recycling network.[26] In a sustainable society markets for products should be developed along with recycling programs.

In the United States, plastics constitute about 10 percent of the municipal solid-waste stream but because of their bulk take up about 30 percent of its volume. With bans on plastic packaging and other products beginning to appear, the plastics industry has voluntarily decided to make some changes. Several major U.S. companies, for example, joined forces to create recycling companies.

The second problem is that many plastic products are composites, and few recycling processes can handle more than one type of plastic.[27] Combining plastics with other materials complicates the recycling process. Packages made of aluminum foil and plastic or paper and plastic are good examples. As the complexity of products increases, their ability to be recycled greatly decreases.

The third problem with plastics is variety. At least 46 different types of plastic are currently on the market. Consumers and recyclers have a hard time telling one type from another. To help solve this problem, manufacturers have begun coding plastic containers and shopping bags, an effort that makes it easier for the recycling industry and for consumers to identify and recycle them.[28]

Limited landfill space and concern over wasted resources have given way to a flurry of recycling programs. Most of the northeastern states have recycling efforts under way that will eventually lead to a 20 to 50 percent reduction in waste streams. By 1997, New York State alone plans to recycle half of its solid-waste stream.

Successful recycling programs, however, can flood the market. Without an accompanying increase in the use of recycled materials, many valuable resources set aside for recycling could end up in landfills. The first law of sustainable solid-waste management is that recycling does not occur until the recycled product is remanufactured and reused. Successful recycling programs hinge on pickup, remanufacturing, and resale.

One surefire way of increasing the market for recycled goods is government procurement. Since state, local, and national government expenditures account for 20 percent of the U.S. GNP, government purchase of recycled products could greatly accelerate the transition to a sustainable society. The U.S. government could become an enormous market for recycled products such as tires, paper, asphalt, and oil. Long-term government contracts would send a signal to manufacturers, encouraging them to make investments in recycling equipment. State and local governments could also help by forming cooperative buying agreements permitting them to acquire recycled products at a better price.

Recycling's success depends as well on developing new businesses to make use of the materials we normally discard, especially, at this time, newsprint and plastics.[29] In the last five years, the amount of newsprint bound for U.S. recycling plants increased 35 percent, but the production of recycled newsprint only climbed 2 percent, according to an official at U.S. Recycling. This mismatch has created a bottleneck in the system and is caused principally by a lack of de-inking facilities. At this writing, about three dozen or so de-inking mills are currently being planned or are under construction in the United States and Canada. They will greatly increase the manufacturing capacity and in turn the supply of recycled paper.

One often overlooked fact is that recycled newsprint can be used to make a variety of useful products other than newspaper, including egg cartons, cereal boxes, tubes, drywall, ceiling tiles, animal bedding, and insulation. Through tax incentives, cities and towns could encourage companies that produce these products to set up operations nearby, putting locally available waste to good use and helping to build stable, self-reliant regional and state economies.

Another novel idea aimed at assisting the recycling industry is life-cycle cost analysis, which takes into account the total cost of a product, including environmental and health costs. In Vermont, where this technique is being tested, life-cycle pricing often gives recycled products an advantage over their competitors.

In summation, successful recycling programs regionally and nationally require a synergistic development of at least three activities: pickup, manufacturing, and purchase. Many states have established programs that require an incremental increase in the amount of recycled products state agencies must purchase. This should give businesses time to increase production capacity gradually.

The output approach: landfills and incineration. Progressive solid-waste management could reduce the output of garbage from cities and towns to a trickle, perhaps as little as 10 percent of the original amount. What's left will have to be dealt with somehow. Two principal options are generally available: incinerators and landfills.

Currently, approximately 350 incinerators or waste-to-energy plants are in operation in countries such as Brazil, Japan, the Soviet Union, and the United States. In some countries, Denmark, Sweden, and Switzerland among them, more than half of household waste is burned.

In the United States, 100 garbage incinerators are currently in operation, most of which burn unseparated municipal solid waste. Another 60 to 70 plants are under construction. If industry has its way, the amount of waste handled by incinerators could grow to 40 percent of the waste stream by the end of the century.

The political and economic push for more incinerators is well-financed and politically savvy. In fact, many companies that once designed and built power plants for the now relatively stagnant electric utility industry have gone into the incineration business and are hawking their wares in economically depressed rural areas. Here and elsewhere, waste-to-energy plants appeal to city administrators because they require no change in the current waste collection system.

Incinerators that produce steam or electricity offer additional economic benefit.

Nonetheless, incinerators are no environmental bargain. They waste potentially valuable resources, capturing only a fraction of the hidden value of our municipal solid waste. According to one study, the value of solid waste as fuel is about 4 or 5 cents per pound, as recycled material is 32 to 40 cents per pound.[30]

Incineration technology has been greatly improved in recent years and is now somewhat more acceptable. One of the major improvements is the separation of glass, metals, and wet organic matter like leaves and grass clippings, which increases the efficiency of incineration. Still, incinerators produce potentially dangerous air emissions. Salt and certain plastics in municipal waste contain chlorine, which when burned combines to form dioxins and furans. Sweden placed a moratorium on the construction of new incinerators in 1985, fearing that dioxins were ending up in the milk of nursing mothers.

Regulators are concerned about acids and heavy metals released by waste-to-energy plants. Although new plants are required to be fitted with stringent pollution-control devices, small quantities of heavy metals may still end up in stack gases and incinerator ash.[31] Because of this, ash from waste-to-energy plants in Sweden is treated as a hazardous waste. California may adopt similar regulations. The U.S. government, however, treats incinerator ash as a normal waste, and municipalities are therefore not required to dispose of incinerator ash in any special way.[32]

Richard Denison of the Environmental Defense Fund asserts that without proper attention to this issue, the growing use of incineration could turn our trash crisis into an even more critical hazardous waste problem. Cities should be warned that if they choose to incinerate trash, they may pay the high cost of proper disposal or cleanup later on.

Incineration should be the last resort, not the first line of attack in the battle against growing mounds of urban trash. Mixed-waste landfills, like incinerators, should be at the bottom of the list of options for reasons alluded to earlier in the chapter.

In a sustainable society, landfills will become a place to bury waste that cannot be recycled, reused, or composted. Cleared of hazardous waste, organic foodstuffs, aluminum, most plastics, paper, and a great many other goods, the garbage ending up in future landfills should be relatively inert.[33]

Retired landfills from the presustainable era could become a source of raw materials like aluminum, cardboard, and steel. Cities may also drill bore holes into old landfills to tap methane gas generated by rotting garbage. In the United States, 70 landfill gas-recovery facilities are currently operating or under construction. The largest of these, on Staten Island, produces five million cubic feet of gas per day, which is sold to the Brooklyn Union Gas Company and provides enough gas to heat 50,000 homes. Methane is produced for decades after a landfill stops receiving garbage, so the 9,000 landfills in the United States may become a valuable source of fuel.

The Household in a Sustainable Future

What's the old saying? "A man's home is his castle." Sexist overtones aside, that's not a bad analogy. As anyone who has ever visited the castles of France, Germany, and Great Britain can attest, these cold, drafty structures are an energy-conscious consumer's nightmare. American homes are a far sight more energy efficient than the castles of medieval times, but they are still far from optimal. According to one estimate, if all of the air leaks in a typical American home were added up, they'd equal a three-square-foot open window. Houses also lose heat through poorly insulated walls, floors, windows, and ceilings as well. One of the first steps to sustainability is making our homes much more energy efficient without poisoning ourselves with indoor pollutants.

MAKING HOMES ENERGY EFFICIENT

According to government statistics, there are about 100 million housing units in the United States.[34] This includes 65 million single-family houses, 7 million mobile homes, and 28 million apartments. Interestingly, only 7 million of the 56 million owner-occupied single-family dwellings have added insulation to cut heating bills.

One of the easiest and most cost-effective ways to save energy in a house is to plug up the leaks around windows and doors and between the house and the foundation by applying caulk and weatherstripping. Reducing air infiltration lowers energy consumption in the average home by nearly 30 percent—and pays for itself in about eight months.[35]

Energy efficiency does not end with weatherstripping and insulation, however. Homeowners can also cut energy demand by insulating water heaters, lowering water heater thermostats by 10° to 20° Fahrenheit, and insulating water pipes. It is a good idea as well to use high-efficiency compact fluorescent light bulbs. Together, these and other simple cost-efficient measures can cut overall energy consumption by 50 to 75 percent.

To promote energy efficiency, cities and towns can sponsor energy-conservation programs. Free infrared pictures of homes and energy audits that show homeowners where they can save energy and money will stretch fossil fuels and ease the transition to renewable energy. Federal tax credits for insulation and weatherstripping would encourage homeowners to make the shift.

Imagine our homes as self-contained units of energy production, an idea promoted by the Institute for Local Self-Reliance. Computer simulations of household photovoltaics, says Morris, suggest that a typical single-family home could generate enough electricity each year to provide all of the energy needed to operate an efficient household with enough left over to power an electric vehicle.[36] Electricity from photovoltaics is not produced at exactly the time it is needed, however. In some climates summer production greatly exceeds demand; winter production may fall short. Excess electricity produced during the sunny months could be sold to utilities and pumped into the electrical grid. During low-sun months homeowners would buy electricity from utilities, energy generated by small-scale hydropower, wind, or some other clean and efficient source. The optimal configuration in Boston, Phoenix, and Seattle, says Morris, would be for the household to export 50 percent of its electricity to the grid and import 50 percent. Power plants would greatly reduce their output in times of surplus and step up production to meet demand when the sun isn't shining. Thus, the home enters into a symbiotic relationship with other sources of electric production.[37]

It is also possible for cities and towns to tap the sun for home heating. New homes should be built facing the south and designed to take advantage of solar heating. Existing homes that face south could be retrofitted with greenhouses or solar additions. Greenhouses are also useful for raising food, which reduces demand for farmland production. Another idea is to compost organic waste from the kitchen and add it to the soil in the greenhouses. Through such steps, the homeowner can help to close the loops on a linear society.

There are enormous opportunities for sustainable design in new construction. A builder in Butte, Montana, for example, has captured 60 percent of the local housing market by building superinsulated passive solar homes that are guaranteed not to require more than $100 a year for electric heat! So far he has had to deliver on his promise only twice, once for $3 and another time for $17.

My wife, two sons, and I live in a 2,500 square-foot passive solar home at 8,200 feet in the foothills of the Rocky Mountains. Winters can be extremely cold, with nighttime temperatures well below freezing several months in a row. Fortunately, the days are often bright and sunny, and we acquire most of our heat from the sun. Our annual heating bill is only about $100.

Even if a climate is not suited for solar energy, high-efficiency construction is essential. In desert regions, for example, good insulation helps to contain cool air during hot summer months when the demand for air-conditioning is high.

Energy-efficient appliances, a topic touched on earlier in the book, bring significant energy savings as well. Many models that use 20 to 50 percent less energy are now available, thanks in part to the National Appliance Energy Conservation Act, which requires manufacturers to produce appliances that consume 20 percent less energy by 1992. As energy prices rise and concern for global warming increases, you can expect still more efficient models. Homeowners, moreover, can wean themselves from their dependence on nonessential gadgets like electric can openers.

Another inexpensive but effective way of reducing energy demand is planting trees around homes. Deciduous trees on the south and east side of a house give shade in the hot summer months, reducing the demand for air-conditioning. In the winter when the leaves are gone, sunlight strikes the house and warms it. Conifers planted on the north and west sides of a house provide shade in the summer and habitat for birds while reducing air-conditioning bills. In the winter, conifers block the wind, helping to reduce heating bills.

Massive urban and suburban tree planting could reduce energy demand and make metropolitan areas more sustainable. Such efforts would help offset global warming while providing habitat for songbirds. In addition, large-scale tree planting could provide work for many unemployed people.

WATER: PROTECTING OUR LIQUID ASSETS

Water conservation efforts are equally important to the task of building a sustainable human habitat. Water is a commodity that is currently squandered by virtually everyone. Cheap and readily available water supplies are a thing of the past, however. Already, dozens of countries are suffering regional water shortages that are bound to grow worse in the coming years.

Using water efficiently reduces pumping costs, chlorine use, and wastewater output, so it's a wise strategy even in areas with abundant supplies. In new homes, water-efficient appliances, faucets, showerheads, and toilets should be mandatory. Low-water grasses or native vegetation should be required in arid and semiarid climates and lawn watering should be restricted to the cool part of the day—early morning and evening—to reduce evaporation and overall demand. By watering late at night or early in the morning, residents in semiarid climates can reduce lawn water demand by 50 percent.

It is possible to design new houses with separate pipes that drain "gray water" from sinks, bathtubs, and showers (not toilets) into special holding tanks. This water is then used to irrigate gardens, trees, shrubs, and lawns.

One of the biggest challenges to making society more water efficient lies in retrofitting existing homes. Fortunately, there are a variety of inexpensive and fairly simple ways to save water in these homes. A clean glass salad dressing bottle fits nicely in a toilet tank and reduces the amount of water required for each flush. More elaborate "toilet dams" are also available. Water-efficient showerheads are readily available and inexpensive. Some showerheads reduce water flow by 70 percent, saving water, energy, and money in the process. Low-flow showerheads are easy to install, and many models provide a vigorous shower. Also on the market are flow restrictors or aerators that screw into faucets and make substantial reductions in water consumption.

As cities and towns are hit by water shortages and as conservationists make the case for protecting in-stream water flow for fish, wildlife, and recreation, urban programs to ensure efficient water use are likely to expand throughout the world. New industries will invariably pop up to assist homeowners in making the changes. As old toilets break down, highly efficient ones will be installed.

A fifty-percent reduction in household water use in cities and towns is well within our grasp. But in order for this to occur, widespread efforts are needed to promote water conservation and ease the transition to a sustainable future. State and federal governments might facilitate the transition by offering small tax credits to those who buy and install low-flow showerheads, flow restrictors, and low-water toilets.

In arid climates, replacing water-thirsty lawns with native vegetation dramatically cuts water use. In northern Marin County, California, for example, lawn irrigation accounts for one-third of household water consumption. One town now offers subsidies of up to $310 to homeowners who will xeriscape their lawns, that is, remove the Kentucky bluegrass and replace it with a water-conserving species. Each converted lawn can save about 120 gallons of water per day during peak months.

BUILDING ENVIRONMENTALLY SOUND HOMES

New home construction is currently being revolutionized by environmental concerns. Recycled carpet, drywall, roofing, insulation, and many other building materials are now available to home builders in the United States, but usually at a slightly higher cost than conventional products. Water-soluble, nontoxic stains, paints, and varnishes are also making their way into the marketplace and gaining wider acceptance, as are oil-based finishes made from renewable citrus oils.

Builders can read up on these products in *The Journal of Light Construction,* which carefully assesses them.[38] A list of energy-efficient, nontoxic, and recycled products is available from The Complete the Cycle Center in Denver, Colorado, or from Architects, Designers, and Planners for Social Responsibility in nearby Boulder.[39] ADPSR can also provide a list of catalogs of environmental products, consultants, and books, as well as example buildings in the United States and abroad.

Combined with efficiency measures discussed above and floorplans that achieve the best ratio of interior volume to exterior space, the home of the future can be a model of sustainable design. With incentives that reward builders who use recycled and high-efficiency products, the occasional experiment in sustainable housing construction could become the norm.

One of the biggest changes over the past century in the industrialized world has been the growing dependency of cities and suburbs on outside sources of food, fuel, water, and other resources—a reliance that is, in the long run, unsustainable. Reducing this dependency and building a more self-reliant way of life require many different actions at all levels of society. Building energy-efficient transportation systems, plugging up the leaks in our homes, growing more of our own food, generating more of our own energy, conserving water, and recycling and composting our garbage, while not dramatic, offer the best hope for a sustainable human presence on the planet. What is more, the technological know-how needed to succeed in this vital task is readily available. All that is lacking is the commitment to a new way of life and the willingness to make this vision a reality.

11 Critical Paths to a Sustainable Society: Population, Food, Agriculture, Energy, and Biodiversity

*Nothing in this world is so powerful as
an idea whose time has come.*

VICTOR HUGO

ON SEPTEMBER 15, 1990, history was made on the Roaring Fork and
Frying Pan rivers near Aspen, Colorado. Organizers of the annual
fishing tournament, concerned about the impact of the event on the
stream's trout population, decided to require participants to measure
the fish they caught, then release them. Prizes were awarded on the
honor system. Given the proclivity of many anglers to—how shall I
say it?—exaggerate their catch, this contest was nothing short of remarkable. The *Denver Post* ran a front-page article entitled "Fishin'
Impossible: Trout Contest Counts on Upright Anglers."

This event illustrates the growing concern for the unsustainability
of human activities; surely it won't change the world, but it typifies a
new way of thinking and acting. This chapter will examine areas of
unsustainable action in need of reform: population, food and agriculture, energy, and biological diversity.

Population: Slowing, Even Stopping, Growth

The problem of population can be summed up in six words: too
many people, reproducing too quickly. Widespread pollution, deforestation, species extinction, food shortages, and desertification,

among other problems, are a reminder that humankind is exceeding the carrying capacity of the planet. With three-fifths of the world's people living in abject poverty or on its edge, very little can be said to convince an objective observer that the human population is not already too big for its own good.

As if that is not bad enough, the world population is growing at a record speed. Each year, approximately 90 million new people are added to the human population. Cities are swelling, and rural areas, which supply resources to urban centers, are being stripped bare in the search for food and fuel.

In 1819, the English poet Shelley wrote that "Hell is a city much like London." If Shelley were alive today, he might have written, "Hell is a city much like Cairo, Calcutta, Shanghai, Bangkok, London, Los Angeles, and Mexico City." In Calcutta, more than 70 percent of the city's 10 million people live at or below the poverty level. In that crowded, dirty city, one water tap supplies 25 slum dwellings on average, and nearly half of the homes in the city have no indoor toilet. By various projections, at least 22 cities will exceed populations of 10 million people by the end of the century. Sixty others will top the 5-million mark, many of them with conditions similar to Calcutta's.

It is not necessary to recount the horrors of overpopulation in this book. What is important is finding ways to solve the problem.

FAMILY PLANNING: FACILITATING THE DECLINE IN POPULATION GROWTH

Like all environmental problems, the human population dilemma will be solved by a variety of actions, each tailored to the culture and religion of a people. Family planning will figure prominently in efforts to slow the growth of the world population.

Family planning is many things to many people. In general, it refers to any measure that helps families determine the number and spacing of their offspring. Successful family planning programs rely on inexpensive and readily available contraceptives. But the world's population problem "will be solved in the mind, not the uterus," reminds Varinda Vittachi, a writer from Sri Lanka. All successful programs require education. The success of China's family planning program, in fact, relies in large part on rural health workers who venture into the villages, talking with women about contraceptive use and the benefits of small families.[1] In Egypt, public education took the form of a popular song played on a government-sponsored commercial. The tune was so popular that it became a national hit. In India and other countries, government-sponsored billboards remind children that small families are desirable. Posters in Vietnam extol the virtues of a one-child family. Schoolchildren in Thailand are introduced to the condom in the hope that when the time comes they will be inclined to use this form of birth control. Thai teachers also spend time discussing the benefits of small families.

SMALL-SCALE ECONOMIC DEVELOPMENT: REDUCING THE DESIRE FOR LARGE FAMILIES

"Family planning cannot exist in a vacuum. You can't just distribute contraceptives and tell people to go ahead and start lowering the birth rate," asserts Aziz el-Bindary, head of Egypt's Supreme Council for Population and Family Planning.[2] "To have an effective family-planning program, you also have to have an effective economy—where jobs are available, where health facilities are adequate."

Numerous countries have found out the hard way that family planning and economic development must go hand in hand. Fifteen years ago, in fact, most Third World countries rallied behind the cry, Development is the best contraceptive. A decade of falling per capita food production and income, however, has changed most minds. Economic gains simply could not keep up with burgeoning population growth.

Small-scale, sustainable economic development of the kind described in chapters 6 and 7 can raise the standard of living of Third World families, which in turn can reduce family size as it has in the West. Slowing population growth also requires good-paying jobs for women, better education, and improved access to contraceptives. Improved health care cuts the birth rate as well. In fact, in most Third World countries couples have large families because of the fear that many of their offspring will die, and children are a kind of insurance policy for parents in their old age. If couples can be sure that their children will survive, they're likely to have fewer.

THE GOOD NEWS AND THE BAD NEWS
ABOUT POPULATION GROWTH

Progress in controlling the growth of the human population has been encouraging. China, for example, has cut its annual growth from 2.5 percent in the 1960s (doubling time 28 years) to 1.4 percent in 1990 (doubling time 50 years). Great strides have been made in Taiwan, Tunisia, Barbados, Hong Kong, Singapore, Costa Rica, and Egypt, but there has been little progress in Africa, Latin America, and parts of Asia. The outcome could be widespread shortages, starvation, and environmental destruction that spreads far beyond the borders of the rapidly growing countries.

POPULATION CONTROL IN THE DEVELOPED WORLD

For many people, overpopulation is an issue for the Third World. Lest we forget, each child born in Canada or the United States has the environmental impact of 25 to 40 children in India because of North America's incredible resource demand. Limiting family size for the sake of the Earth is, therefore, just as important in Great Britain, France, Canada, and the United States as it is in Thailand, India, and Kenya, perhaps even more important.

Currently, developed countries are growing at an average rate of about 0.5 percent per year. Eighteen countries in Europe now have near-stationary populations. Three European countries are experiencing what demographers call negative growth, in other words, their populations are shrinking.[3] While this is reason for celebration, we must remember that developed countries already consume 75 percent of the world's resources and produce three-quarters of the world's pollution and waste. A growth rate of 0.5 percent means that the population of macroconsumers and macropolluters will double in 140 years. If current trends continue, there will be two billion of us devouring resources and spewing out waste in a little over a century.

Given the state of the environment in the developed world, the only eco-logical step is to stop growing altogether. Instead of replacement-level fertility, we should be striving for below-replacement-level fertility. Our immediate goal should be to halt population growth, then find ways to reduce our numbers over time through attrition. Only then can we live within the carrying capacity of the environment. Without such efforts, attempts to make the developed world more efficient may well prove useless.

Declines in fertility in the developed world should occur across all socioeconomic classes. No one should be excluded. Education programs could be started in *all* school districts, explaining the importance of small families from a personal and global viewpoint. Health clinics can provide information on family planning and show the poor and disadvantaged how they gain by contraception. In the United States, Planned Parenthood, working in conjunction with local civic leaders, could disseminate information and contraceptives in poor neighborhoods.

More active measures may be required to curb population growth in the industrial world. In the United States, eliminating the standard tax deduction for children after the second child would send a signal that discourages larger families. Another way is to alter property taxes by levying an additional tax for public education on parents with more than two children.

THE ECONOMIC CHALLENGE OF NO GROWTH

The phrase "no growth" sends chills down the spines of politicians and business people because, as noted in chapter 4, economic growth is often mistakenly equated with economic health. In the industrialized world economic growth relies chiefly on two forces: increasing per capita consumption and rising population. Take away population growth and you threaten economic growth.

Clearly, stabilizing or declining populations alter the economic prospects of many industrial countries, but the changes need not be disastrous, and, in fact, could be beneficial in the long run. Great lessons are to be learned from Germany and other European countries where population growth has slowed or stabilized. Despite a decline in population growth, Germany has built a vigorous economy.

Efforts to stabilize or decrease population give countries an opportunity to create sustainable economies and get off the economic growth treadmill that is so damaging to the environment. When a country's population ceases to grow, a number of changes occur. The workforce stabilizes, then shrinks. Economic output may stabilize, too. Projects justified in large part to create jobs will no longer be necessary. Further economic growth would be justified only to improve the economic conditions of the poor. Thus, a more equitable sharing of the wealth would be possible without requiring growth.

A stable economy based on a stable population does not spell stagnation. Opportunities for personal gain abound. In a sustainable society, as noted in chapter 10, some activities such as oil production and automobile manufacturing will inevitably decline, while others such as energy auditing, solar energy, and recycling will flourish. There will always be opportunities for people to benefit from innovation and hard work.

Feeding the People, Protecting the Planet

Thomas Jefferson once wrote that "civilization itself rests upon the soil." Judging from the way we treat our soil, it is clear that few among us recognize the importance of the land to the present welfare and the long-term future of humanity. History has shown repeatedly that a society that abuses its soil is a society that restricts, sometimes forecloses on, its own future.

MODERN AGRICULTURE: DESTROYING THE FOUNDATION OF LIFE

Each year, most countries lose topsoil to wind and water erosion in amounts that far exceed soil regeneration. In addition, millions of acres of farmland and rangeland are destroyed annually because of desertification caused by overgrazing and intensive agriculture. Worldwide, an area the size of Belgium (about 15 million acres) turns to desert each year. According to the UN Environment Program, if current trends continue, one-third of the world's cropland will become desert by the end of the century.

Soil erosion and desertification are key factors in the destruction of arable land. Another more subtle problem is the loss of soil nutrients. Harvesting a crop removes nutrients from the soil in much the same way that mining extracts minerals from the Earth's crust. In many locations, valuable nutrients are extracted from cropland soils year after year, and only a few are replaced by fertilizer.

Still another problem facing agriculture is a growing shortage of irrigation water. Much of the world's cropland is dependent on irrigation. But groundwater supplies are quickly running out in many regions. In the midwestern United States, the giant Ogallala aquifer is pumped far faster than it is replenished. Parts of the aquifer that took about 25,000 years to fill have been depleted in only a few decades. In heavily irrigated regions, the water table (the uppermost level of the groundwater) is falling one meter per year and being replenished at a rate of one millimeter (1/1,000 meter).

Another problem facing agriculture is waterlogging, the saturation of poorly drained soils by excessive irrigation water. Waterlogging blocks the flow of air to roots, killing crops. About one-tenth of the world's irrigated cropland suffers from waterlogging. Productivity has fallen about 20 percent on these 53 million acres (an area the size of Idaho).

Irrigation water applied to poorly drained land also raises the water table; groundwater then evaporates from the soil, leaving behind salts. Salinization poisons the soil, reducing crop production. When salt buildup is considerable, the soil may become lifeless. An estimated 20 percent of the world's farmland (100 million acres) is suffering from salinization.

Further losses of arable land are brought about by farmland conversion—a relatively innocuous name for the insidious spread of cities, suburbs, highways, airports, and shopping malls onto once productive farms and pastures. Each day the United States loses approximately 7,000 acres of farmland, pasture, and rangeland to activities like these. In one year, that is equivalent to a strip of land one kilometer (.6 mile) wide extending from New York City all the way to San Francisco. Year after year after year the assault continues, not just in the United States but everywhere the population is expanding.

The loss of productive farmland from erosion, desertification, waterlogging, salinization, and farmland conversion is a trend that cannot continue. While frontierists argue that improvements in crops, fertilizers, and pesticides could offset the losses, the facts suggest otherwise. From 1950 to 1970, for instance, improvements in agricultural production and the expansion of land under cultivation increased world per-capita grain consumption 30 percent. From 1971 to 1984, however, world food production barely kept pace with population growth. Between 1984 and 1988, food production per capita fell 15 percent.

It is doubtful that improvements currently under development will reverse the decline. Nor will efforts to expand arable land help in the long run, because most continents have little reserve land. Those that do run the risk of invading ecologically valuable forestland and fragile grassland ecosystems. Even if they do, the gains would be transitory, for world population growth will soon outstrip any marginal gains achieved by expanding the farmland base.

SUSTAINABLE AGRICULTURE

Massive efforts are needed to make agriculture sustainable. For a farm to be sustainable, says John Reganold and the coauthors of an article in *Scientific American,* it must produce adequate amounts of high-quality food, protect its resources (especially soil and water), and be environmentally safe and profitable.[4] Sustainable agriculture does not necessarily represent a return to pre–industrial revolution methods; rather, it combines traditional conservation-minded farming techniques with modern technology.

Interestingly, sustainable agriculture addresses many serious environmental problems afflicting the world: declining fossil fuel supplies, groundwater contamination, groundwater depletion, soil erosion, loss of wildlife, deforestation, surface-water pollution, and even global warming.

To build a sustainable system of agriculture, we first need measures to reduce, then stop, the growth of the human population. Second, we must find ways to put an end to soil erosion. The 1985 U.S. Farm Bill was a good start. It provided subsidies for farmers to remove highly erodible land from production, and since its passage approximately 34 million acres has been retired from crop production.[5] Farmers have planted grass or trees on this land, cutting average annual erosion from 21 tons per acre to 2 tons per acre. Nationwide, this measure has cut erosion by about 600 million tons a year. Similar measures are needed throughout the world.

The 1985 Farm Bill also calls on farmers to develop erosion control plans for farmland in production. If farmers are to keep federal subsidies and crop insurance, they must implement their plans by 1995. At this writing, 1.5 million farmers have developed soil conservation plans with the Soil Conservation Service, covering 134 million acres of farmland or about 30 percent of U.S. farmland. When these plans are in place they could reduce erosion by another 700 million tons per year. The Department of Agriculture recently weakened its requirements for erosion control, citing economic hardship of farmers. The department estimates that reductions in erosion will therefore only amount to 300 to 500 million tons per year.

U.S. government subsidies currently discourage farmers from practicing crop rotation and planting soil-building crops like peas and clover. Subsidies that promote unsustainable activity are prime candidates for legislative reform. Promoting crop rotation and other measures that reduce soil erosion and maintain or build soil fertility are essential for the long-term health of American farm soil.

Crop rotation is one of the most important requirements of sustainable agriculture. As organic farmers will attest, crop rotation can be used to increase soil organic matter, which, in turn, makes soil more porous, allowing air and water to penetrate to the roots of a crop. Organic matter also holds moisture like a sponge and decreases the water required to grow a successful crop. Additionally, organic matter helps to hold soil in place, reducing erosion by wind and rain.

Crop rotation has an additional, often overlooked advantage: it diversifies a farmer's crops and thereby limits risk. A hail storm that damages a wheat crop, for example, could wipe out a farmer's entire year's earnings. But if that farmer has planted corn, alfalfa, beans, and lettuce in addition to wheat, the damage would be greatly reduced since hail does not affect all crops equally.

One of the most widely appreciated benefits of crop rotation is the dramatic reduction in insect pests. Planting the same crop year after year creates a virtually unlimited supply of food for pest species. Each year as infestations grow worse farmers apply more and more pesticide in a cycle often referred to as the pesticide treadmill. Making matters worse, about 5 percent of an insect population will be genetically resistant to a given pesticide. This 5 percent survives and reproduces. To control them farmers must use a higher dose of the same pesticide or apply a different one. The new treatment again usually kills 95 percent of the pests, but leaves behind a genetically resistant subpopulation that can flourish again, perpetuating the cycle no farmer ever wins. In the meantime, soil and groundwater are contaminated with toxic chemicals and a farmer's drinking water becomes a health risk. Birds and wildlife perish.

When crops are alternated every year, pest populations remain relatively low. In a crop rotation scheme that alternates corn, beans, and clover, insects that attack corn the first year lay their eggs in the soil, but their offspring find little food when they hatch among newly sprouting bean plants. Insects that feed on the bean crop face a similar dilemma in year three in the clover crop.

A variety of other environmentally benign measures are available to organic farmers. Predatory insects like ladybugs can be released into fields where they quickly go to work on pesty insects. Farmers can take steps to encourage predatory insects to take up residence on their farms. One farmer in California, in fact, found that by not killing the weeds that grew between his fruit trees, he attracted birds and predatory insects; they in turn helped to control insect pests and eliminated the need for insecticides.

A number of organic farmers are finding that they can plant several different crops in a field side by side to control insect pests. Alternating strips of corn, soybeans, and wheat, for example, creates conditions favorable to predatory insect species. This technique also reduces insect pests by providing substantially less food for any one species.

This technique can be used to increase crop yields as well. In a recent study in Nebraska, farmers planted corn and sugar beets in the same field. Two rows of corn were planted between every 15 rows of sugar beets, providing protection from the wind. The corn windbreaks increased the sugar beet yield by 11 percent, and the corn yield was increased by 150 percent as a result of increased sunlight penetration and carbon-dioxide replenishment.

To control insects, farmers can also spray their fields with a bacterial insecticide consisting of nothing more than the inert spores of a microbe called BT. In the stomachs of crop-eating larvae (caterpillars), BT spores hatch and begin to produce a lethal protein that kills their unsuspecting prey.

The exciting thing about sustainable agriculture is that there are so many options. All that's needed is a long-term view of the value of farmland and the political will to make farming a sustainable human endeavor. As in other areas, economic incentives would advance the move toward sustainable practices, as would the elimination of outdated laws and harmful subsidies that encourage environmentally shortsighted farming.

Equally important are measures to stop the spread of deserts. Like soil erosion, desertification must be attacked on many fronts. One of the first steps is a drastic reduction in the release of greenhouse gases and deforestation, both of which could curb global warming. Tree planting in rural and urban areas is also essential to this effort.

Countries would be wise to reduce the overgrazing and exhaustive farming practices that lead to desertification. In Ethiopia, for example, farmers once plowed and planted marginal (arid) land, then let the land lie fallow for seven years. During that time, natural vegetation took over, rejuvenating the soil and making it arable once again. Today, shortsighted government policies force farmers to till marginal land year after year. In an act of ecological suicide, the Ethiopian government confiscates land if farmers do not replant within three years.

The spread of desert can be offset by replanting recently desertified land with native, drought-resistance species. China launched a massive program to plant a 4,300-mile green wall of vegetation to stop the spread of desert in the northern provinces. Similar efforts are under way in other countries, but in most places tree cutting and overgrazing far exceed the rate of revegetation. In China, for example, 4,000 square miles of trees are planted every year, but twice that amount is still being cut.[6]

Sustainable agriculture means using irrigation water much more wisely, for example watering early or late in the day, even at night, when evaporation is minimal. More efficient irrigation systems can cut demand. Farmers who line their irrigation canals with concrete or plastic cut water losses by as much as half. Irrigation pipes reduce water loss even more. Farmers can install systems that capture irrigation water flowing off their crops; this water can be diverted to ponds and used over and over again. Another idea is to improve the organic content of soil, since organic matter retains soil moisture. Special drip irrigation systems are useful in orchards and some row crops. In irrigated cornfields, farmers can lower the height of pivot irrigation systems to reduce water loss by wind and evaporation.

Each year, approximately 42 million people die of starvation and diseases worsened by malnutrition. For many people, the challenge is to find ways to feed these people. But many short-term solutions ignore the long-term health of the soil and, therefore, could ruin the sustainable resource base upon which billions of people will depend in the coming decades. The more pressing challenge is how we create a system of agriculture that can survive in the long haul.

There are a great many other measures for managing land sustainably. But the point is clear: we cannot continue along the current path. Destroying farmland and grazing land while allowing the population to swell is ecological suicide. Feeding the world's people sustainably surely complicates today's shortsighted practices, but it is our only hope for the future.

Powering a Sustainable Society

To achieve a sustainable relationship with the planet, humanity must also find new ways of providing energy, ways that do not destroy the planet's climate or wreak some other havoc. For most students of sustainability that means phasing out nonrenewable resources such as oil, natural gas, coal, and nuclear energy and replacing them with more environmentally compatible renewable supplies, such as wind and solar energy. As we pursue these options, every effort must be made to use energy more efficiently. The costs and benefits of energy conservation, discussed at length in previous chapters, can be further explored in numerous books and magazine articles.[7]

Energy conservation will buy us time to develop alternatives to fossil fuels and to switch to them. According to one estimate, making the transition to renewable fuels on the scale required for sustainability could take 50 years or longer. Using current resources more efficiently is essential if the transition is to be smooth.

WHAT'S DRIVING THE SWITCH TO RENEWABLE FUELS?

Projections of world oil supply and demand suggest that this fuel is on the fast track to oblivion. So besides making more efficient use of oil, we must find substitutes. The chief candidates will probably be ethanol and methanol, derived from specially grown crops and from wood.

The prospects for natural gas reserves are better than for oil. According to several sources, proven reserves of natural gas will last about 57 years at the current rate of consumption. Unproven resources, natural gas we think is in the ground, will last another 53 years. In other words, there is a 110-year global supply of natural gas at the current rate of consumption, provided reserves are as big as we think. Increasing demand will undoubtedly reduce the supply of this vital resource, but natural gas will probably remain in use far longer than oil.

That's fortunate in some respects. Natural gas burns much more cleanly than oil, producing only one-fourth as much carbon dioxide per BTU.[8] Eventually, though, it too will need to be replaced. Since much of the natural gas consumed by industrial nations is for heating buildings and offices, a logical replacement is passive solar energy—sunlight streaming through south-facing windows and captured inside a building in thermal mass where its energy is gradually released into the internal environment. Combined with efficiency, passive solar heating can supply 100 percent of a home's heating requirements. Two additional renewable substitutes for natural gas are hydrogen, a combustible gas produced from water, and methane, an equally flammable gas released from garbage dumps and other organic matter. Both fuels are clean, relatively abundant, and neither adds to global warming.

Coal is the world's most abundant nonrenewable fuel. According to several estimates, the total recoverable reserves will last about 1,700 years at the current rate of consumption. Even though increasing use could cut the supply substantially, these large surpluses suggest that coal could be with us for many years to come.

Unfortunately, coal is a dirty fuel. It produces enormous amounts of carbon dioxide, sulfur dioxide, and nitrogen dioxide, and is a major contributor to global warming and acid deposition. A coal-powered future would require extensive mining, disrupting farmland, rangeland, and wildlife habitat. It would produce significant amounts of toxic waste, especially from smokestack scrubbers. That waste would end up in landfills and in our water. A coal-powered future would likely be much warmer, since controlling carbon dioxide emissions from coal combustion is next to impossible.[9] Clearly, it is a future we cannot afford. But given the massive reserves and the political muscle of the coal industry, I suspect that advocates of a sustainable energy system will have a tough time in the coming years convincing governments *not* to tap into this resource.

The rising controversy over the future of coal demonstrates that building a sustainable society requires decisions made *not* just on the basis of supplies but also on the need for a healthy, well-functioning ecosystem. The challenge lies in convincing the world's leaders and businesses to consciously shift to environmentally benign fuels, even though other fuels are available and in some cases abundant. The challenge is all the more difficult because the industrialized world is built on a foundation of nonrenewable fossil fuels, structurally, politically, and economically. Those who wield power are often those who benefit from maintaining a system hooked on fossil fuel.

The Coming Solar Age

The massive shift to wind energy in California and the shift to renewable energy sources elsewhere may prove to governments that renewable fuels are indeed a bargain, both economically and environmentally. In fact, large-scale wind farms produce electricity at rates competitive with coal, about five cents per kilowatt hour. The cost of solar thermal electricity is competitive with nuclear power rates.

Moreover, wind and solar thermal have minuscule external costs, which makes them far more desirable than coal or nuclear.

Continued environmental deterioration and the troubles associated with getting oil out of the Middle East may convince governments to shift to home-grown and infinitely more reliable energy sources. One of the most important is solar energy. Solar is a diverse source. It can provide space heating for buildings or produce electricity, and it can heat water for washing dishes and bathing. It is even possible to cool buildings with solar. The sunlight that falls annually on an area the size of the state of Connecticut would supply all of the power needs of the United States for one year.

The sun generates wind that can be tapped for electricity. By one estimate, the globe's windiest spots, in fact, could provide 13 times the electricity now produced worldwide.

Sunlight is captured in plants through photosynthesis, then trapped in organic molecules. Burned or distilled, plants might provide additional energy in the coming solar age.

The sun is also responsible for evaporation and cloud formation. Water falling on mountains flows down rivers, releasing energy that can be tapped by hydroelectric facilities. Thus, even hydroelectric power is a kind of solar energy. Carefully sited and protected from erosion, hydroelectric facilities can provide relatively clean electricity.

Direct solar energy, wind energy, biomass (plants), and hydropower could supply all the energy needs of our society, easily replacing the oil, coal, natural gas, and nuclear fuel in use today.[10] In the residential and commercial sector, for example, space heating could be provided by passive solar energy combined with measures to cut energy loss. Active solar systems would heat water. Electricity from sunlight or wind could power electric stoves, high-efficiency lights, and high-efficiency motors. Methane produced from plant matter could be used to provide energy for gas stoves. Ethanol from sustainably managed fuel farms could serve as liquid fuel for energy-efficient trucks, cars, trains, and planes. Farmers could plant 10 percent of their land in sunflowers, whose seeds produce a renewable oil that can be burned in diesel engines. Photovoltaic cells could supply electricity to power trains that take commuters to and from work or that speed passengers from one city to another. Plastics, currently made from petroleum, could also be made from ethanol and methanol.

Hydrogen might also become a fuel of great importance in years to come. Produced from water, hydrogen fuel burns cleanly. It can be used in vehicles and in stoves. Power to split water molecules to produce hydrogen could come from sunlight and wind energy.

Making the shift to a renewable energy system requires an investment in renewable energy resources by governments and people. The shift to renewable energy will not occur without a revolution in American politics spurred by a massive outpouring of public sentiment. Public pressure stirred by environmental and citizen groups may be the only antidote powerful enough to loosen the fossil fuel industry's grip on public policy. Given the massive supplies of renewable energy and their many environmental benefits, solar, wind, biomass, and other similar sources are not just important to a sustainable future, but its essential building blocks.

Critics, nonetheless, are quick to point out their weaknesses. One of the most obvious targets is price. As noted above, some renewable sources are cost-competitive while others, like photovoltaics, are far more expensive than conventional fuels in most applications. Proponents of renewable energy are asking not that countries convert to photovoltaics (the electricity from which would cost approximately 27 cents a kilowatt hour), only that they switch to cost-competitive renewable energy sources where feasible. Proponents are asking that the cost of *all* fuels be based on full-cost pricing, that is, a price structure that takes into account economic externalities such as the one billion dollars per year spent by the federal government on disability payments to coal miners suffering from black lung disease and a variety of subsidies described earlier in the book. And lastly, proponents are asking that subsidies be removed from nonrenewable energy resources so that renewable sources can compete on a level playing field. These changes would boost the application of technologies currently deemed uncompetitive.

The second target of critics is storage. Wind generators, for example, produce electricity only when the wind blows. Photovoltaics operate only during the daytime and, of course, only when the sun is out. A coal-fired power plant can operate day and night as long as there is plenty of fuel available. This discrepancy suggests to opponents of renewable energy that fossil fuels are a more reliable source. Wind and solar proponents, however, point out that batteries store electricity to bridge the gaps between nonproduction periods. Some suggest that fossil fuels could be used as a backup for renewable energy resources. My home is a perfect example. While most of my heat comes from the sun, I use my high-efficiency gas furnace on cloudy winter days or on extremely cold evenings when stored heat proves inadequate. I get by with a fraction of the nonrenewable energy of a typical household. Codependent systems promise to wean us from our fossil fuel dependency, and with enormous benefit to the biosphere.

The third problem critics like to raise is that the availability of solar energy varies from one location to another. Maine, it is assumed, receives far less sunlight than Arizona. Interestingly, the differences are not as great as some would have you believe. In fact, Maine receives 70 percent as much sunlight as Arizona, which is located in the heart of America's sunbelt. A map showing the availability of solar energy across the United States indicates that except for two small regions—part of Washington State, and northern New York State and Vermont—the sun can be tapped at least 60 to 70 percent of daylight hours in the course of a year. And when the sun doesn't shine, there's wind or wood or hydroelectric or geothermal. Each region, in other words, comes up with the mix of renewable energy resources that works best for it.

SOME SUCCESS STORIES

A world powered by renewable energy, especially sunlight, is not a pipe dream. Already efforts are under way to make the shift.

- Brazil, for example, currently gets about half of its automobile and truck fuel from ethanol derived from sugarcane.
- The state of California currently has over 1,400 wind generators producing enough electricity to meet the needs of one million people.
- The U.S. Coast Guard has installed more than 11,000 photovol-

taic systems to harness electricity from sunlight. These systems power navigational aids and telecommunications.[11]

- More than 10,000 homes in the United States are using photovoltaics for all of their electricity or as supplemental power.
- Sweden has vowed to eliminate nuclear power and derive its energy from conservation efforts, hydroelectricity, and other renewable fuels.
- In China's Inner Mongolia, 2,000 small wind turbines provide electricity for lighting, televisions, and other needs. Portable wind turbines are carried by nomadic herders. Three Chinese factories produce several thousand wind generators each year for use in Tibet and other remote areas.[12]
- In French Polynesia, over 2,000 solar electric systems installed from 1982 to 1987 supply electricity to homes, hospitals, radio stations, and water pumps.
- The Philippines has reduced oil-generated electricity from 78 percent in 1978 to 46 percent in 1984 by developing hydroelectric and geothermal sources.

Despite these successes, the world's people tap only a tiny fraction of the full potential of renewable fuels. Far more effort is needed to make the shift to a sustainable energy system. Businesses and countries can contribute by making a major commitment in money and time to renewables, for example, by purchasing photovoltaic modules in quantities that help factories to improve mass production and drive costs down. Rising dependence on renewable energy technologies may help free the economy from the epileptic fits that occur every time the price of oil rises a few dollars, and they tap into local sources of energy that help to clean up our air, our water, and our land.

Protecting Biodiversity

A shift to a sustainable way of life would nudge the human economy into alignment with the economy of nature and also relieve pressure on our fellow creatures, the plants and animals living in the path of bulldozers and draglines. But as I noted in chapter 7, additional efforts are needed if we are to protect biodiversity in wildlands. That chapter focused on ways of protecting biodiversity in Third World development projects; not surprisingly, many of these ideas apply to the industrialized world. Accordingly, industrialized countries would be well advised to do the following:

1. Protect all wildlands of "special concern" from development. Estuaries, wetlands, old-growth forests, and other valuable habitats should be off-limits to development and given permanent protection for the services they provide to humanity and the Earth.

2. Establish buffer zones around wildlands of special concern to further protect them from the impact of development. Limited human use, such as sustainable tree harvesting, might be permitted as long as it didn't affect protected areas.

3. Shift development to lands already cleared, cultivated, logged, or otherwise converted. By concentrating development on these lands, we can ease the pressure on forests, fields, and other such areas. Development on these lands would have to be accompanied by strict measures to prevent pollution and other environmental damage.

4. Protect valuable lands near projects such as dams and reservoirs. By actively controlling soil erosion, we can increase the life span of reservoirs and reduce the need to build on new dams. A well-protected watershed would yield a sustainable supply of clean water for irrigation, livestock, or human use.

5. Provide funding and staffing to protect wildlands in the long term. Sustainability requires a commitment to manage and protect preserves, buffer zones, and ecologically important lands surrounding development projects.

6. Improve the productivity of existing land. By reducing soil erosion, desertification, salinization, waterlogging, and land conversion, and by adopting measures to rebuild soils, we would greatly decrease the need to tap into farmland reserves—grasslands, forests, and other lands that can be plowed and planted.

7. Work closely with farmers and other land users to develop plans that benefit people, wildlife, and the environment.

8. Offset necessary development by establishing additional wildland preserves.

CONNECTING CORRIDORS

There are additional measures to take if we are serious about protecting wildlife. One of the most important new ideas is the wildlife corridor, strips of land that connect isolated patches of habitat set aside to protect species.

Ecologists refer to these patches as ecological islands. Existing amid crops, cities, pastures, towns, and mines, ecological islands have proved only marginally successful in protecting biodiversity, much to the surprise of many. Ecologist William Newmark studied the loss of mammal species in national parks and reported an alarming decline in the number of species in all but the very largest parks. Bryce Canyon National Park, one of the nation's smallest parks, has lost 36 percent of its species. Yosemite, nearly 20 times larger than Bryce, has lost 23 percent. Even mammoth parks such as Yellowstone suffer losses, though they are lower.

Why do protected areas fail to protect species? Ecological islands rarely contain enough habitat for all of the species that live within them. Roaming animals are especially hard hit. Ecological islands may also reduce populations below levels needed for successful reproduction. And islands lead to interbreeding among members of a small population, which may result in offspring less capable of surviving.

Wildlife corridors allow species to migrate from one island to another and breed with members of previously isolated subpopulations. This increases genetic diversity within a species and gives it a better chance of survival. Corridors also open up new habitat. Food shortages encountered in one region might be offset by animals migrating to another area.

The state of Florida and the Nature Conservancy are currently planning a series of wildlife corridors to protect the Everglades panther, an endangered species that has been relegated to a few patches of land widely dispersed throughout the state. If efforts to connect them are successful, the panther may someday roam more freely in search of food and mates, living in relative harmony with the human population and infrastructure that surrounds it.

Besides setting aside new habitat and connecting ecological islands via wildlife corridors, industrial societies can help improve the fate of wildlife by improving existing habitat, a point made several times in earlier chapters. Replanting forests and denuded grasslands, for example, could help boost wildlife populations. Stabilizing stream banks, clearing logs from trout and salmon streams, and dredging sediment that is eroded into spawning beds can also help heal the Earth. These efforts combined with others discussed earlier could pay enormous dividends in the long run, helping forge a synergy between humankind and the rest of the living world.

12 Sustainability: More Than a Semantic Solution

*Humanity seeks self-sufficiency, while
nature demands relationship. Humanity
wants to be invulnerable, but nature
reminds it that it is bonded to all other
things.*

JEREMY RIFKIN

IN JULY 1989, the leaders of seven major industrial nations called for worldwide adoption "of policies based on sustainable development." Had a reporter asked for a definition of sustainable development, I suspect few, if any, of the so-called leaders could have offered much more than a vague explanation.

This announcement shows us that the concept of sustainability is trickling into the mainstream of environmental thought. It is a germinal idea at best, begging to be fleshed out and incorporated more fully into our thinking.

Al Bartlett, a physicist from the University of Colorado who has spent much of the past twenty years describing the dangers of exponential population growth, is concerned that the term *sustainable* may become part of a semantic whitewash. Inserted into phrases such as "economic development" and "economic growth," the adjective creates the illusion of positive change. If individuals, businesses, and governments embrace this new term yet continue along old, destructive pathways, little if anything will be gained.

The term *sustainability* is rich with meaning and possibility. Creating a sustainable society requires an intimate understanding of this term—what it means and what it requires of us. Those who have studied sustainability at any length realize that it means finding a way of fostering an enduring human presence. It requires of us a profound shift in our thinking and our way of life, a revolution of sorts to reverse many dangerous trends set in motion by the agricultural and industrial revolutions.

My purpose here is to piece together the sustainability puzzle and offer a few additional insights that arise out of this synthesis.

Living within the Carrying Capacity

In natural ecosystems, sustainability implies the ability to live within the carrying capacity of the environment. For humans, that means creating a society that lives within ecological limits. If we are smart, we can even thrive within what may appear to be constraints imposed by nature.

Mindful of limits of resources and the laws of ecology, a sustainable society seeks ways to cooperate with nature and protect the natural resource endowment so vital to the survival of all living things. It pursues balance and relationship rather than domination, control, and isolation. A sustainable society safeguards ecosystems not solely for immediate self-interest but to benefit other living organisms and future generations. By recognizing the rights of all living things, present and future, the citizens of a sustainable society live in ways that honor future generations and other species. In a sustainable society, the Earth is viewed as a priceless heirloom, bequeathed to the present by the past and handed on to future generations in a condition as good as, or better than, it was received. Present generations are a bridge that joins the past and the future. Treating the planet as an heirloom means accepting a basic ecological reality—the Earth is finite—and tempering our seemingly endless lust for more.

Living within the carrying capacity of the environment requires a major revision of critical activities from agriculture to industry to home life. For agriculture, it means creating systems that provide food in ways that protect and enhance the long-term health and productivity of the soil. A sustainable agricultural system minimizes or eliminates the use of pesticides by finding biological controls, and it minimizes the use of artificial fertilizers as well, relying on soil-nurturing practices such as crop rotation and heteroculture—methods that do not just protect but rather enhance the quality of soil. Recognizing that it is part of a larger whole, sustainable agriculture furthermore seeks to protect rivers, groundwater supplies, and the many species that live with us on this planet.

Living sustainably on the planet calls for a marked change in the way we satisfy our demand for resources such as water, energy, and building materials. For most countries, the greatest opportunities lie in tapping into our most abundant resource, waste. Efforts to reduce unnecessary consumption, to improve efficiency, recycle, and reuse materials all figure prominently in the waste-reclamation strategy and could be the source of a steady stream of resources for present and future generations, helping us to minimize our impact on the environment.

An enduring human presence also depends on significant strides in the management of renewable resources upon which human civilization's long-term future rests. Renewable resources are no panacea. They must be managed carefully with the long-term health of the system in mind. Without dramatic improvements in the management of these resources, our days are surely numbered.

Living within the carrying capacity demands that we close the distance between producer and consumer, creating locally or regionally self-reliant economies that operate within the sustainable productivity of the bioregions they occupy.

Living sustainably also requires continuing efforts to mobilize energy and finances to put an end to pollution. Of the many strategies available to us, pollution prevention heads the list. In a sustainable world, end-of-pipe solutions, while important, should be a last resort, for they merely shift pollution from one medium to another in a kind of toxic shell game that does little to reduce the planet's overall pollution burden.

A New, Practical Earth Ethic

As noted earlier, building a sustainable society requires revolution in our way of life, a revolution as far-sweeping as the agricultural and industrial revolutions. This reformation must be based on sustainable ethics, the core principle of which is that a healthy, well-functioning ecosystem is essential to all life and economic well-being. Sustainable ethics recognizes the limits of the ability of the planet to supply resources and handle wastes, encouraging us to be frugal, and it acknowledges the rights of other species to share with humans in the Earth's bounty. A sustainable ethic sees people as part of the economy of nature, not separate from nature. It reminds us that we are subject to the laws of nature and that to prosper on the planet we must find ways of cooperating with it.

To be effective, the new ethics must be a synthesis of theory and action. At least five broad actions, which I've called the operating principles of a sustainable society, permit us to put this ethics to work: conservation, recycling, renewable resource use, restoration, and population control. As you have seen throughout this book, decisive action on a large scale in each of these areas is needed if we are to live sustainably on the planet.

Treating the Disease, Not the Symptoms

Creating a sustainable future requires systemic change, but for most of the past 20 years, industrial nations have treated the symptoms of the environmental crisis by installing smokestack scrubbers, catalytic converters, sewage treatment plants, and other similar measures. This approach ignores the root causes of our present crisis: overpopulation, overconsumption, linearity, inefficiency, fossil fuel dependency, frontier thinking, and the frequent failure to restore ecosystems damaged in our push to feed, shelter, and clothe the world's people.

The actions prescribed by the biological principles of sustainability confront these problems head on, providing humanity with a practical strategy to reach effective, long-lasting solutions to the modern dilemma. Root-level solutions cut across the issues, solving a variety of problems at once and represent our greatest hope for redirecting the course of modern society.

Economies Designed with Nature

To achieve sustainability, we must alter our priorities. Nowhere is this need more evident than in the economic life of nations whose machinations threaten to destroy the economy of nature.

In a sustainable world, economies must be designed in sync with nature rather than in opposition to it. This, of course, requires vision. Mechanisms that help businesses identify their impacts then fold the external costs into the price of goods and services promote vision and ecological responsibility. Efforts to modify supply and demand economics are also crucial to this task, as are changes in ethics that shift our time frame in ways that may, at times, convince us to accept lower immediate returns for long-term sustainability.

In a sustainable economy, new measures of human success will focus on the quality of life rather than economic growth. These may end before our obsession with growth, which leads to the erosion of life on Earth. We must find ways to reduce, eventually eliminate, our exploitation of people and the planet. Closing the loops in the industrial economy by recycling and reusing virtually all waste will brighten the long-term human prospects.

Businesses are key to the success of sustainability. Fortunately, many businesses now recognize that they play a significant role in solving the environmental problems gripping the world. But environmental consciousness is not enough. Businesses must reorganize around the concept of sustainability. In other words, sustainability must be a central component of the business ethic, on equal standing with profitability.

To make business practices sustainable, companies are going to have to use resources much more efficiently, practice recycling, and wherever possible draw on renewable resources like solar and wind energy. Products are going to have to be designed for ease of recycling and manufactured from recycled materials. Wherever possible, businesses should introduce new products in conjunction with recycling programs.

Since consumers are an integral part of the economic system, they too are vital to the success of the sustainable revolution. They do their part by becoming conscientious consumers—buying green products but also buying less.

Sustainable Third World Development

In the Third World, economic development projects are essential to raise the standard of living and end the grip of poverty that contributes to environmental deterioration. The first rule of economic development in the Third World is that all efforts to improve the economy must promote ecological health concurrently.

Unfortunately, until recently, environmental considerations have taken the back seat to economic considerations, and much of what passed for development actually worsened the lives of those it was intended to help. Recognizing the fundamental failure of Western-style development projects, the development community has begun to rally behind the idea of sustainable economic development.

In the Third World, sustainable economic development requires greater self-reliance in food production and in the production of goods and services. Attempts to encourage self-reliance are more likely to succeed if they draw on local resources and tap into local knowledge and skills. Outside knowledge, while valuable, should be woven into the indigenous cultural fabric, supplementing rather than attempting to displace what already exists. Put another way, sustainable economic development means augmenting, where possible, centuries-old cultural practices with novel Western ideas, for example, introducing solar ovens to dry fruit harvested in rain forests.

To encourage local self-reliance, industrial nations will inevitably have to relieve at least part of the tremendous debt incurred by Third World countries, debt that currently obligates them to pursue a policy of environmental pillage. Flexibility is another prerequisite of sustainable economic development. Without it, well-intentioned projects stand little chance of working. Permitting nongovernmental agencies to manage development projects may provide flexibility. Finally, in the Third World, as elsewhere, massive restoration projects are needed to reclaim deserts, forests, and grasslands subjected to human abuse.

The Systems Approach: A Holistic, Participatory, and Anticipatory Government and Citizenry

Efforts to manage the interaction between people and the environment are as old as human civilization. Today, however, because of an uprecedented increase in the complexity of interaction and the enormous consequences of mismanaging it, the problem has reached a critical stage. What was once local pollution has become global, and what was once provincial and (relatively) reversible damage has assumed a global impact with irreversible consequences. Now more than ever people are beginning to understand that the interaction between people and the environment should be managed with the goal of sustainability.

Sustainability requires systems thinking—a recognition that everything is connected in space and time. Systems thinking is anticipatory, that is, it seeks to understand and to avoid systemwide impacts now and in the future. Holistic systems thinking helps advance social and ecological justice.

A humane, sustainable future also requires a system of government that is participatory and a citizenry that plays an active role in shaping the world. The concentration of wealth and influence in the hands of a few leads to exploitation of people and resources and crippling economic dependency. In a sustainable society, government strives to serve people and the planet.

The Question of Scale, A Question of Restraint

In nature, the size and scale of a given species are regulated by internal and external factors such as predation and disease. Humans, once subject to the forces of nature that control population size, have developed a remarkable technological capacity to override nature's limits. Technology, in fact, has permitted us to build a society whose size and scale exceed the Earth's carrying capacity. To many observers, advances in technology have led to an erroneous definition of humankind. The current definition is ecologically inaccurate and—many think—genocidal. Author Wendell Berry asserts that humankind sees no wisdom in restraining itself. Few people recognize that the success of modern civilization lies in reestablishing a balance with nature, reining in our technological prowess, and modifying it to fit the dictates of sustainability.

Building a sustainable society calls for a new definition of humanity, one that seeks proper scale. A new definition of humanity will invariably lead to restraint—curbing our desires and technology for the sake of the planet's future.

In a properly scaled society, humans and nature are partners, not adversaries. In such a world a diverse range of creatures coexists peacefully with humans, in part because resources are used efficiently and with little pollution. Such a world will not be all pristine wilderness, although there is ample room for untouched land, nor will it be an entirely human dominated world. In many places, it will be a blend of both humankind and nature that works to benefit both.

The biggest challenge of the sustainable revolution is to transform human endeavors so grossly out of balance with nature—agriculture, energy use, waste disposal, water use, transportation, and housing—into sustainable systems. Fortunately, this task is not so daunting as many observers would have us believe. By following the biological principles of sustainability, citizens, businesspeople, and government officials can refashion each sector of society.

One World, One People: The Need for Massive Global Cooperation

Today all nations have a stake in the security of their neighbors, and each nation has a stake in security of the whole world. But security requires much more than a large militia or a massive arsenal of high-tech missiles. It depends ultimately on a healthy, well-functioning global ecosystem. Lest we forget, it also depends on freedom from the tyranny of crime and war, and on economic opportunities, education, and other social gains.

In today's world, widespread cooperation is needed to ensure global environmental balance. Through regional and international accords, nations can work together toward common environmental goals. To achieve global sustainability, however, it may also be necessary to strengthen international regulation by giving more money and additional authority to the UN Environment Program.

Global cooperation cannot come about without a new kind of leadership—men and women with vision who can bridge the differences among the world's people and forge shared concern for the environment into strong working relationships. Vital to the sustainable revolution are leaders who understand the problems and want to work for root-level solutions rather than add to the useless bandaids that only pass problems on to future generations. Each of us, too, can serve as a leader—in our communities, in our families, and within our circle of friends.

Critical Paths

Much of this book has attempted to outline systemic changes in ethics, economics, and government. As noted earlier, achieving a sustainable society also requires systemic changes in many vital sectors of human life, each of which is a critical path on the journey to a sustainable society.

Perhaps no greater challenge lies before us than making our cities and towns sustainable. This obliges us to redesign urban transportation systems, making them much more efficient in their use of energy and land. It obligates us to find ways to reduce energy demand in homes, offices, and factories. It means that we must increase recycling and composting of solid wastes in a substantial way and build local industries to put these materials to good use. Critical to our success will be efforts to tap into wind and solar energy. Lastly, this mammoth undertaking will require us to use water more sparingly and wisely.

Another vital path in the journey to a sustainable future is energy. Developing a sustainable, environmentally safe energy supply system requires efforts on two fronts. First and foremost, we need to dramatically improve the efficiency of our energy use, and second, we need to replace most of our fossil fuel and nuclear energy with renewable sources.

Sustainable agriculture poses a massive challenge. Steps must be taken to protect and enhance the soil and water upon which farming depends. In addition, we must slow, even halt, population growth through family planning and sustainable economic development. If we don't, nature will. And finally, we'll have to protect and enhance biodiversity.

Sustainability . . . A Question of Survival

An exploration of the term *sustainability* reveals it to be a rich and inviting concept, one full of promise. Founded on undisputable biological principles, sustainability is finding acceptance in economics, politics, and ecology. As an overarching goal applicable to all human activity, sustainability has the potential to bind disparate factions in a common struggle to remake the world. So powerful is this concept that it could, in fact, seed a revolution in human civilization.

In closing, building a sustainable society is clearly more than an academic question, it is a question of survival. We ignore the sustainable imperative at our own peril and at the peril of the biosphere upon which all life depends. We rise to the challenge of sustainability because the stakes are so high and time is so short. In the words of Wendell Berry, "To cherish what remains of the Earth and to foster its renewal is our only legitimate hope of survival."

In fact, it is the only hope we have of saving the entire planet from ecological ruin. Whether we like it or not, we have become the custodians of an entire planet. Its fate, along with the fate of our children, and of theirs, and of all living things, lies in our hands.

Notes

Chapter 1

1. G. Tyler Miller, Jr., *Resource Conservation and Management* (Belmont, California: Wadsworth, 1990).
2. Based on an estimate by the UN Food and Agricultural Organization of about 800 million people who are malnourished and undernourished.
3. Jim MacNeill, "Strategies for Sustainable Economic Development," *Scientific American* 261, no. 3 (1989): 155–165.
4. Based on estimates from the *BP Statistical Review of World Energy* (London, England: British Petroleum Company, 1989). For an explanation of my calculations, see chapter 11 in Daniel D. Chiras, *Environmental Science: Actions for a Sustainable Future,* 3d ed. (Redwood City, California: Benjamin/Cummings, 1991).
5. G. Tyler Miller, Jr., *Living in the Environment,* 5th ed. (Belmont, California: Wadsworth, 1988).
6. Locally, many societies have pushed grasslands beyond their capacity to produce, resulting in desertification and erosion. Societies have also altered the capacity of the air and streams to absorb pollutants. Globally, we have exceeded the Earth's capacity to absorb acid precursors, resulting in widespread acid deposition. We have also exceeded the Earth's capacity to absorb carbon dioxide, resulting in global warming.
7. Tighter regulations have reduced the outflow of noxious pollutants from factories and sewage treatment plants, helping to clean waters. Nevertheless, many lakes and rivers have shown little improvement over the past decade. Many bodies of water contain hazardous levels of pollutants from lawns, golf courses, parking lots, farm fields, and precipitation.

Chapter 2

1. For a more detailed discussion of exponential growth, see Chiras, *Environmental Science.*

2. Frank P. Davidson, "Macroengineering: Some Next Steps," *The Futurist* 24, no. 2, (1990): 16–21.

3. Paul Hawken, James Ogilvy, and Peter Schwartz, *Seven Tomorrows: Seven Scenarios for the Eighties and Nineties* (New York: Bantam, 1982).

4. See James E. Lovelock, *Gaia: A New Look at Life on Earth* (Oxford: Oxford University Press, 1979).

5. Norman Myers, *A Wealth of Wild Species: Storehouse for Human Welfare* (Boulder, Colorado: Westview Press, 1983).

6. Mary McCommon, "A Blooming Boom in Texas," *National Wildlife* 21, no. 5 (1983): 4–5.

7. Lester W. Milbrath, *Envisioning a Sustainable Society: Learning Our Way Out* (Albany, New York: State University of New York Press, 1989).

8. There's ample evidence to support the notion that our own health is dependent on a healthy physical, chemical, social, and psychological environment. For some examples, see the environment and health sections in Daniel D. Chiras, *Human Biology: Health, Homeostasis, and the Environment* (St. Paul: West, 1991).

9. Arne Naess, "Identification as a Source of Deep Ecological Attitudes," in *Deep Ecology*, M. Tobias, ed. (San Diego: Avant Books, 1984).

10. Daniel D. Chiras, "Lessons From Nature," *Colorado Outdoors* 35, no. 3 (1986): 19–21.

11. Robert L. San Martin, "Renewable Energy: Power for Tomorrow," *The Futurist* 23, no. 3 (1989): 37–40.

12. In part because of conservative pressure, the Reagan administration terminated U.S. financial backing of the UN Fund for Population Activities, which has financed nearly 5,000 family-planning projects since the late 1960s in 150 developing countries.

13. I'd say we hold it in common with other species as well.

14. The NWF amendment is on hold because it is not clear how to get it passed.

15. Comprehensive Environmental Amendment Project, Environmental Amendment Circular No. 4. (June 1991) (Denver: Comprehensive Environmental Amendment Project). This contains a summary of all of the proposals currently being offered.

16. Presented in Bill Devall, *Simple in Means, Rich in Ends: Practicing Deep Ecology* (Salt Lake City, Utah: Peregrine Smith, 1988).

Chapter 3

1. Roderick F. Nash, *The Rights of Nature: A History of Environmental Ethics* (Madison, Wisconsin: University of Wisconsin Press, 1989).
2. We broaden ourselves through watching nature and by reading. Education broadens our image of the self.
3. Developing my own "ecological self" has come in part from years of backpacking, extended river trips, and quiet contemplation. This sense was also fostered by reading about ecosystems and the dependence of humankind on nature. Poetry and music have helped strengthen my ecological self.
4. Steve Van Matre and Bill Weiler, *The Earth Speaks: An Acclimatization Journal* (Warrenville, Illinois: Institute for Earth Education, 1983). Good sources of writing on the environment that may help you develop your ecological self.
5. William D. Ruckelshaus, "Toward a Sustainable World," *Scientific American* 261, no. 3 (1989): 166–74.
6. The most popular was the Earth Works Group, *Fifty Simple Things You Can Do to Save the Earth* (Berkeley: Earthworks Press, 1989).
7. Chapter 3 of Chiras, *Beyond the Fray,* focuses on this issue, offering specific ways that we can create a more cooperative, socially cohesive response.
8. Quoted in Andrew Bard Schmookler, "Why Are We Devouring the Earth?" *In Context* 26 (1990): 22–23.
9. Cynthia Pollock Shea, "Environmental Investing," *World-Watch* 3, no. 1 (1990): 8–9.

Chapter 4

1. Representative Claudine Schneider, cited in *World-Watch* 3, no. 4 (1990): 8.
2. Assuming electrical costs of about seven to ten cents per kilowatt hour.
3. A 100-megawatt power plant provides enough electricity to serve approximately one million people.
4. The law of supply and demand describes the behavior of markets for all goods, and it's a pretty good predictor of price in the short run. People who invest in futures use it to determine buying patterns. If a drought destroys the wheat crop of the Midwest, investors quickly buy up futures in wheat, believing that the fall in supply will increase prices.

5. Paul A. Samuelson and William D. Nordhaus, *Economics,* 12th ed. (New York: McGraw-Hill, 1985).
6. Study cited in Marlise Simons, "Europeans Begin to Calculate the Price of Pollution," *The New York Times,* December 9, 1990.
7. Hazel Henderson, "Toward a New World Order," *The Christian Science Monitor* (April 8, 1991): 19.
8. Some trends toward globalization will continue, for example, global communications and global cooperation through governmental agencies such as the UN.
9. Cited in Facts Out of Context, *In Context* 28 (1991): 5. Original source Benjamin Friedman, *The Washington Spectator,* February 1, 1991.
10. James Robertson, "A New Economics for the 21st Century," *The Egg: A Journal of Eco-Justice* 9, no. 1 (1989): 4–5.
11. For a more detailed discussion, see John Okay, "Economic Forces," in *Renewable Natural Resources: A Management Handbook for the 1980s,* edited by Dennis L. Little, Robert E. Dils, and John Gray (Boulder, Colorado: Westview).
12. Farmers may use artificial fertilizers to boost soil fertility, but they replace only three of several dozen nutrients needed by plants.
13. One suggestion for easing the pain of transition is to have government support during transition periods.
14. Jim MacNeill, "Strategies for Sustainable Economic Development," *Scientific American* 261, no. 3 (1989): 155–65.
15. David Haenke, "Ecological Economics," *The Egg: A Journal of Eco-Justice* 9, no. 1 (1989): 5–7.
16. Hazel Henderson, "Introduce Green Tax," *The Christian Science Monitor* (July 6, 1990).
17. This belief is no doubt based on the frontier belief of unlimited resources and undying technological optimism—the belief that technological developments will get us out of any mess we get ourselves into.
18. Hazel Henderson, "Economics in the Solar Age: An interview with Alan AtKisson," *In Context* 25 (1990): 13–17.
19. One could argue that this is the result of businesses following one another rather than taking the lead in a competitive marketplace.
20. Milbrath, *Envisioning a Sustainable Society.*
21. When NEW and GNP are nearly identical, one can rest assured that human economic activity is less damaging and more sustainable.
22. Herman E. Daly and John B. Cobb, Jr., *For the Common Good* (Boston: Beacon Press, 1988).

23. For more, see Henderson, "An Interview with Alan AtKisson."
24. Jacksonville Chamber of Commerce, *Life in Jacksonville: Quality Indicators for Progress* (Jacksonville, Florida: The Jacksonville Community Council, 1990).
25. Marlise Simons, "Europeans Begin to Calculate the Price of Pollution," *The New York Times,* December 9, 1990.
26. It is a term I borrowed from the folks at the Rocky Mountain Institute. See William D. Browning and L. Hunter Lovins, *Energy Casebook,* casebook no. 2 (Snowmass, Colorado: Rocky Mountain Institute, 1989).
27. Cited in ibid.
28. Cited in Environmental Defense Fund, *Coming Full Circle: Successful Recycling Today* (New York: Environmental Defense Fund, 1988).
29. Peter Borrelli, "Can Earth Day Be Every Day?" *The Amicus Journal* 12, no. 2 (1990): 22–26.

Chapter 5

1. In my view, the movement toward frugality is inevitable. Declining resource supplies, rising prices, and environmental decay caused by global warming, deforestation, acid rain, and so on will oblige industrial societies like ours to act with much greater restraint.
2. Eric Hirst, "Demand-Side Management: An Underused Tool for Conserving Electricity," *Environment* 32, no. 1 (1990): 5–8, 27–31.
3. Christopher Flavin, "Yankee Utilities Learn to Love Efficiency," *WorldWatch* 3, no. 2 (1990): 5–6.
4. According to federal law, a utility is guaranteed a 10 percent return on its capital investment. Unbeknownst to many people, that guarantee may have facilitated the decision of certain utilities to build a nuclear power plant, whose capital cost is at least four, often as much as ten times greater than the capital cost of a new coal-fired power plant.
5. Cited in Browning and Lovins, *Energy Casebook,* casebook no. 2, Economic Renewal Program.
6. Recreation is prohibited on some reservoirs to protect water quality.
7. An acre-foot is an acre of water one foot deep, or about enough water to supply the needs of a family of four for a year.
8. These examples were published in the *Rocky Mountain Institute Newsletter* 6, no. 2 (1990): 4.

9. For more, see Cynthia Pollock Shea, "Doing Well by Doing Good," *World-Watch* 6, no. 2 (1989): 24–30.

10. Debra Lynn Dadd and Andre Carothers, "A Bill of Goods? Green Consuming in Perspective," *Greenpeace* 15, no. 3 (1990): 8–12.

11. Peter Weber, "Green Seals of Approval Heading to Market," *World-Watch* 3, no. 4 (1990): 7–8.

12. West Germany began a program in 1977; Japan began its program in 1988; Canada started a program in 1989. Sweden, Switzerland, and several other countries also have green-labeling programs.

13. Ken Sternberg, "Earth Day 1990," *Chemicalweek* 146, no. 15 (1990): 20–21.

14. This section adapted with permission from Daniel D. Chiras, *Beyond the Fray: Reshaping America's Environmental Response* (Boulder, Colorado: Johnson Books, 1990).

15. Cynthia Pollock Shea, "Environmental Investing," 8–9.

16. They also consist of the Interfaith Center for Corporate Responsibility, which is an investment advisor to the National Council of Churches.

17. I have paraphrased the Valdez Principles to make them more understandable.

18. One would also have to look at the energy cost of manufacturing and building such systems when determining their net energy efficiency.

19. Waste minimization has been stimulated by tighter regulations on hazardous waste. As landfill costs for hazardous waste increase, more and more manufacturers are finding it profitable to sell their waste as raw material or recycle it themselves, or redesign the manufacturing process to produce less waste.

20. These strategies have several payoffs. First, they reduce waste-disposal costs. They also make the company money in potential revenues and reduce liability associated with cleaning up hazardous waste sites.

21. The estimated optimal recycling rate is about 60 to 80 percent, since some material will be lost along the way—as a result of disposal or permanent use (copper wiring in houses and buildings).

22. We need companies that recycle plastic and we need companies that use products locally.

23. Recent years have seen the construction of numerous steel mills. The new generation of mills use an electric-arc furnace and consume scrap steel almost exclusively. However, electric-arc furnaces are found only in relatively low-volume steel mills and currently produce only a small percentage of the steel. Electric-arc furnaces would be perfect for regional facilities. Unfortunately, they produce steel for only a limited

range of products, many of which must be made from scrap containing few impurities.
24. Ken Sternberg, "Earth Day 1990."
25. Cynthia Pollock Shea, "Doing Well by Doing Good."

Chapter 6

1. Helena Norberg-Hodge, "The Cost of Development," *In Context* 25 (1990): 28–32.
2. Ravi Sharma, "Assessing Development Costs in India," *Environment* 29, no. 3 (1987): 6–11, 34–38.
3. Catherine Caufield. *In the Rainforest: Report from a Strange, Beautiful, Imperiled World.* (Chicago: University of Chicago Press, 1991).
4. For a more detailed description, see Chiras, *Environmental Science*, 8.
5. Waterlogging reduces plant growth and often kills crops by cutting off their oxygen supply.
6. Fertilizers only partially replace nutrients lost in soil.
7. Fortunately, successful development projects do exist, and a great deal can be learned from them.
8. With little regard for the long-term impact on our soil, water, and wildlife.
9. Many governments encouraged farmers to shift to export crops to reduce growing trade imbalances.
10. Thailand's marine fishery production represents about 90 percent of the total activity.
11. Overfishing is the result of technological development and also the increasing cost of operations. Fishermen are pressured to catch more and more fish, and some resort to the use of illegal nets with a smaller mesh. Furthermore, the fish meal and animal feed industries have induced the harvest of species considered less desirable.
12. The decree ending the tax breaks also requires Brazilian industry to manage forest resources more sustainably.
13. I use the term "sustainable economic activity" for industrialized countries, suggesting that continued growth is ultimately a prescription for disaster. In the Third World, some economic growth is essential to the elimination of poverty.
14. Quoted in Arianthé C. Stettner, "Considerations for Sustainable Economic Development in a Mountain Resort Community," Master's thesis, University of Phoenix, 1991.

15. Trevor Burrowes, "Does the Third World Point to the Future?" *In Context,* 26 (1990): 6–7.
16. Norman Myers, "Making the World Work for People," *International Wildlife* 19, no. 6 (1989): 12–14.
17. Information from Myers in this chapter comes largely from ibid.
18. Mark Kurlansky, "Haiti's Environment Teeters on the Edge," *International Wildlife* 18, no. 2 (1988): 35–38.
19. Sir Edmund Hillary, ed., *Ecology 2000: The Changing Face of Earth* (New York: Beaufort Books, 1984).
20. Environmental abuse in Haiti started 300 years ago when French colonists cleared forests to plant sugarcane. In 1791 a violent slave rebellion started fires on the island, and for more than a decade plantations were burned and the countryside was devastated.

    In 1804, Haiti gained independence from the French, but retained a French custom that today creates enormous problems. In France land is bequeathed to all offspring. A man who owns 40 acres for instance, divides his land up and gives one portion to each offspring. In Haiti, where families are large, this form of property inheritance has divided the land into tiny farms, each barely able to sustain its owners.
21. M. Anjali Sastry, "Improving Efficiency: Opportunities and Hurdles in India," *Rocky Mountain Institute Newsletter* 6, no. 2 (1990): 1 and 3.
22. Nicholas Lenssen, "Ray of Hope for the Third World," *World-Watch* 4, no. 3 (1991): 37–38.

Chapter 7

1. This material is adapted from Walter V. C. Reid, "Sustainable Development: Lessons from Success," *Environment* 31, no. 4 (1989): 7–9, 29–35.
2. Some remote homes in the United States are more economically served thanks to photovoltaics. For more information on this technology, see Richard J. Komp, *Practical Photovoltaics: Electricity from Solar Cells* (Ann Arbor, Michigan: aatec., 1984), and Joel Davidson, *The New Solar Electric Home: The Photovoltaics How-To Handbook* (Ann Arbor, Michigan: aatec., 1990).
3. Pierre R. Crosson and Norman J. Rosenberg, "Strategies for Agriculture," *Scientific American* 26, no. 13 (1989): 128–35. A rather sanguine view of the future of agriculture but nonetheless contains some good ideas on sustainability.

4. Catherine Caufield. *In the Rainforest: Report from a Strange, Beautiful, Imperiled World.*
5. William N. Ellis and Margaret McMahon Ellis, "Cultures in Transition: What the West Can Learn from Developing Countries," *The Futurist* 23, no. 2 (1989): 22–25.
6. I am not suggesting that they be used. This calculation is simply intended to show the vast potential.
7. For a thoughtful and detailed description of the value of wildlands and ways to protect them, see Robert Goodland and George Ledec, "Wildlands: Balancing Conversion with Conservation in World Bank Projects," *Environment* 31, no. 9 (1988): 7–11, 27–35.
8. The money for building the park went mainly toward establishing boundaries, developing a management plan, hiring and training personnel, and providing the infrastructure and equipment to improve production on already converted land.
9. William Ruckelshaus, "Toward a Sustainable World," *Scientific American* 261, no. 3 (1989): 166–74.
10. Carla Cole, "Ending Hunger," *In Context* 25 (1990): 36–37.
11. Trevor Burrowes, "Does the Third World Point to the Future?"
12. Ellis and Ellis, "Cultures in Transition."

Chapter 8

1. *Greenpeace* 13, no. 5 (1988): 5.
2. Robert Schaeffer, "Trading Away the Planet," *Greenpeace* 15, no. 5 (1990): 13–16.
3. Kenneth W. Hunter, "Big Messes: Problems That Grow Bigger and Bigger," *The Futurist* 25, no. 1 (1991): 10–17.
4. Cited in Daniel M. Fields, "Government with Foresight," *The Futurist* 24, no. 4 (1990): 17–19.
5. Chiras, *Beyond the Fray.*
6. Devall, *Simple in Means, Rich in Ends.*
7. Albert Gore, Jr., "Futurizing the United States Government," *The Futurist* 24, no. 2 (1990): 22–24.
8. William E. Halal, "A New Planning System Is Fine, But We Need to Plan a New System," *The Futurist* 24, no. 2 (1990): 27–28.
9. Herman E. Koenig, "Energy, Ecology, and Economics," *Phi Kappa Phi Journal* 55, no. 1 (1975): 4–8.
10. Two-year terms were designed, of course, to make government more

responsive to people's needs. But the House is an outdated organization. The demands of the job and the complexities of the issues require
longer terms of office.

11. I should hasten to add that the constitutionality of a state law that limits
    federal legislative terms is questionable. Most authorities on law believe
    that the limits on U.S. congressional representatives will be overturned
    in the courts.

12. One might argue that the reductions in sulfur-dioxide emissions would
    be much the same in either scenario, so why worry? The answer is that
    toxic sulfur compounds extracted by pollution-control devices on facil-
    ities burning high-sulfur coal must be disposed of somewhere. If low-
    sulfur coal had been used, there would have been less waste.

13. In a society powered by ethanol, the rate of absorption by plants would
    probably equal the rate of carbon-dioxide production from ethanol
    combustion. In a society powered by methanol, carbon-dioxide levels
    would increase, since a huge storehouse of carbon was locked away in
    coal millions of years ago.

14. Hazel Henderson, cited in Fields, "Government with Foresight."

15. Depletion allowances are tax breaks given to mining companies. As a
    company depletes its reserves, it is given a tax credit to stimulate further
    exploration. This gives the virgin ore industry an unfair advantage over
    recycling. Moreover, many companies are using the money to diversify,
    that is, to invest in other ventures.

16. Largely due to cold temperatures and frequent temperature inversions.

17. This section is adapted with permission from Daniel D. Chiras, *Beyond
    the Fray: Reshaping America's Environmental Response* (Boulder, Colo-
    rado: Johnson Books, 1990).

18. This section is adapted from Chiras, *Beyond the Fray.*

19. Bruce Brown, *Mountain in the Clouds: A Search for Wild Salmon* (New
    York: Simon and Schuster, 1982).

20. Kai N. Lee, "The Columbia River Basin: Experimenting with Sustain-
    ability," *Environment* 31, no. 6 (1990): 6–11, 30–32.

21. In addition, regulations are often pierced by unforeseen loopholes.

22. In fiscal year 1990, nearly $2 billion was allocated for construction
    grants for water treatment, while $1.6 billion went to the Superfund.

23. Adapted with permission from Daniel D. Chiras, *Environmental Science:
    Action for a Sustainable Future* (Redwood City, California: Benjamin/
    Cummings, 1991).

24. Sandra Postel, "Toward a New 'Eco'-nomics," *World-Watch* 3, no. 5
    (1990): 20–28.

25. Robert Gilman, "Economics, Ecology, and Us," *In Context* 26 (1990): 10–12.
26. Lee, "The Columbia River Basin."
27. There is some rather compelling evidence that fish hatcheries aren't so desirable after all. For example, diseases spread in the close confines of a hatchery may also spread to native species.

Chapter 9

1. Based on 1990 data from the Population Reference Bureau.
2. Hazel Henderson, "Toward a New World Order."
3. Karl-Henrik Robert, "Educating a Nation: The Natural Step," *In Context* 28, (1991): 10–13.
4. Subsistence whaling continues in some parts of the world, but subsistence harvests are still regulated. Some whaling also continues in the name of science.
5. The emissions-offset policy was established in the 1977 amendments to the Clean Air Act.
6. The new company is permitted to release an amount of pollution smaller than the cutbacks achieved by emissions offset.
7. Quoted in Harlan Cleveland, "The Future of International Governance: Managing a Nobody-in-Charge World," *The Futurist* 22, no. 3 (1988): 9–12.
8. Cleveland believes that governments and international organizations cannot be expected to initiate this kind of rethinking.
9. Although the environmental consequences of their actions leave much to be desired.
10. The World Constitution and Parliament Association is located at 1480 Hoyt Street, Suite 31, Lakewood, Colorado 80215.
11. Quoted in Robert Gilman, "Gaian Leadership: An Interview with David Gershon," *In Context* 22 (1989): 54–55.
12. I discuss these myths much more fully in chapter 3 of *Beyond the Fray*.
13. John W. Gardner, "Leadership and the Future," *The Futurist* 24, no. 3 (1990): 9–12.
14. For more information, contact the Elmwood Institute, P.O. Box 5895, Berkeley, California 94705.
15. Quoted from Richard D. Lamm, *Mega-Traumas: America at the Year 2000* (Boston: Houghton Mifflin, 1985).

16. Steven C. Lundin and Lynne C. Lancaster, "Beyond Leadership . . . The Importance of Followership," *The Futurist* 24, no. 3 (1990): 18–22.

Chapter 10

1. Lester R. Brown and Jodi Jacobsen, "The Future of the City," *The Amicus Journal* 9, no. 1 (1987): 21–28.
2. Sim Van der Ryn and Peter Calthorpe, *Sustainable Communities: A New Design for Cities, Suburbs, and Towns.* (San Francisco: Sierra Club Books, 1985).
3. This section adapted with permission from Daniel D. Chiras, *Environmental Science: Action for a Sustainable Future* (Redwood City, California: Benjamin/Cummings, 1991).
4. Population-Environment Balance, "The Myths of Growth," *Balance* 24 (1987): 1–2.
5. When farmland was taxed as if it were residential, farmers could no longer stay in business. The only way out was to sell it to developers.
6. The material on the myths of growth management is adapted from Population-Environment Balance, "The Myths of Growth."
7. The section on transportation is adapted from Chiras, *Environmental Science.*
8. Michael Renner, *Rethinking the Role of the Automobile,* Worldwatch Paper 84 (Washington, D.C.: Worldwatch Institute, 1988).
9. Quoted in Francesca Lyman, "Rethinking Our Transportation Future," *E Magazine* 1, no. 5 (1990): 34–41.
10. Rocky Mountain Institute Annual Report, Snowmass, Colorado, 1990.
11. Lyman, "Rethinking Our Transportation Future."
12. Nancy Shute, "Driving beyond Our Limit," *The Amicus Journal* 13, no. 2 (1991): 10–17.
13. Ibid.
14. The Worldwatch Institute recently published statistics on the caloric consumption of various modes of transportation. Bicycles turn out to be the most efficient means of transportation. Per passenger mile bicycles consumed 35 calories; walking, 100; rail transit, 885; bus transit, 920; and automobile single-occupant, 1,860.
15. Today, 20 cents of every dollar spent in the United States goes directly or indirectly to the automobile industry and its suppliers. Eighteen cents of every tax dollar the federal government collects comes from automobile manufacturers and their suppliers.

16. To increase the efficiency of the breakdown process, SERI researchers focused attention on enzymes that break down certain components of wood.
17. Concern, *Waste: Choice for Communities* (Washington, D.C.: Concern, 1988).
18. According to experts, industries are driven by price considerations to use a minimum amount of packaging. It benefits them to economize on packaging.
19. Carl Lehrburger and Rachel Snyder, "The Disposable Diaper Myth: Out of Sight, Out of Mind," *Whole Earth Review* Fall (1988): 60–66.
20. Single-use diaper manufacturers recommend rinsing feces in the toilet, but for most parents this is too much trouble. Rinsing in the toilet, moreover, significantly increases the water content of the diaper. It is doubtful that more than 10 percent of parents actually rinse out disposable diapers routinely.
21. Based on a $27 per ton fee for disposing in a landfill and an average transportation cost of about $48 per ton, or a total average of about $75 per ton, although this is much higher in some areas.
22. The EPA, which has announced its official goal to reduce solid waste by 25 percent by 1992, suggests that recycling, reuse, and source reduction could go a long way in helping us cut solid waste. Composting two-thirds of all yard waste, for instance, would meet half the target. At this writing, the EPA is thinking about increasing the goal to 40 percent.
23. According to Ray Hoffman, president of Washington Citizens for Recycling, a nonprofit group that struggled for ten years to convince the city to recycle its garbage.
24. The city can charge less because it is saving money on landfill fees and is earning income on the sale of recyclable materials.
25. This is especially true if landfill costs are high, say, over $80 per ton.
26. Sales of plastic have grown almost 5 percent a year since 1977, according to Cynthia Pollock-Shea of the Worldwatch Institute.
27. Cynthia Pollock, *Mining Urban Wastes: The Potential for Recycling*, Worldwatch Paper 76 (Washington, D.C.: Worldwatch Institute, 1987).
28. The voluntary identification system was devised by the Society of the Plastics Industry. It calls for number codes on all plastic bottles 16 ounces or larger, and on other containers of 8 ounces or more.
29. For example, that means making new milk bottles from old ones, not frivolous or unnecessary items.
30. From G. Tyler Miller, *Living in the Environment* (Belmont, California: Wadsworth, 1988). The current decline in the value of recyclables,

caused by a dramatic increase in supply, may alter these estimates.

31. Interestingly, test data compiled by the Environmental Defense Fund shows that incinerator ash contains toxic metals such as lead and cadmium in concentrations that the EPA considers hazardous.

32. The industry generally argues that waste incinerator ash is exempt from RCRA disposal regulations. The Congress and the EPA have been struggling for a number of years to determine whether waste from municipal incinerators should be regulated by RCRA provisions.

33. I'm talking about an ideal state. Considerable effort is needed to make this happen.

34. According to the Statistical Abstracts of the United States, 1989.

35. Peter Steinhart, "Who Turned Out the Lights?" *National Wildlife* 27, no. 1 (1989): 46–49.

36. David Morris, "Local Self-Reliance: A Response to the Changing Rules of the Game," in *Sustainable Communities,* edited by Sim van der Ryn and Peter Calthorpe (San Francisco: Sierra Club Books, 1986).

37. For more on photovoltaic systems, see Joel Davidson, *The New Solar Electric Home.*

38. Published by Builderburg Partners, Ltd., 1025 Vermont Ave, N.W., Washington, D.C. 20005.

39. Complete the Cycle Center's address is 3600 48th Avenue, Denver, CO 80216 and their phone number is 303/333–3434. ADPSR's address is 2546 15th Street, Denver, CO 80211.

Chapter 11

1. China relies on a number of economic incentives as well to encourage couples to have small families.

2. Cited in Pranay Gupte, *The Crowded Earth: People and the Politics of Population* (New York: Norton, 1984).

3. We can't even get away from growth terminology here.

4. John P. Reganold, Robert I. Papendick, and James F. Parr, "Sustainable Agriculture," *Scientific American* 263, no. 6 (1990): 112–20.

5. Peter Weber, "U.S. Farmers Cut Soil Erosion by One-Third," *WorldWatch* 3, no. 4 (1990): 5–6.

6. L. Ming, "Fighting China's Sea of Sand," *International Wildlife* 18, no. 6 (1988): 38–45.

7. The Worldwatch Institute and the Rocky Mountain Institute have been

champions of energy conservation. The economic virtues of energy conservation are well presented in Christopher Flavin and Alan Durning, "Raising Energy Efficiency," in *State of the World 1988,* edited by Linda Starke (New York: Norton, 1989).

8. Natural gas may be phased out earlier if global warming worsens and if the public demands a conscious shift in policy.

9. Some engineering schemes have been developed to remove carbon dioxide from smokestack gases, but this technology is still largely on the drawing boards.

10. H. W. Kendall and S. J. Hunt, *Energy Strategies: Toward a Solar Future* (Cambridge, Massachusetts: Ballinger, 1980).

11. Christopher Flavin, Rick Piltz, and Chris Nichols, *Sustainable Energy* (Washington, D.C.: Renew America, 1989).

12. Christopher Flavin, "Electricity in the Developing World," *Environment* 29, no. 3 (1987): 12–15, 39–44.

Bibliography

Adams, John H., et al. 1985. *An Environmental Agenda for the Future*. Washington, D.C.: Island Press. Excellent reading, but limited principally to legislative and regulatory solutions.

Agran, Larry. 1990. "Local Politics, Global Issues: An Interview with Will Swaim." *In Context* 25: 25–27. Offers some important insights on how politics can affect global issues.

Anderberg, Robert K. 1988. "Wall Street Sleaze." *The Amicus Journal* 10 (2): 8–10. Excellent overview of the effect of junk bonds and takeovers on natural resource management.

Atlee, Tom. 1990. "The Conversion of the American Dream." *In Context* 26: 15–19. Extraordinary analysis of consumerism.

Benton, R. 1986. "Economics and the Loss of Meaning." *Review of Social Economy* 44 (3): 251–63. Iconoclastic look at economics, well worth the reading.

———. 1987. "Work, Consumption, and the Joyless Consumer." In *Philosophical and Radical Thought in Marketing,* edited by A. F. Firat, N. Dholakia, and R. P. Bagozzi. Lexington, Massachusetts: Lexington Books. Penetrating look at one of the chief causes of wasteful consumption.

Berger, John J. 1985. *Restoring the Earth: How Americans Are Working to Renew Our Damaged Environment*. New York: Knopf. Superb and uplifting book on efforts to repair damage to the earth.

Berry, Wendell. 1977. *The Unsettling of America: Culture and Agriculture*. San Francisco: Sierra Club Books. Incisive look at some of society's weaknesses.

———. 1987. *Home Economics*. San Francisco: Northpoint Press. Collection of important essays on a variety of topics.

Borelli, Peter, ed. 1988. *Crossroads: Environmental Priorities for the Future*. Washington, D.C.: Island Press. Valuable collection of essays on environmentalism.

Borrelli, Peter. 1988. "Debt or Equity?" *The Amicus Journal* 10 (4): 42–49.

Explains early efforts to trade international debt for conservation in Third World countries.

———. 1988. "The Ecophilosophers." *The Amicus Journal* 10 (2): 30–39. Interesting look at the major philosophical factions of the environmental movement.

———. 1990. "Can Earth Day Be Every Day?" *The Amicus Journal* 12 (2): 22–26. Look at the kinds of changes needed to build a sustainable future.

Brown, Lester R. 1981. *Building a Sustainable Society.* New York: Norton. A book way before its time. Outlines goals in the effort to build a sustainable society.

Brown, Lester R., Christopher Flavin, and Sandra Postel. 1989. "No Time to Waste: A Global Environmental Agenda for the Bush Administration." *World-Watch* 2 (1): 10–19. Outlines key goals for the transition to a sustainable society.

Brown, Noel J. 1989. "The Rights of Earth: An Interview by W. R. Prescott." *In Context* 22: 29–34. Describes some international efforts to protect the environment and ensure sustainability.

Browning, William D., and L. Hunter Lovins. 1989. *Energy Casebook.* Snowmass, Colorado: Rocky Mountain Institute. Exceptional guide to economic revival through energy conservation.

Brundtland, Gro Harlem. 1989. "Global Change and Our Common Future." *Environment* 31 (5): 16–20, 40–44. Describes some of the challenges of building a sustainable society, especially for the scientific community.

Burrowes, Trevor. 1990. "Does the Third World Point to the Future?" *In Context* 26: 6–7. Frank discussion of the need to consider the lessons that can be learned from the Third World.

Callenbach, Ernest. 1990. "The Green Triangle." *In Context* 26: 13–14. Interesting look at the connections between environment, health, and economics.

Caufield, Catherine. 1991. *In the Rainforest: Report from a Strange, Beautiful, Imperiled World.* Chicago: University of Chicago Press. Gripping account of the atrocities occurring in tropical rain forests.

Chandler, W. U. 1985. *Energy Productivity: Key to Environmental Protection and Economic Progress.* Worldwatch Paper 63. Washington, D.C.: Worldwatch Institute. Detailed treatise on energy efficiency.

Chiras, Daniel D. 1980. "Models for Evaluating Environmental Issues in the Classroom." *American Biology Teacher* 42 (8): 471–73. Presents ways to promote critical thinking.

———. 1982. "Risk and Risk Assessment in Environmental Education."

American Biology Teacher 44 (8): 460–65. Overview of the risk-assessment process.

————. 1986. "Lessons from Nature." *Colorado Outdoors* 35 (3): 19–21.

————. 1990. *Beyond the Fray: Reshaping America's Environmental Response.* Boulder, Colorado: Johnson. Examination of the environmental response with numerous suggestions for ways to broaden and deepen it.

————. 1991. *Environmental Science: Actions for a Sustainable Society.* 3d ed. Redwood City, California: Benjamin/Cummings. Describes current environmental problems and solutions, emphasizing ways to build a sustainable society.

Cleveland, Harlan. 1988. "The Future of International Governance: Managing a Nobody-in-Charge World." *The Futurist* 22 (3): 9–12. Nice overview of some of the challenges to increasing global cooperation.

Cole, Barbara A. 1988. *Business Opportunities Casebook.* Snowmass, Colorado: Rocky Mountain Institute. Extraordinary presentation of ways communities can revitalize sagging economies, with special emphasis on environmentally sound methods.

Cole, Carla. 1990. "Ending Hunger." *In Context* 25: 36–37. Concise description of some of the solutions needed to end hunger by changing current policies, programs, and practices.

Commoner, Barry. 1989. "Why We Have Failed." *Greenpeace* 14 (5): 12–13. Questions deeply cherished views of risk assessment.

————. 1990. *Making Peace with the Planet.* New York: Pantheon. Wonderfully written analysis of the environmental crisis with timely advice on ways to solve it.

Comp, T. Allan, ed. 1989. *Blueprint for the Environment: A Plan for Federal Action.* Salt Lake City: Howe Brothers. List of recommendations for federal reform.

Dadd, Debra Lynn, and Andre Carothers. 1990. "A Bill of Goods? Green Consuming in Perspective." *Greenpeace* 15 (3): 8–12. Sobering look at green consumer passion.

Daly, Herman E. 1987. *The Steady-State Economy: Alternative to Growthmania.* Washington, D.C.: Population-Environment Balance. Good overview of Daly's views on the steady-state economy.

Davidson, Frank P. 1989. "Macroengineering: Some Next Steps." *The Futurist* 24 (2): 16–21. Instructive view of technological optimism that is blind to sustainability.

Devall, Bill. 1988. *Rich in Means, Simple in Ends: Practicing Deep Ecology.* Salt Lake City: Peregrine Smith. Thoughtful discussion of environmental values and ways to put those values into action.

Durning, Alan B. 1988. *Building on Success: The Age of Energy Efficiency.* Worldwatch Paper 82. Washington, D.C.: Worldwatch Institute. Detailed discussion of energy efficiency.

———. 1989. *Action at the Grassroots: Fighting Poverty and Environmental Decline.* Worldwatch Paper 88. Washington, D.C.: Worldwatch Institute. Incisive survey of grassroots movements throughout the world.

The Earth Works Group. 1989. *50 Simple Things You Can Do to Save the Earth.* Berkeley: Earth Works Press.

Easwaran, Eknath. 1990. "The Lesson of the Hummingbird." *In Context* 26: 30–35. Engaging article on a variety of issues of importance to sustainability.

Ehrlich, Paul R., and John P. Holdren, eds. 1988. *The Cassandra Conference: Resources and the Human Predicament.* College Station: Texas A & M University Press. Collection of essays on the environment.

Elgin, Duane. 1981. *Voluntary Simplicity: Toward a Way of Life That is Outwardly Simple, Inwardly Rich.* New York: William Morrow. Superb coverage of a topic of grave importance to the building of a sustainable society.

Flavin, Christopher. 1987. "Electricity in the Developing World." *Environment* 29 (3): 12–15, 39–44. Helpful survey of activities to produce electricity in Third World countries.

———. 1990. "Last Road to Shangri-La." *World-Watch* 3 (4): 18–26. Interesting look at a country on the verge of economic development choosing to protect its ecological health.

———. 1990. "Yankee Utilities Learn to Love Efficiency." *World-Watch* 3 (2): 5–6. How environmentalists have forced New England utilities to promote consumer efficiency, and how utilities have found that efficiency can be profitable.

Flavin, Christopher, Rick Piltz, and Chris Nichols. 1989. *Sustainable Energy.* Washington, D.C.: Renew America. Excellent survey of renewable energy options and their prospects for future energy production.

French, Hilary. 1989. "An Environmental Security Council?" *Worldwatch* 2 (5): 6–7. Discussion of the Declaration of the Hague.

Frosch, Robert A., and Nicholas F. Gallopoulos. 1989. "Strategies for Manufacturing." *Scientific American* 261 (3): 144–52. Proposes a strategy by which manufacturers can greatly reduce their impact on the environment.

Gardner, John W. 1990. "Leadership and the Future." *The Futurist* 24 (3): 9–12. Addresses the need for leaders who can inspire people to believe in themselves, individual action, and a new future.

Gershon, David. 1989. "Gaian Leadership: An Interview by Robert Gilman." *In Context* 22: 54–55. Describes the need for a new kind of leadership that inspires individual responsibility and action, and efforts under way to create new leaders.

Gilman, Robert. 1990. "Sustainability: The State of the Movement." *In Context* 25: 10–12. Attempts to define the key tenets of sustainability.

Goodland, Robert, and George Ledec. 1988. "Wildlands: Balancing Conversion with Conservation in World Bank Projects." *Environment* 31 (9): 7–11, 27–35. Excellent piece on the World Bank's efforts to make economic development more sustainable in Third World nations.

Gore, Jr., Albert. 1990. "Futurizing the United States Government." *The Futurist* 24 (2): 22–24. Describes a bill that would create a presidential commission to study critical trends and government policies.

Gupte, Pranay. 1984. *The Crowded Earth: People and the Politics of Population.* New York: Norton. Superb discussion of the overpopulation problem and solutions to it.

Guttman, Astrid. 1989. "Urban Releaf." *World-Watch* 2 (6): 5–6. Brief account of U.S. efforts to plant urban trees to offset global warming.

Haenke, David. 1989. "Ecological Economics." *The Egg: A Journal of Eco-Justice.* 9 (1): 5–7. Interesting discussion of ecological economics.

Hagerman, Erik. 1990. "California's Drive to Mass Transit." *World-Watch* 3 (5): 7–8. Looks at California cities and counties that are tackling traffic problems by building mass transit.

Hall, Bob and Mary Lee Kerr. 1991. *1991–1992 Green Index: A State-by-State Guide to the Nation's Environmental Health.* Washington, D.C.: Island Press. Very useful rating of environmental conditions and policies.

Hardin, Garrett. 1985. *Filters against Folly.* New York: Viking. Delightful discussion of ecological wisdom.

Harvey, Joe. 1990. "Outgrowing Growth." *Rocky Mountain Institute Newsletter* 6 (2): 3. Delightful essay on the myths of economic growth.

Hawken, Paul, James Ogilvy, and Peter Schwartz. 1982. *Seven Tomorrows: Seven Scenarios for the Eighties and Nineties.* New York: Bantam. Thorough and interesting analysis of possible futures.

Henderson, Hazel. 1990. "Americans Want Energy Retrofit." *The Christian Science Monitor* (September 21): 18. Prescription for government actions to encourage the transition to a sustainable energy system and a sustainable economy.

———. 1990. "Economics in the Solar Age: An Interview with Alan Atkisson." *In Context* 25: 13–17. Presents some ways to alter the human economy, making it more humane and sustainable.

———. 1990. "From Economism to Systems Theory and New Indicators of Development." *Technological Forecasting and Social Change* 37: 213–33.

Critical rethinking of debt, aid, ecological destruction, and other topics within the context of a new view of progress.

————. 1990. "Introduce Green Tax." *The Christian Science Monitor* (July 6). Frank discussion of taxes on pollution, returnable containers, and depletion of resources.

————. 1991. "Beyond the Traditional 'Bottom Line' of Business and Government." *Providence Journal Bulletin* (June 8). Thoughtful analysis of Project 88, a measure to tap market forces in order to protect the environment.

————. 1991. "Population: Its Rights and Resources." *The World Paper* (April): 12. Discussion of some of the limits of GNP-based economic development.

————. 1991. "Toward a New World Order." *The Christian Science Monitor* (April 8): 19. Offers some thoughts on strengthening the global response to environmental and economic problems.

Henderson, Hazel, and Robert Theobald. 1988. "Money vs. Wealth: The Need for New Economic Tools." *The Futurist* 22 (2): 34–35. Discusses some interesting new concepts for economic activity.

Hillary, Sir Edmund, ed. 1984. *Ecology 2000*. New York: Beaufort Books. Highly readable collection of essays on environmental problems and solutions.

Hirst, Eric. 1990. "Demand-Side Management: An Underused Tool for Conserving Electricity." *Environment* 32 (1): 5–9, 27–31. Important discussion of ways utilities can conserve electricity by offering incentives and disincentives to customers.

Holdgate, Martin W. 1989. "Planning for Our Common Future." *Environment* 31 (8): 14–17, 38–41. Outlines a strategy for coping with and lessening the impact of global warming, with special attention to government responses.

Hunter, Kenneth W. 1991. "Big Messes: Problems That Grow Bigger and Bigger." *The Futurist* 25 (1): 10–17. Insightful look at the reasons behind America's inability to solve social, economic, and environmental problems.

Johnson, Lynell. 1987. "Children's Visions of the Future." *The Futurist* 21 (3): 36–40. Study of children's attitudes toward their personal future and the future of the world.

Johnson, Warren. 1978. *Muddling toward Frugality*. San Francisco: Sierra Club Books. Important book with an interesting section describing human history from an ecological perspective.

Kazis, Richard, and Richard Grossman. 1982. "Environmental Protection:

Job-Taker or Job-Maker?" *Environment* 24 (9): 12–20, 43–44. How jobs are often used to convince people of the need for projects and how environmental protection often creates far more jobs than it eliminates.

Koenig, H. E. 1975. "Energy, Ecology, and Economics." *Phi Kappa Phi Journal* 55 (1): 4–8. Interesting discussion of consumerism and the environment.

Lamm, Richard D. 1985. *Mega-Traumas: America at the Year 2000.* Boston: Houghton Mifflin. Important reading for anyone interested in a wide range of social, economic, and environmental issues.

Lee, Kai N. 1989. "The Columbia River Basin: Experimenting with Sustainability." *Environment* 31 (6): 6–11, 30–33. Instructive look at efforts to achieve sustainability.

Leman, Christopher K. 1988. "Bringing Environmental Policy Home." *Environmental Forum* 5 (4): 19–22. Looks at the ways law can be used to affect individual behavior.

Lenssen, Nicholas. 1990. "Ray of Hope for the Third World." *World-Watch* 3 (5): 37–38. Interesting discussion of the use of high-efficiency light bulbs to help to solve the growing power demands of Third World countries.

Little, Charles, E. 1987. "Letting Leopold Down." *Wilderness* 30 (177): 45–48. Examines society's failure to heed Aldo Leopold's advice.

Lovelock, James E. 1979. *Gaia: A New Look at Life on Earth.* Oxford: Oxford University Press. Early description of the Gaia hypothesis.

Lovins, Hunter S. 1990. "Abundant Opportunities: An Interview with Robert Gilman." *In Context* 25: 20–24. Describes the work of the Rocky Mountain Institute and the potential for energy and water savings through efficiency measures.

Lundin, Stephen C., and Lynne C. Lancaster. 1990. "Beyond Leadership: The Importance of Followership." *The Futurist* 24 (3): 18–22.

Lyman, Fracesca. 1990. "Rethinking Our Transportation Future." *E Magazine* 1 (5): 34–41. Describes the cost and impact of the global automobile society.

MacNeill, Jim. 1989. "Strategies for Sustainable Economic Development." *Scientific American* 261 (3): 154–65. Outlines ways to reduce poverty and restore ecological balance. These are sound, but his thesis that we can greatly expand economic activity and achieve ecological balance seems blind to environmental realities.

McCommon, Mary. 1983. "A Blooming Boom in Texas." *National Wildlife* 21 (5): 4–5. Delightful account of Texas' attempt to cooperate with nature in roadside landscaping.

McCoy-Thompson, M. 1989. "Saline Solution." *World-Watch* 2 (4): 5–6.

Discusses how the Australian government is working with individuals to put a halt to salinization.

McKibben, Bill, et al. 1990. "How We Can Save It." *Greenpeace* 15 (1): 4–8. Excellent collection of thoughts by leaders in the environmental movement on how to save the planet.

McPhee, John. 1989. *The Control of Nature.* New York: Farrar Straus Giroux. Engaging account of human attempts to dominate nature and their catastrophic backlashes.

Meadows, Donella H. 1990. "Four Not-So-Easy Things You Can Do to Save the Planet." *In Context* 26: 9. A strategy for solving some of the endemic problems that contribute to the current state of environmental affairs.

Meadows, Donella H., et al. 1972. *The Limits to Growth.* New York: Universe Books. Classic study on exponential growth in a finite world.

Meeker-Lowry, Susan. 1988. *Economics as if the Earth Really Mattered: A Catalyst Guide to Socially-Conscious Investing.* Philadelphia: New Society Publishers. Contains an enormous amount of information and a compelling analysis of the economy.

Milbrath, Lester W. 1984. *Environmentalists: Vanguard for a New Society.* Albany: State University of New York Press. Interesting look at public attitudes and the role of environmentalists in reshaping American society.

———. 1989. *Envisioning a Sustainable Society: Learning Our Way Out.* Albany: State University of New York Press. Candid discussion of the author's vision of a sustainable society and some ways to achieve it.

Miller, Annetta. 1991. "Japan's Window of Opportunity." *International Wildlife* 21 (1): 12–17. Examines the environmental impact of a leading industrial power.

Miller, G. Tyler. 1988. *Living in the Environment.* 5th ed. Belmont, California: Wadsworth. Authoritative textbook on general environmental issues.

———. 1990. *Resource Conservation and Management.* Belmont, California: Wadsworth. Excellent source on resource conservation and management.

Moore, Curtis. 1989. "Does Your Cup of Coffee Cause Forest Fires?" *International Wildlife* 19 (2): 39–45. Traces individual contributions to global environmental problems.

———. 1989. "Will Changing Your Light Bulb Save the World?" *International Wildlife* 19 (3): 18–23. Offers ideas on what environmentalists can do to protect the environment.

Muckleston, Keith W. 1990. "Striking a Balance in the Pacific Northwest." *Environment* 32 (1): 10–15, 32–35. Discussion of an attempt to reach a more equitable relationship with nature.

Myers, Norman. 1985. *A Wealth of Wild Species: Storehouse for Human Wel-*

fare. Boulder, Colorado: Westview Press. Comprehensive view of ways wild species enrich our lives.

————. 1989. "Making the World Work for People." *International Wildlife* 19 (6): 12–14. Well-written essay on sustainable development in the Third World.

Naess, Arne. 1985. "Identification as a Source of Deep Ecological Values." In *Deep Ecology,* edited by Michael Tobias. San Diego: Avant Books. Speaks of the importance of expanding our concept of the self to include the world of which we are a part.

Nanus, Burt. 1990. "Futures-Creative Leadership." *The Futurist* 24 (3): 13–17. Description of the role of future-sensitive leadership.

Nash, Roderick. 1985. "Rounding Out the American Revolution: Ethical Extension and the New Environmentalism." In *Deep Ecology,* edited by Michael Tobias. San Diego: Avant Books. Incisive look at the expansion of ethics.

————. 1989. *The Rights of Nature: A History of Environmental Ethics.* Madison: University of Wisconsin Press. Intriguing study of the rights of animals and nature.

Norbert-Hodge, Helena. 1990. "The Cost of Development: An Interview with Alan Atkisson." *In Context* 25: 28–32. Describes some of the problems with conventional Third World development programs and offers suggestions for a new model of development.

Okay, John. 1982. "Economic Forces." In *Renewable Natural Resources: A Management Handbook for the 1980s.* Edited by Dennis L. Little, Robert E. Dils, and John Gray. Boulder, Colorado: Westview. Excellent discussion of economic factors that block efforts to reach a sustainable state.

Orr, David. 1991. "What Is Education For?" *In Context* 27: 52–55. Interesting insights on American education with recommendations for an emphasis on "earthwise" education.

Owen, Oliver S., and Daniel D. Chiras. 1990. *Natural Resource Conservation: An Ecological Approach.* 5th ed. New York: Macmillan. Introductory textbook on natural resource conservation.

Patterson, Alan. 1990. "Debt for Nature Swaps and the Need for Alternatives." *Environment* 32 (10): 4–13, 31–32. Analysis of the shortcomings of debt-for-nature swaps and of infrequently discussed alternatives.

Phantumvanit, Dhira, and Khunying Suthawan Sathirathai. 1988. "Thailand: Degradation and Development in a Resource-Rich Land." *Environment* 30 (1): 11–15, 30–32. Another account of environmental destruction in the name of economic development.

Postel, Sandra. 1990. "Toward a New 'Eco'-nomics." *World-Watch* 3 (5): 20–

28. Excellent overview of some of the issues discussed in the economics chapters of this book.

Prescott, W. R. 1990. "Sustainability in an Uncertain World." *In Context* 25: 57. Presents an interesting hypothesis on the inevitability of transitional instability.

Raloff, Janet. 1988. "Energy Efficiency Means More: Fueling a Sustainable Future." *Science News* 133 (19): 296–98. Good summary of ways of achieving energy efficiency.

Reganold, J. P., R. I. Papendick, and J. F. Parr. 1990. "Sustainable Agriculture." *Scientific American* (June): 112–20.

Reid, Walter V. C. 1989. "Sustainable Development: Lessons from Success." *Environment* 31 (4): 6–9, 29–35. Important reading on the nature of sustainability.

Renner, Michael. 1989. "Forging Environmental Alliances." *World-Watch* 2 (6): 8–15. Describes the need for international cooperation to prevent environmental deterioration and outlines some important progress in this area.

———. 1989. "What's Sacrificed When We Arm." *World-Watch* 2 (5): 9–10. Excellent account of the cost of arming a nation and how funds could be used to create a sustainable environment.

———. 1990. "Hot Air on Global Warming." *World-Watch* 3 (3): 35–36. Analysis of expenditures on renewable energy resources and of improved efficiency among members of the International Energy Agency.

Robert, Karl-Henrik. 1991. "Educating a Nation: The Natural Step." *In Context* 28: 10–16. Delightful essay on one man's successful effort to change the thinking of an entire nation.

Robertson, James. 1989. "A New Economics for the 21st Century." *The Egg: A Journal of Eco-Justice* 9 (1): 4–5. Discussion of the dangerous assumptions underlying the modern economy.

Robin, Vicki. 1990. "How Much Is Enough?" *In Context* 26: 62. Delightful article that addresses consumption.

Ruckelshaus, William D. 1989. "Toward a Sustainable World." *Scientific American* (September): 166–75. Excellent introduction to sustainability.

Russell, Peter. 1983. *The Global Brain: Speculations on the Evolutionary Leap to Planetary Consciousness.* Los Angeles: J. P. Tarcher. Beautifully written treatise on the role of humanity in global affairs.

Sancton, Thomas A. 1989. "What on Earth Are We Doing?" *Time* 133 (1): 24–30. Sobering look at the planet in peril.

San Martin, Robert L. 1989. "Renewable Energy: Power for Tomorrow."

The Futurist 23 (3): 37–40. Valuable estimates of the potential of nonrenewable and renewable energy resources.

Sastry, M. Anjali. 1990. "Improving Efficiency: Opportunities and Hurdles in India." *Rocky Mountain Institute Newsletter* 6 (2): 1–3. Superb discussion of the problems India faces in meeting its growing electrical demands and ways to solve them.

Schaeffer, Robert. 1990. "Car Sick: Automobiles Ad Nauseam." *Greenpeace* 15 (3): 13–17. Intriguing description of subsidies for automobiles and the lack of support for mass transit.

———. 1990. "Trading Away the Planet." *Greenpeace* 15 (5): 13–16. Describes some international trade negotiations that could set environmental protection back 20 years.

Schmookler, Andrew Bard. 1990. "Why Are We Devouring the Earth?" *In Context* 26: 22–23. Engaging view of the thinking about our obsession with economic growth.

Schumacher, E. F. 1973. *Small Is Beautiful: Economics as if People Mattered.* New York: Harper and Row. Classic reading on economics and appropriate technology.

Scudder, Thayer. 1989. "Conservation vs. Development: River Basin Projects in Africa." *Environment* 31 (2): 4–9, 27–31. Looks at the impact of river basin development projects and offers suggestions for making future projects sustainable.

Sharma, Ravi. 1987. "Assessing Development Costs in India." *Environment* 29 (3):6–11, 34–38. Documents the impact of unsustainable development.

Shea, Cynthia Pollock. 1990. "Doing Well by Doing Good." *World-Watch* 6 (2):24–30. Survey of progress toward a more sustainable economy.

———. 1990. "Environmental Investing." *World-Watch* 3 (1): 8–9. Looks at the growth in environmental investing in the United States and its benefit to the environment.

Solkoff, Joel. 1985. *The Politics of Food: The Decline of Agriculture and the Rise of Agribusiness in America.* San Francisco: Sierra Club Books. Engaging account of agricultural subsidies.

Speth, J. G. 1989. "Dedicate the '90s to the Environment: International Commitment Could Be Our Gift to New Century." *Los Angeles Times,* February 16. Call for international action to heal the environment.

Stavins, R. N. 1989. "Harnessing Market Forces to Protect the Environment." *Environment* 31 (1): 4–7, 28–35. Survey of ways to reduce pollution without regulation.

Steinhart, Peter. 1989. "Who Turned Out the Lights?" *National Wildlife* 27 (1): 46–49. Describes the benefits of conservation.

Stettner, Arianthe. 1991. "Considerations for Sustainable Economic Development in a Mountain Resort Community." Master's thesis, University of Phoenix. Excellent review and synthesis of the literature on sustainable thinking.

Todd, John, and Nancy Jack Todd. 1990. "The Restoration of Waters: An Interview by Robert Gilman." *In Context* 25: 42–45. Delightful introduction to the work of the Todds.

Turner, Tom. 1988. "The Legal Eagles." *Amicus Journal* 10 (1): 25–37. Excellent history of environmental law.

Van der Ryn, Sim, and Peter Calthorpe. 1985. *Sustainable Communities: A New Synthesis for Cities, Suburbs and Towns.* San Francisco: Sierra Club Books. Offers detailed information on ways to create sustainable communities.

Van Matre, Steve, and Bill Weiler. 1983. *The Earth Speaks: An Acclimatization Journal.* Warrenville, Illinois: The Institute for Earth Education. Collection of environmental poetry and prose that's well worth reading.

Vaughan, Christopher. 1988. "Disarming Farming's Chemical Warriors." *Science News* 134 (8): 120–21. Review of efforts to control insect pests without pesticides.

Wann, David. 1990. *Biologic: Environmental Protection by Design.* Boulder, Colorado: Johnson Books. Calls for a revolution in our way of life to include nature-compatible designs.

Weber, Peter. 1990. "Green Seals of Approval Heading to Market." *World-Watch* 3 (4): 7–8. Discusses the impact and importance of programs to label consumer products.

———. 1990. "U.S. Farmers Cut Soil Erosion by One-Third." *World-Watch* 3 (4): 5–6. Discusses reductions in soil erosion made as a result of the 1985 Farm Bill.

Weiner, Edith, and Arnold Brown. 1990. "Exonomics: What Economics Fails to Explain." *The Futurist* 24 (4): 36–39. Interesting view of noneconomic forces that help to determine economic reality.

Weis, Edith Brown. 1990. "In Fairness to Future Generations." *Environment* 32 (3): 7–11, 30–31. Stimulating article on principles of economic activity that ensure the rights of future generations.

Well, Malcolm. 1991. "Notes from Underground: An Architect's Sketchbook." *The Futurist* 25 (1): 28–32. Engaging description of earth-sheltered construction.

Will, Rosalyn, et al. 1988. *Shopping for a Better World: A Quick and Easy*

Guide to Socially Responsible Supermarket Shopping. New York: Council on Environmental Priorities. Important reference for consumers who want to make a difference.

Willers, Bill, ed. 1991. *Learning to Listen to the Land.* Washington, D.C.: Island Press. Important collection of essays for anyone interested in delving deeper into environmental values.

Williams, Joy. 1989. "Save the Whales, Screw the Shrimp." *Esquire* (February): 89–95. A satirical look at human responsibility or lack thereof.

Wood, Wilbur. 1990. "Holistic Resource Management." *In Context* 25: 48–51.

Youth, Howard. 1990. "Ecotourism: Loving Nature to Death." *World-Watch* 3 (5): 36–37. Summarizes some of the problems associated with the potentially sustainable ecotourism industry.

About the Author

Dan Chiras holds a Ph.D. in biology and teaches courses on sustainability at the University of Denver and University of Colorado, Denver campus.

A leading advocate of personal action and responsibility, Dr. Chiras cofounded Friends of Curbside Recycling, a group that helped to convince the city of Denver to begin its curbside recycling program. He also cofounded Speakers for a Sustainable Future, which operates a successful speaker's bureau in Colorado, offering slide programs on recycling and water conservation to civic groups, schools, and businesses. Dr. Chiras is president of the Colorado Environmental Coalition, a coalition of 40 statewide conservation/environmental groups.

Dr. Chiras speaks on environmental issues, especially sustainability, and is the author of numerous articles and books on the environment. His college textbooks include *Environmental Science: Action for a Sustainable Future*, *Natural Resource Conservation: An Ecological Approach*, and *Human Biology: Health, Homeostasis, and the Environment*. He is also author of *Beyond the Fray: Reshaping America's Environmental Response*, which offers numerous ideas on strengthening the environmental movement.

An avid kayaker, bicyclist, organic gardener, and aquarist, the author lives in a passive solar home in the Foothills of the Rocky Mountains with his wife and two sons where they strive to live by the principles of sustainability.

Index